The Tangled Web

The Tangled Web

The Life and Death of Richard Cain—
Chicago Cop and Mafia Hitman

Michael J. Cain

Skyhorse Publishing

www.skyhorsepublishing.com

10 9 8 7 6 5 4 3 2 1

Library of Congress Cataloging-in-Publication Data
    Cain, Michael J.
    The tangled web : the life and death of Richard Cain—Chicago cop and Mafia hitman / Michael J. Cain.
        p.   cm.
    ISBN-13: 978-1-60239-044-7 (hardcover : alk. paper)
    ISBN-10: 1-60239-044-4 (hardcover : alk. paper)
    1. Cain, Richard, d. 1973.   2. Police—Illinois—Chicago—Biography.
3. Mafia—Illinois—Chicago.   4. Organized crime—Illinois—Chicago.
I. Title.

HV7911.C35C35   2007
364.1092—dc22
[B]   2006102869

Printed in the United States of America

Dedicated to my sons, Aaron and Jason,
in the hope they may learn that chasing a dream
is always a worthwhile pursuit.

ACKNOWLEDGMENTS

It takes the support of many people to write a book, especially one that happens over as many years as this one. I'd like to thank Bill Roemer for his encouragement and his friendship, Bunny Porter for being my best friend when I most needed one, and Lydia Cain, who opened her home and her heart to me.

I am grateful to my father, John Cain, for teaching me how to tell a story and to Phyllis Mueller for teaching me how to write one. A special acknowledgment is due the dedicated staff at the National Archives in College Park, Maryland, and the Gerald R. Ford Library in Ann Arbor, Michigan, who helped far beyond the call of duty.

Also, Lamar Waldron, a fellow writer who understands. The Village Writers Group in Atlanta, whose members offered support, advice, and timely criticism. Virginia Velleca, who found books for me. Martin McGaffey, who read an early draft and showed me the holes. Paul Newey, Jim Malcotte, Tom Foran, Antoinette Giancana, and many more who can't be named—and still more who should be, but I've forgotten.

And my editor at Skyhorse, Jay McCullough, who deftly made my work better; Skyhorse publisher Tony Lyons, who took a chance on me; and Erik Laidhold, who asked him to.

CHAPTER

1

It was Christmastime, 1973. I had recently been transferred to Memphis to work as the controller of Eller Outdoor Advertising. My wife and I were flying from our new home there to spend the holidays with my family in Bay City, Michigan. We made an intermediate stop at O'Hare with a two-hour layover, so I decided to call some relatives in the area to wish them a Merry Christmas. First on the list was my Aunt Virginia.

"Isn't it awful what happened to Dick?" she said.

"What are you talking about?" I asked.

"Oh my God, you haven't heard. Just go buy a Chicago newspaper and you can call me back if you like."

I hurried down the concourse until I found a *Chicago Tribune* vending machine. The headline read: EX-COP CAIN SHOT TO DEATH. My hands were trembling as I dropped a dime in the slot and pulled a copy of the paper. Then I bought the *Sun-Times* and walked back to the waiting area to sit there and read the news about my brother.

I wasn't so much surprised that he'd been killed—I knew he'd been living life on the edge—but the public nature of his death stunned me. I recall wondering if he was killed as a lesson for someone else, or whether he was really involved in something big enough to have caused his murder in broad daylight in a West Side Chicago diner.

By the time we arrived in Bay City, I was pretty much up to speed on what the public knew and was anxious for more details. My father picked us up at the airport and, as we drove away, I waited for him to say something about the death of his first-born son, and perhaps an explanation for why no one had told me. How could that be? How could they not tell me? But he simply drove on, silent, impassive. Finally I asked, afraid that maybe he didn't even know.

That wasn't the case at all. It was just something he'd filed away already. This was how John (J. B., as we called him) dealt with difficult issues. When we had a discussion about almost any sensitive topic, he shut down, clammed up. His lips got thin, his jaw set; that was the signal. In other words, you deal with it by not dealing with it at all.

I was furious; how could he not have told me? But fury wasn't an emotion the children of John Cain were allowed. He'd only really seen me angry with him once, and that was the day I moved out of his house. Anger, rage, and fury; that was his turf, not ours. He refused to discuss Dick's death with me. Worse yet, my siblings seemed reluctant to talk as well, though their silence was born more of a lack of information, since my father wouldn't talk with them about it, either. So we went on with Christmas pretending that nothing had happened.

J. B. had called my sister, Mary Ellyn, who was living in Ann Arbor at the time. Maybe because Dick had been closer to her than to the rest of us, or perhaps she was just the first one on his list. She asked where Dick had been killed, and when J. B. told her in Chicago, she asked, "What was he doing in Chicago?"

"Where else would he be?" was his reply. She realized then that J. B. hadn't any idea what Dick had been up to lately. Mary Ellyn had recently gotten a postcard from Brazil, so she knew he'd been out of the country and thought it was permanent. She was surprised he would have gone back to Chicago, since she assumed he'd left because he sensed some danger there.

The next day she drove to Bay City, anxious to talk about it, and was frustrated by J. B.'s reticence. It was as if he believed if he didn't talk about it, didn't address the death of his son in any way, he wouldn't hurt. He knew at the time that Dick had chosen the road less traveled, but he couldn't have known with any certainty that his son was a bad guy. Even if he did, Dick was still his son.

In an effort to talk about it with someone, Mary Ellyn went to the home of a close friend in town whose husband was a reporter for the *Bay City Times*. The wife offered an empathetic shoulder while her husband took notes. And as reporters are wont to do, he called in a story about the son of a local resident who was a mobster in Chicago and had been murdered there. J. B. was angry beyond words when he read the story a few days later, and Mary Ellyn was furious with herself. She hadn't gone to her friend to become part of a story; she'd gone to share her grief. She felt betrayed, and still does.

The following week, the *Chicago Tribune* declared that thieves had killed Dick. Their story was that he had been involved with a burglary ring and that something had gone terribly wrong amongst the burglars, resulting in Dick's murder.

I was determined to understand who killed him and why, but then and there was neither the time nor the place for me to press it. As it turned out, the time and place wouldn't present themselves for several more years, after I'd moved to the Bay Area of Northern California.

My father's relationship with Dick had always been a mystery to me. Dick was seventeen years older than I, and he joined the Army before I was born. When I was a kid we'd see him frequently, or so it seemed to me. He lived near us for a time, and when he was a Chicago cop he'd drive to Michigan on occasion. He'd have one wife or another in tow and a couple or three kids, depending on which wife. Everyone was happy to see him, especially me. He'd tell stories about chasing the bad guys and we'd all listen with rapt attention. Dick was not only a great storyteller; he had great stories to tell. He'd lived in Bay City for a brief period with his first wife. Ultimately, he began to face the reality that he would never be very close to his father. They would disagree on almost every topic, and underlying it all was John Cain's deep-seated hatred for Dick's mother, Lydia, who had been his first wife. I've never known anyone who carried that level of contempt for so many years. She apparently deserved it, if one is to believe the stories my father told about her.

John and Lydia had been married in 1930, just as the depression was kicking off, but John Cain had the good fortune of having a steady, secure job. He was a bricklayer at Republic Steel, keeping the furnaces working. It was hard work and sometimes dangerous, but it was good work at a time when a lot of people were selling apples on street corners. So he had money when others were struggling, and that was likely part of what drew Lydia to him. That, and his devil-may-care attitude about life in general. But she had a mean streak that dug into him like a hot poker.

One story he told me was about a radio he'd saved for and bought. He'd paid a hundred dollars for it, no small purchase in those days. He loved listening to the radio, and in the days before television it was great entertainment. One day, Lydia decided he was listening to the radio when he should have been listening to her and she threw it out the window of their second-story apartment. He told me that it took all the power of his will not to kill her that day. He left for three days to calm down.

So I went home to Memphis after that Christmas of 1973 with a million questions. I hadn't seen Dick for more than ten years, but he was still family. I bought all the Chicago papers, I even found an article about his death in the *New York Times*. I didn't talk about him much at work. I figured that if he was actually in the Mafia, spreading that news would only complicate my own life.

I'd done some volunteer work for St. Jude's Hospital during my Memphis days, and received an invitation to a fund-raising dinner in Chicago. The featured speaker at the event was Jack Mabley, famed Chicago columnist and a man I knew from his writing to have been a friend to Dick. I couldn't make the event, but a friend who was going agreed to pass a note to Mabley on my behalf. The note, written on the back of my business card, read, "I'm Dick Cain's brother and I'd like to talk with you."

Jack called me the next week and said that he was surprised to hear from me. He'd been told about our side of the family, but assumed we were well out of Dick's life. He had some information to share with me, but he was uncomfortable telling me about it on the phone. When could I come to Chicago?

It took a couple of weeks to work it out, but I flew to Chicago. My brother Bill and I met with Jack at the *Chicago Tribune*. He told me that on the day after Dick died, FBI agent Bill Roemer visited Mabley and told him, "Dick Cain died a martyr, he was working for us." Mabley was clearly pleased to share this with me, but I was skeptical and could tell he wasn't exactly buying it either. He was trying to bring a measure of peace to a guy dealing with his brother's murder and he didn't think I was ready for the real truth. I asked him if he thought Dick had ever killed anyone.

"Well, yes, I suppose," he said, "but I'm certain he never killed anyone that didn't deserve it."

I was still skeptical of Dick's martyrdom, but still couldn't wait to share Mabley's comment with my father, thinking it would make him feel better.

"What the hell are you poking around in that mess for?" was his response. It seems my brother Bill had already told him what I'd been up to.

That was the last discussion J. B. and I had about the research that would consume parts of the next twenty years of my life. I would occasionally ask him questions about Dick to test the current climate, but he was steadfast in his refusal to discuss it, so I just carried on without his knowledge. Sometimes I felt a little guilty, especially as I got to know Lydia, J. B.'s first wife, but I always found ways to rationalize it. My one concession to his feelings was a private one—that I wouldn't publish the book until after his death—but that didn't apply to research.

I was transferred to California in 1974, and shortly thereafter Congress passed the Freedom of Information Act (FOIA). In the course of my work I'd gotten to know a freshman congressman from San Jose, Norman Y. Mineta, and asked if Norm would write to the FBI and the CIA on my behalf requesting a release of Dick's file. As it turned out, that wasn't the best strategic move. I was naïve and only just beginning to learn about research. Both agencies resented the passage of FOIA and generally didn't respond well to congressional requests because it had been Congress that foisted this burden on them in the first place. They eventually sent me about ten pages, 90 percent of which had been redacted. What was left convinced me that it was worth digging further. Over time I got better, and new laws aided my research. Eventually, I'd get nearly five thousand pages from the FBI alone.

At the time, though, the FBI reacted by making me a target. They began casually following me, and ultimately planted an agent inside the company I worked for to investigate me. On one occasion, an agent from the San Francisco office called me and asked for a meeting. He eventually admitted that he'd thought I was a member of organized crime and was hoping he could flip me as an informant. He didn't much appreciate my hearty laughter.

The inside guy represented himself as a former FBI agent and offered to help me get information, but I was to tell him what I knew. I became skeptical of his intentions when he suggested to me once that the FBI didn't like my digging around much, and they might scoop me up one day and take me "out to the rail yard and beat the crap out of me." He wondered what my reaction to that would be.

I was incredulous, and suggested that the only reason I could think of that they'd do such a thing was to cover some wrongdoing on their part. If that was the case, I was more determined than ever to proceed, and my guess would be that if they ever carried out this threat I'd be sure to sell ten to fifteen thousand more copies of this book. I told him I didn't think they'd be stupid enough to kill me, so they could bring it on; I'd take a beating for the additional sales. It wasn't long after that he left the company, never to be heard from again.

When Bill Roemer, a retired FBI agent, published his autobiography, *Man Against the Mob,* I wrote him a letter and thanked him for the kind things he'd said about Dick. Over time, Roemer and I became friends; he encouraged me to "keep punching," a favorite phrase of his that carried over from his boxing days at Notre Dame.

Along the way I've met some fascinating people. Good guys, bad guys, cops, and robbers. No one (except for the FBI) ever threatened me. I was cautioned to "be careful" more times than I can remember, but I never really felt unsafe.

I was constantly amazed at the impact Dick had on the people who knew him. I interviewed a federal judge, just for background, because I knew he had been a criminal defense attorney in the fifties and sixties. I wanted to get a sense of the times. It turns out that the judge had met Dick once, at the Playboy Club on Michigan Avenue in Chicago. He was having lunch with several colleagues when Dick walked up to say hello to George Callahan, another defense attorney at the table. As the judge told me, "George introduced him around the table and, of course, we all knew who he was. We were very impressed with his demeanor, his dress, everything about him." The judge went on to tell me the names of all six men at the table with him and what they'd had for lunch that day. From my perspective the amazing thing about that story is that more than forty years had passed since then and the judge could recall the minutest detail about meeting Dick Cain. I asked him what he'd had for lunch the following day, and he hadn't a clue.

Dick had a demeanor about him, a savoir-faire that people remembered for years. Even the people who hated him remembered him with the same clarity as the judge. There isn't any changing who Dick Cain was. He was many things to many people, and always a master manipulator, a gangster, a crooked cop—but he was a truly interesting character.

The high drama of his public and private adventures was defined by his work as vice cop, international spy, bodyguard to presidential candidate Barry Goldwater, and Chief of the Special Investigations Unit for the Cook County Sheriff's Department. And that's just the beginning. He was also married and divorced four times, a made member of the Outfit (Chicago's version of the Mafia), and a convicted felon.

CHAPTER

2

The Outfit. That's how they came to be known.

Al Capone hailed from Naples, as did his predecessor and first cousin, Johnny Torrio. When they arrived in New York they became gangsters, but they knew they could never become "made" members of the Mafia because they were not Sicilian. When they each, in turn, seized the opportunity to run things in Chicago, their rule was that all Italians could be members, not just Sicilians. Since they had never participated in the Sicilian ceremony for induction, they didn't know how it worked, so they just declared a guy to be made when they wanted it done. Over time, when the Sicilians attempted to wrest control from Capone, he'd simply have them killed and send word back to New York that he would kill them all if he had to. Eventually they got the message and Chicago stood on its own, answering to no one.

Dick Cain's story begins in the era of Al Capone, when Dick's grandfather, Ole Scully, lived and worked in Chicago. It was the best of times, and the worst of times.

In the fall of 1928, Herbert Hoover had defeated Al Smith in the presidential race. From humble beginnings, Smith had worked hard and had become first a feared prosecutor in New York City, then governor of the state. Smith's presidential campaign had nearly put the country on end. He favored repeal of the Eighteenth Amendment, and many people were genuinely concerned that a Catholic president would run the White House as an extension of the Papacy. So real were voters' fears that four southern states recorded not a single vote for Al Smith, and Hoover was swept in by a margin of six million votes. Being Catholic hurt Al Smith at the polls. Being a Democrat cost him the election. In 1928, no Democratic candidate could have won.

In 1928, the stock market was booming and the voters were supportive of a government that sought most of its tax revenues from the rich. There were changes going on, though—farmland was losing value and the Great War had brought the boys off the farm. Many didn't want to return to the farms at the end of the war. They'd seen a new way of life and they wanted more of it. High school enrollment was up sixty-six percent, and college enrollment was up by more than seventy percent over pre-World War I enrollments. As a country, Americans were becoming better-educated and less willing to do the menial jobs they had left behind when they went off to fight the War to End all Wars. Household income, while having grown steadily, was less than $2,000 a year.

Politicians in Chicago watched the presidential race with detached interest. It didn't much matter to them; they were in a world of their own. They felt secure, but recognized Al Smith had a reputation for being tough on crime in his home state. There could be trouble in Chicago if he were elected. Big Bill Thompson had been re-elected mayor of Chicago in 1926, almost at the command of Al Capone. Thompson was crooked, and he made no attempt to hide his relationship with Capone.

Prohibition, in effect since 1920, had helped solidify the mob's hold on Chicago by providing a breeding ground for corruption and creating a situation that gave the mobsters a positive standing in the community. Speakeasies got their illegal alcohol from the mob, but the customers came from the neighborhoods. Much of the alcohol was made by families in The Patch, the Italian section of Chicago, roughly two blocks on either side of Taylor Street from Clark Street to Halstead. Scores of bathtubs and stills in rundown apartments had become moneymakers for poor families. Bootlegging of bonded liquor from Canada was becoming a huge business, and Chicago controlled a great deal of the traffic. The mob provided a valuable service to the community, so it was accepted, even embraced by the masses.

Murder was commonplace, but as long as it was confined to the ranks of mobsters, the public simply ignored it. The Chicago mobsters had a curious willingness to treat the police as their enemy, and it wasn't unusual for the mob to attack an aggressive cop. Their favorite tactic seemed to be to bomb the homes of police captains who wouldn't accept regular payoffs.

By 1928, organized crime in Chicago had evolved. Al Capone had taken over the reins from Johnny Torrio two years earlier, when Capone was just twenty-six years old. Capone had come to Chicago from New York in 1920, at Torrio's request, and Torrio himself came from New York to Chicago in 1910 to help his uncle Big Jim Colosimo, the undisputed head of the Mafia in Chicago at the time. He ran it like a country club from a table at the back of his restaurant, Colosimo's, at 2126 South Wabash. Unlike the thugs who came later, Big Jim thought of himself as a gentleman gangster. In reality, he was a pimp, and with his diamonds and flashy clothes, he set the style for pimps that endures to this day. He enjoyed the easy money and the respect, but he wasn't much for getting his hands dirty with messy crimes and delegated these tasks to his underlings, who committed murder on his behalf.

Big Jim especially wanted his nephew, Johnny Torrio, to deal with the Black Hand. The Black Hand was an organization of Sicilian miscreants, unrelated to the Mafia. They kidnapped people, usually Italians, often children, and held them for ransom. The Black Hand had operated for many years in Chicago with virtual impunity. Once they had a victim, they tried to extort ransom money from the family. In many cases they would carry out the crime without actually kidnapping anyone—they would simply express a threat to kidnap.

They knew the many thousands of immigrant families would be unlikely to report a crime to the police. Immigrant Italians felt isolated in America and seemed to have only each other to turn to. The Irish dominated the Police Department. They were not very warm toward the Italians and not at all sensitive to their language problems. Worse than that, many were on the take and simply couldn't be trusted. In fact, most other ethnic groups felt the same way about the police. The more they were victimized, the more they closed ranks in their own neighborhoods. They would stay together, and everything would be all right.

Since most Italian immigrant families were poor working-class people, the Black Hand often included an entire neighborhood in its ransom demands. Big Jim Colosimo himself had been victimized by the Black Hand, so he asked his nephew Johnny Torrio to put an end to the harassment. Big Jim wasn't particularly bothered that the Black Hand was kidnapping children, but he was incensed that they would include him in their ransom demands.

Johnny Torrio got the Black Hand under control. He murdered their leaders and explained to those who remained that if they wanted to continue doing "business" in Chicago, they would not only stop extorting money from his uncle, but also they would pay tribute to Big Jim by giving him a cut of future ransom money.

Torrio was impressed with how easy it was to make money in Chicago, but he resented Colosimo's laying claim to the lion's share of the new income when it seemed to him that he was doing most of the work. After sixteen years of working with his uncle, he had Big Jim Colosimo murdered so he could claim control. Torrio saw his opportunity when Colosimo divorced his wife, Victoria, to marry Dale Winter, a dance hall vixen. Soon after they returned from their honeymoon, Big Jim was killed by a single shot to the back of the head. It was almost certain that Al Capone arranged the hit for Torrio.

In order to deflect suspicions about his involvement in the murder and to make his own garish statement about the respect due Colosimo, Torrio staged an elaborate funeral that would set the standard for mob funerals for years to come.

Over six thousand people attended Big Jim's funeral, including the First Ward Democratic Club, three judges, a congressman, nine city alderman, and an assistant state's attorney. Several limousines transported the flowers alone. The funeral procession included a stop at Colosimo's Café, where two bands played a funeral dirge. But for all his friends in high places, Big Jim could not be buried in consecrated ground. The Catholic Church could overlook the pimping, the gambling, and the murders, but the Catholic Church could not forgive the fact he had divorced his first wife and married again.

After Big Jim's death, Torrio ran the mob as if it were a real business. He didn't hang out with mobsters. He lived in a posh apartment with a wife who may not have even suspected (for a time, anyway) that her husband was a mobster. Prohibition was in full swing, and Al Capone began to see the opportunities Torrio was missing. Now it was *his* turn, so

Capone set in motion a plan to wrest control of Chicago from Torrio. First, he set Torrio up to be caught in one of his breweries when it was raided. This was an important arrest for the Chicago police and played well in the news. Torrio was convicted of running an illegal brewery and sentenced to a year in prison. While he was awaiting appeal, his car was attacked one day in what is now the classic Chicago-style hit: a black limo pulled up alongside Johnny's car, and its occupants opened fire with Tommy guns. Johnny's chauffeur and his dog were killed instantly. Johnny Torrio, uninjured, but in shock, was painfully aware of what had just happened as he sat in the car looking at his hat, staring at the two bullet holes in it. A few days later, while he was returning to his home in the evening, another attack felled Johnny with three bullets, but he survived. After a month in the hospital, it became clear to Johnny it was time for him to change his life.

He withdrew the appeal of his earlier conviction and was sent to serve time in the state penitentiary at Waukegan. Distrustful of the prison guards, he supplemented their protection with several of his own men. When Johnny was released, he negotiated to turn over all of his operations to Capone (who was clearly behind the assassination attempts) in return for allowing him safe passage to Italy. Thus ended the reign of Johnny Torrio.

During Capone's rise to power, most Italian families were powerless to fight the scourge of the Black Hand. Capone offered protection to the kidnappers as long as they continued to pay him a share of their profits and never tried to cut in on any of his rackets. They continued to kidnap, preying mostly on the Italian community. Eventually, a small group of neighborhood businessmen formed an alliance called the White Hand. The White Hand worked mostly behind the scenes, applying pressure where they could to secure the release of kidnap victims. Occasionally, they negotiated for lower ransoms: first, through Torrio's men, and later Capone's. Their only goal was the safe release of the victim. Although they weren't opposed to paying ransom, they tried to minimize it. They refused to resort to violence. When they ran out of options, they turned to the police.

One well-known member and early organizer of the White Hand was Ole Scully. A roughly handsome man with a huge handlebar mustache, Ole lived a comfortable life with his wife Vincenza, daughter Lydia, and two sons. He had immigrated to America as Olympio Scalzitti from his native Italy. He worked hard as a sewer contractor, but he had trouble understanding the "American way." In 1925, his business failed and he filed for bankruptcy. Determined to learn from his mistakes, he resolved to start afresh. The first part of his fresh start was a new name.

Selecting Ole Scully served two purposes for Olympio Scalzitti: First, it allowed him to disguise his past to a certain degree so that his former creditors would have difficulty finding him. Second (and perhaps most important to him), it provided the opportunity to Americanize his name and gain a slight edge on his Italian competitors—an edge to combat the prejudice against Italians in the 1920s.

Ole became a successful sewer contractor this time and was respected in the community. Ole's community was Taylor Street in Chicago. The neighborhood got its name, The Patch, from the quality of life on Taylor Street. There was a great deal of poverty, and the tenement apartments and flats were dank and dingy. The children ran wild in the streets. In school they were taught to speak English and came to learn that their Italian-speaking parents were behind the times.

On September 6, 1928, ten-year-old Billy Ranieri was abducted. He was walking home from school in the alley behind his home when a car pulled up alongside him. Billy stepped aside to let the car pass but, instead of passing, the car stopped at Billy's side, and a man snatched him up and put him in the back seat. Billy cried out for his mother as a neighbor looked on in horror.

That evening, a note was delivered from the kidnappers promising that Billy would be killed unless the family paid a $60,000 ransom. Although Frank Ranieri was a successful sewer contractor, like Ole Scully, he and his wife, Teresina, just didn't have that kind of money. Ranieri immediately reached out to Anthony Lombardo, the Mafia boss in The Patch. Lombardo agreed to meet with Ranieri the next night, September 7. Frank Ranieri was optimistic that Lombardo could be persuaded to intercede on his behalf and at least get a reduction in the ransom.

They were to meet at seven o'clock Friday evening at a tavern they both knew. As Lombardo was leaving the offices of the Italo-American National Union in the Hartford Building at 85 South Dearborn, about 4:30 P.M. that afternoon, he was approached by two gunmen on the sidewalk and gunned down, taking two .45-caliber slugs in his head. Both his bodyguards were shot as well. Lombardo was killed instantly. When police arrived they immediately identified him by his unusual deformed right hand.

Frank Ranieri was devastated when he heard a news report on the radio that Lombardo had been gunned down. It could be weeks before a replacement would be named, and there was no telling how willing the new boss would be to help. For five agonizing days, Frank Ranieri tried to stay calm, tried to work the system, but there was no help available. The mob was in turmoil, and there was no one to take an interest in the matter of Billy Ranieri.

In a last-ditch effort to save his son, Frank called the police on Wednesday, September 12. He told them everything he knew. He showed them the ransom note and told them about the phone calls he'd received threatening to kill young Billy. Working with the police, Frank made arrangements with the kidnappers to leave the money in a package at the "El" station (the elevated train) at Chicago Avenue and Wells. He was ordered then to take the southbound train to Randolph and Wells to wait for his son. The police set up surveillance of the bench where the bundle of money was to be left. No less than six people picked up the package and tried to take off with it, only to be collared by the police. None, however, was the kidnapper. The real kidnappers had been scared off, possibly by the several struggles and arrests at the site.

On the following Saturday, ten days after the abduction, the Ranieri family received another ransom note. In it, the kidnappers asked if they would recognize their son's head if it were in a paper sack. They were mortified. What would become of their son?

The White Hand began to get involved after Lombardo's murder. They questioned neighbors, being certain this kidnapping had been carried out by someone who knew Billy Ranieri, or at least knew his father. The Ranieri family received a new ransom note that said, "You have the money and if you don't put it here, you will receive a nice little package, and see if you know who it is. You will never find the other part of your son."

Young Billy was Ole Scully's godchild, and Frank was his best friend. Scully was mad. Though he hadn't actually witnessed Billy's kidnapping, he found witnesses who pointed the finger at Angelo Petiti, whom Scully had known to be involved in other kidnappings.

Petiti owned a saloon in the neighborhood, a saloon that in those dry times of Prohibition could only serve soft drinks, which he seemed only rarely to have on hand. People in the neighborhood told Scully they had seen Petiti addressing envelopes in his saloon in such numbers that they all suspected him of being a kidnapper mailing ransom notes. Frequently, ransom demands would be mailed to friends and neighbors as well as to the family of the victim. His saloon seemed a total failure, yet he owned two cars and wore nice clothes. Scully shared his information with the police, and on the strength of Ole Scully's sleuthing and his declaration that he would testify against Angelo Petiti, the police arrested Petiti on September 16.

Petiti's attorney, Nuncio Bonelli, maintained this kidnapping could not have been done by Italians. Italians, he said, would first send a Black Hand letter with a threat of kidnapping and then do the actual kidnapping only after the family had failed to pay the ransom. It wasn't a very effective defense strategy, and Petiti was scheduled for trial in December.

Three days later (thirteen days after his abduction), Billy Ranieri was released unharmed. Two men who had not been involved in the kidnapping had held him at a farm near Lockport, Illinois. Their job was only to keep Billy out of sight. After Petiti's arrest they got frightened and decided to turn Billy loose. At about midnight on September 18, they dropped Billy on a lonesome road, gave him a ten-dollar bill, and pointed him in the direction of a gas station about a mile away. When he arrived at the gas station, Billy asked the owner to call the police, who called Frank Ranieri. Frank drove out to pick up his son and went with him to the police station to support and comfort him as he told his story to the police.

Despite the defense attorney's logic, Billy was certain his abductors were Italian, but that's about all he knew for certain. The people who'd kept him on the farm were French, he thought, and they had been very kind to him.

On December 17, the day the trial began, Ole Scully was sitting in a neighborhood tavern, Nash's Place, with some friends when three men burst through the front door. Instinctively, Scully knew they were after him, and he ran for the back door. He was dead before he made his third step, cut down by two shotgun blasts. His killers then turned on the other patrons and the tavern's owner with baseball bats. They fractured the skulls of three of the men and inflicted less serious injuries on two others. The beatings were intended not to kill, but rather to keep the witnesses from talking about what they had seen.

But at the age of 47, Ole Scully now lay dead on a tavern floor. The court convicted Petiti without Ole Scully's testimony, while Scully's wife, Vincenza, vowed vengeance against the people who murdered her husband. It was a vow she repeated every day for the rest of her life.

Life changed for the Scully family, but they carried on. Vincenza's daughter, Lydia, who had turned seventeen on the day her father died, befriended a neighbor named Dooley, who introduced her to a cousin, Genevieve Cain. Lydia and Genevieve became fast friends, despite a seven-year difference in their ages, because Genevieve had a crush on Lydia's brother, Larry, and hoped being close to Lydia would help her get close to Larry.

In March of 1930, Genevieve Cain invited Lydia to join her on a trip to Michigan, where Genevieve would visit her family on their farm in Owosso. Lydia asked her mother for permission and was told it was shameful for a single girl of eighteen to travel out of state with another single woman and no chaperone. Lydia went anyway and stayed a week or so. Genevieve's brother, John, was also visiting at the time, and he and Lydia hit it off quite well.

Lydia returned the following month for another visit and again spent time with John. In late July, Genevieve and Lydia made the trip a third time. This time, Lydia had left Chicago in a huff, following a violent argument with Vincenza about her behavior, her rejection of the Catholic Church, and her lack of respect for her mother. Vincenza had not actually invited her to leave, but had threatened, "If you can't follow my rules, young lady, you'll just have to leave." Lydia, angry over the many tedious and repeated arguments with her mother, threw up her hands and said, "OK then, I'm leaving." And off she went to Michigan.

The Cain's farm had never been prosperous. With nine children to feed and only a hundred acres to farm, the Cain's main focus had been on survival. The Depression hadn't changed their lives much; they had been dirt-poor before the crash and were not heavily invested in the market, so the Crash's aftermath was just more of the same. Genevieve's parents, William and Margaret Cain, had themselves tried to make it in Chicago. For a time, they ran a hardware store, but did not have enough experience and skill to run such a business. Their Irish ancestors

had been farmers for centuries and shunned the cities of Ireland that
had been founded and were generally inhabited by the English. But
when the Irish began to immigrate to America, most of them headed
for the cities to find work. Still flinching over the devastation of the
potato famine, they were apprehensive about farming and had no
money to buy farmland; however, they had neither the experience nor
the social skills to blend smoothly into city life. They were considered
suitable for menial labor and police work, but not much more. Many
eventually retreated to farms, and so did the Cains in 1914, when their
hardware store was lost to bankruptcy.

By 1930, when Lydia was visiting, some of the Cain children had
moved away. John Cain had been gone for five years and was living in
Chicago working as a brick mason in the massive ovens of Republic Steel.
Brash and tough, John, twenty-three at the time, drove a flashy car and
clearly had a lust for life. He swept Lydia off her feet. When he proposed
marriage, though, after only their third meeting, she hesitated, for she
knew her mother would disapprove. A traditional Italian, Vincenza wanted
her daughter to marry a nice Italian boy.

When she arrived at the farm, Lydia had written her mother asking
forgiveness for the terrible fight they'd had the day she left. She told herself if Vincenza did not reply within a week, she would marry John Cain.
When the week passed, Lydia and John drove to Lima, Ohio, and were
married there by a Justice of the Peace. They agreed to keep their marriage
a secret. The only other people who knew were John's sister, Winifred, and
her husband, Harvey Gorte, who were witnesses at the wedding. When
they got back to the farm, though, they learned Genevieve had found
Lydia's diary, read it, and told the rest of the family about the wedding.

To make matters worse, Vincenza's letter, offering forgiveness and her
own apologies, arrived at the farm in their absence. The newlyweds left for
Chicago, stopping on the way at a telegraph office where Lydia wired her
mother, "Have married John Cain stop Please forgive me stop Lydia."
Lydia later retrieved the telegram from Vincenza, and it was among the
many things she gave to me nearly fifty years later.

Vincenza was not forgiving. Lydia had married an Irishman, an
unspeakable act. Vincenza Scully had a new mission: to harass John Cain
until he left the family so that Lydia could be with a nice Italian boy.
Vincenza wanted Lydia to marry Pasquale Cozzone, a man who had

worked closely with Ole Scully before his death. Cozzone was Scully's right hand man and so much a part of Ole Scully that people referred to him as "Little Scully." After Scully's death, they dropped the "Little", and simply referred to him as Scully. It has long been rumored Scully Cozzone personally avenged the death of his friend and mentor by killing the men who were in Nash's Place that day.

Catholicism would be a major factor in the family for years to come. The Catholic Church made Lydia feel constrained, and she felt it held her back from living the kind of life she preferred for herself, yet guilty for feeling that way. Having been raised in an Irish Catholic home myself I can attest to the Church's development of guilt as a tool. Guilt may have been invented by the Jews, but it was perfected by the Catholics.

Vincenza was at mass every morning praying for revenge for her fallen husband. When Lydia stopped going to mass, Vincenza blamed John Cain, the heathen Irishman, even though Lydia's enthusiasm for the Church had waned years before she met her husband. Vincenza knew this, but preferred to deceive herself.

But, at a time when the Depression was crushing so many families, John Cain had a bricklaying trade, steady work, and the money to enjoy life. He and Lydia planned a trip to Hot Springs, Arkansas, in the fall of 1930. Hot Springs was the Las Vegas of its day, crawling with casinos to entertain the many tourists, and, of course, there were hot mineral baths as well. "Sort of a honeymoon," the Cains called it. John related to me years later that it might have been a wonderful, renewing trip, except for Vincenza's insistence she come along and bring Lydia's brother, Al, a loner and a homosexual. Vincenza and Al were always there to know of every disagreement, to express disapproval, and to antagonize John.

Lydia was not strong or self-confident enough to stand up to her mother, and she felt guilty about marrying John because she knew she had betrayed her mother and the memory of her father by marrying outside of her Italian heritage. Following the trip to Arkansas, the marriage went downhill. The only photographs showing John and Lydia together that survived the marriage were those taken in Hot Springs.

A son, Richard Scully Cain, was born in Chicago on October 4, 1931. After that, life was never the same for Lydia and John. Their marriage, already a stormy one, was laced with frequent and sometimes violent fights that became intolerable to them both. Many of their disagreements involved Vincenza, and most were about her or their son, Richard. Finally, after seven years of mutual agony, they separated—and divorced six months later, in 1938.

As was the custom, Lydia was given custody of young Richard, though her inability to deal with Richard had been a major factor in causing the marriage to fall apart. Lydia felt the responsibilities of motherhood were overwhelming, and she resented having to spend so much of her time caring for her child. Many years later, she admitted to me that she abhorred children, including her own. She pleaded with John to take Richard, but John worked the night shift at the steel mill and could not care for Richard adequately. In the fall of 1939, Richard was sent to Owosso, Michigan, to live on the farm with John's parents.

Richard was enrolled in St. Paul's Catholic School in Owosso and, for the next ten years, was shuttled between Lydia in Chicago and the farm with John's parents. When Lydia's guilt got the most of her, she would send for Richard, and he would come to Chicago for a while, but never for longer than six months.

In Chicago, Richard learned about the streets and about being tough. Lydia gave him neither love nor direction. He had no curfew and no restrictions of any kind. He learned to shoot pool, wield a knife, and fight as fiercely as someone twice his size. He brought that knowledge back to the little farm community that didn't know what to make of him. He used to go down to the public school in Owosso and pick fights with the Protestants, the "proddy dogs," he called them. When he was enrolled in public school in Chicago, he would go to the Catholic school in the neighborhood and pick fights by taunting the kids there and calling them "Catlickers." He spent nearly every summer at the farm.

Dick enjoyed the farm and bonded with the Cains, especially his grandmother. Several of his aunts and uncles still lived on the farm and they treated him like a little brother. He'd return to Chicago once in a while, but never felt as welcome with his mother as he did on the farm. My own mother told me one time that she rode the train with Dick once when he was returning to Chicago and he told her that he wished she'd been his mother. It made her quite happy to hear that, even though she never talked about it until thirty years later.

In 1942, John remarried. His new wife, Catherine Hanlon, was known as Kay. She was a registered nurse, having attended training at Little Company of Mary Hospital on Ninety-fifth Street with one of John's sisters. Soon after they were married, Richard was visiting and casually referred to his new step-mother as Kay. John tried to correct him, saying, "This is your mother."

Richard's reply, "I already have a mother," was taken by John as a slap. Kay understood where she fit, but John thought he could change reality simply by saying it was so.

Two years later John and Kay moved to Owosso themselves with their two small children. They bought a small restaurant in nearby Perry. Soon there were two more children, and it seemed to Richard there was no place for him in his father's home.

Richard, who by now was called Dick, was still attending Catholic school in Owosso and living at the farm, about ten miles out of town. When Dick was in the tenth grade, he tired of school and Owosso and took off for Chicago again to live with his mother, never to return.

During the next year, he roamed the streets of Chicago with virtually no supervision and wasn't enrolled in school. He lived with Lydia, but they generally avoided one another. In July 1947, when he was sixteen years old, he got in trouble with the law, though the nature of the trouble is unclear. He told his mother he wanted to join the Army. Since he was underage, he had to have written permission from both parents. Lydia was delighted. It was the best idea the boy had ever had. She thought she could finally really get him out of her hair, and with a clear conscience at that. John Cain, on the other hand, was opposed to the idea and fought it very hard. He loved Richard and felt his joining the Army was an escape (which, of course, it was) and that, as such, it pointed out John's failure as a father. He wasn't prepared to change anything about his relationship with Dick; he just didn't like his failures revealed to him.

Eventually, John grew tired of fighting with Lydia over the matter; after all, he was busy raising his new family. With great reluctance, he signed the consent forms. Dick was off to the Army. He wrote his father from boot camp at Fort Knox, Kentucky, in August 1947 and told him he wanted to come for a visit when he got his first furlough. John Cain never answered the letter.

I first met Lydia in 1978 in the early days of my efforts to learn more about Dick's remarkable life. One of Dick's twin daughters was staying with me in California at the time, and she arranged the introduction. I flew to Chicago and went to Lydia's South Side apartment on a Saturday afternoon. We hit it off right away, partly because of the number seventeen. Lydia had a fixation with the number seventeen, beginning with the fact that her father, Ole Scully, was murdered on her seventeenth birthday, December 17, 1928. He had given her a birthday present that morning, a check for $50.00. Check number seventeen. She never cashed the check; she gave it to me when she realized that Dick was seventeen years older than I. To Lydia, that was proof I was OK.

On that first visit, she gave me some newspaper clippings about Dick and we talked for thirteen hours straight, interrupted only by a short trip to the liquor store for a bottle of bourbon and a six-pack of Old Style beer. She was a charming, if manipulative lady, in her seventies when we met. She made it clear that if I would return for another visit, she would find more things to give me. In truth, she didn't have to look, she knew where everything was. She just wanted to ensure that I *would* return.

Among other things, she told me that she had known the mobster Sam Giancana most of her life. They'd grown up in the same neighborhood and though he was three years older and they didn't become friends until later, they knew one another. When Dick was growing up, he came to know Sam as well. They weren't particularly close, but they were aware of one another and Sam was a guy who watched what was going on in The Patch.

Over the course of the next several years Lydia and I met every couple of months, whenever I could make the trip from California. She told me stories and she gave me clippings, photos, and every letter Dick had ever written to her—almost 400 in all. She gave me stories that Dick had written. One day she handed over his passport, which she'd hidden at the bottom of her hamper since his murder. Some of the things she'd ask me to copy and return to her, the passport she asked me to keep because she felt she was in danger just having it.

I was curious to learn her side of the story about her marriage to my father, and she admitted that she'd been a difficult wife. She only married him in the first place to spite her mother, but the thing that finally broke their marriage was Richard. She told me that she didn't like children and, though she tried, the fact that he was her own child didn't seem to make a difference. So Richard was sent to his paternal grandparents, who lived on a farm in Owosso, Michigan, and Lydia felt liberated. She felt guilt as she was telling me, but not at the time it happened.

CHAPTER

3

After basic training at Fort Knox, and training as a radioman at Fort Hood, Texas, Dick was sent to Japan for a short stay. While stationed in Japan, he got involved with a local woman and hinted to his mother that their relationship was getting serious. He called home one day and announced he was going to marry her and wanted to know what his mother thought of the idea. "That's fine," she said, "if that's what you want to do."

"But what will I do with her when I return to the States?" he wondered aloud to his mother.

"Why, you can bring her to my apartment, I suppose."

"But where would she sleep, Mom? Your apartment has only one bedroom."

"She can have my bed," was Lydia's terse reply, "because the minute you bring that yellow bitch through my door, I'm leaving."

Dick cancelled his Japanese wedding plans and returned to the States shortly thereafter to undergo eye surgery at an army hospital in Philadelphia. Following his recuperation from surgery, he was posted to St. Thomas, in the Virgin Islands, where he worked as a full-time supply clerk and a part-time MP. He found the work to be boring, so he took an off-base job as manager/bartender for a small tavern. It was there that he met his first wife.

She was a native of the Virgin Islands and a single mother, rare in those days. Her child's father was an American sailor who'd left before he knew she was pregnant. Her daughter was four years old by the time Dick Cain came into their lives. The courtship with Dick was brief; she was looking for a husband to help care for her child, and Dick was ripe for the picking.

It's not important how it happened, but they fell in love. It never occurred to her to question Dick about his age. It was years before she realized he had lied to her. He'd added seven years in order to match her age. He was just eighteen years old when he married her, yet he had passed himself off as twenty-five.

This seven-year bonus he'd given himself quite by chance to avoid losing his Virgin Islands sweetheart became a permanent part of Dick's life in the years to come. It served him well, by projecting an illusion of maturity, as well as an accounting for time with which to pad his resume. Working backward, he calculated the time he needed to account for, and he then invented activities to fill that time. Three extra years in the military, where he claimed he served in the OSS and was trained in counter-intelligence. Copier technology in those days was pretty limited, but he experimented with what was available to modify his Honorable Discharge certificate to claim a later release from the Army, from June 1950 to July 1953.

His new resume also included three more years to finish high school, which he had never done, and finally a year at Loyola University where he studied criminal psychology. So firm had he been about his age that at the time of his death, every newspaper, as well as the Chicago Police Department, reported his age to be forty-nine. He was actually just forty-two years old.

It was in 1949 they married. He loved her as well as an eighteen-year-old could, but his motivation for marrying at such a young age was partly a desire to strike out at his father. He knew "the old man" would flip out when he heard about it, and that made it all the more attractive to him. John had lost control over his son's life and while John blamed himself, it seemed to the eighteen-year-old that Dick was taking the blame. Dick felt his father had rejected him, but rather than be angry with his father and deal with that anger, he chose to reject his father and punish him when he could. That way, their lack of a relationship was Dick's decision and not his father's. He could tell himself he was rejecting his father so he wouldn't have to deal with explaining (to himself or anyone else) why his father rejected him.

In reality, rejection of his son was the furthest thing from John Cain's mind. He loved Dick to the best of his ability. What Dick saw as rejection from his father was intended for Dick's mother, Lydia, for whom John held the deepest contempt. So strong was John's hatred for Lydia that he never spoke a kind word about her, even forty years after their divorce. He blamed everything bad that ever happened in his life on this woman, and certainly he held her responsible for "the way Dick turned out."

Marrying not only gave Dick a shot at hurting his father, but it also, in Dick's mind, trumped his lack of maturity. As a married man, he would surely have to be treated with respect. Marrying an older woman who was unaware of their age difference ensured she would respect him. Now he just had to work on his father.

Dick wrote to his mother on February 24, 1949, one month after his wedding:

Hi Mom—

Well—it sure seems that it's the old story—but I'm sorry I didn't write sooner—I just didn't have time! We can tell from your handwritten letter just received that you're strained at receiving the news that we have a daughter. I hope we're wrong. You see, Mom, when we first went out, and I learned she had a child, I rather took the position (unconsciously maybe) of a man who'd be going with you. I carefully took note of my feelings toward the child . . . did I feel jealous because of its father? Did I resent the child for interfering with my love life! NO! I love the child as much as my wife! True, she made a mistake. Lots of people do. Would it be correct for me to shun her because her husband was a louse? The whole affair is a sore spot in her, which is why her letter explaining the child is hard to understand. It's your first grandchild, Mom!

Now I MUST explain the enclosed clipping. When I joined the Army, I gave my name as Richard Sculzitti Cain. Why, I don't know. Anyway, that's what's on the records. Also, that is the name I was married in and also the name I'm adopting Jackie in. I guess I really bit off more that I could chew, but as you realize the circumstances surrounding my enlistment, I was liable to do most ANYTHING. (I bet this rising generation leaves you dumbfounded.) Anyway, I'm adopting Jackie, which is now getting on paper. I've also been supporting her until now. Really, Mom, the child is wonderful. Being rather spoiled when she came, she sat in the corner the first day and has given me no trouble. I've trained her to say "Daddy" & not Dick—but must watch myself because people sometimes note the similarity between training and dogs.

All I can say is "it's been wonderful til now, and I wish them both luck."

About Dad—well, I wrote him, but *what* a letter. I got drunk (not because of that) on a party, came home & wrote him a letter. I didn't stop at NOTHING. I told him- from what I can remember- I was married and if he didn't like it he could go to _____. Wonder what now?

I like this MP duty, but bad hours.

Oh yes, sorry. I got the Airmail package OK. *THANKS A LOT*. Let me know what it cost. Will write Gram tomorrow. I've got to sign off now.

Love,
Dick

Dick was asserting himself against his father. He felt cheated, robbed of a childhood. If he couldn't be his father's son, maybe he could be his father's peer, a family man who surely deserved respect for his hard work and loving attitude toward his wife and child.

None of those are good reasons to get married, but they seemed to make sense to Dick at the time. His wife was of Dutch descent, her ancestors being among the first white settlers in the Virgin Islands five generations earlier. Dick moved into the family home at Charlotte Amalie, a sprawling two-hundred-year-old house that had survived countless tropical storms and would hopefully survive the storm that was sure to ensue. His mother-in-law was in charge, and Dick knew not to challenge her. He'd have his day when he was able to move away from the island.

After being discharged from the army on June 23, 1950, Dick took his family to Miami where he hoped he could start a meaningful career. A Chicago friend introduced him to a private detective named John Buenz, who owned a small private investigations firm. Buenz hired him right away, sensing Dick's ambition and intelligence. Dick decided to continue the ruse about his age. At nineteen, he knew he didn't have a prayer of finding a real job, so he told Buenz he was twenty-six, had been in the OSS, and had fought in Burma.

Buenz taught Dick a number of important skills, chief among them wiretapping and surveillance. Dick also learned to speak Spanish while he worked with Buenz. He'd grown up speaking Italian, so it wasn't too big a stretch for him, but it was an important part of the work he did there. Much of the work was related to divorce cases, but there's a lot of downtime in a private investigator's office, so they filled some of that time by doing car repossessions for banks and finance companies. Buenz, who was a Cuban national, had many contacts in Havana and eventually used Dick as a fresh face to send into Cuba to monitor government activity for various clients in the Miami area.

Dick made numerous trips into Cuba to gather information and install wiretaps. It was during this time he decided espionage was a line of work he could really enjoy. Buenz was a friend of Fulgencio Batista, the future president of Cuba, who at the time was living in self-imposed exile in Ft. Lauderdale. Batista became a valued client, leaning on Buenz to keep him apprised of the situation back home in Cuba while he prepared to return.

Dick learned a great deal during his three years in Miami and certainly had no regrets, but maybe it was time to move on. Miami didn't suit Dick. He wanted something different, but he didn't really know what it was. His friends told him he could do better in Chicago; there was no end of wealth awaiting him there. A guy with his ambition and skills could really do well, but he'd have to relocate.

He counted among his blessings at the time that he had an opportunity to rebuild a relationship with his mother. Late in 1952, at the age of forty-one, Lydia had gotten pregnant. The father was a police captain who was never told of the pregnancy. To avoid the shame of dealing with such a thing at home, she took a leave of absence from her job with the Chicago Police Department and went to Florida for six months. She stayed with Dick and his family until it was time to deliver the child.

Lydia had known from the start that she couldn't possibly raise another child. She had made arrangements with an adoption agency to take the baby immediately after its birth. She'd made the right decision for herself and her newborn child; she never doubted it, even thirty-five years later when they were reunited.

Lydia returned to Chicago as soon as she could travel. Dick began making plans himself to pull out of Miami and build a new life with his family.

CHAPTER

4

In 1953, they moved. Dick's wife was angry and scared. She hated the thought of being farther away from the Islands than they already were, and she knew she would hate it even more once she got there. It didn't matter where "there" was; she simply hated being so far from her home. She was very close to her family and tolerated Miami only because it was close enough to the Islands so that she could get home regularly to visit.

The first stop was Bay City, Michigan, where Dick's father then lived with his new family. Dick had matured since going into the army in 1947, and he desperately wanted to reconcile with his father and get a fresh start. He was twenty-two years old with a wife and a nine-year-old stepdaughter. They took an apartment near his father's house, but not so near that they could interfere with one another. Dick got a job, tending bar, at the BonTon, a neighborhood dive on the West Side of Bay City.

Dick learned two important things there: First, it was no place for a man with his kind of ambition. Secondly, he discovered that he was so much like his father in temperament that they couldn't be together for longer than thirty minutes before an argument would break out. Dick wanted, needed, some adventure in his life, and that wasn't going to happen in Bay City, Michigan. He'd stick it out for a while, for the sake of his relationship with his father. He made it six months, but his heart had moved on well ahead of that.

John would ask, "Are you going to work in beer joints for the rest of your life?" In hindsight it was a stupid question. Dick had not come to

Michigan to be a bartender; he had come to be with his father. Bartending was just a job. But, in unfortunate, albeit typical John Cain fashion, he saw only what he saw. What he saw was his son, whom he loved deeply although he never told him so, tending bar in a jerkwater town with a dead-end past and a dead-end future.

John Cain couldn't say "Dick, I love you, and I want better things for you than to spend your life pouring whiskey for bozos." So what he said was, "Are you going to work in beer joints for the rest of your life?" And so, with the best intentions, with heartfelt love he couldn't show, John Cain drove his son away. Dick fell back on his childhood escape route and, six months after arriving in Bay City, he packed up his family and moved to Chicago.

His first job was with United Parcel Service as a security officer. During his time at UPS, Dick perfected some skills he had learned in Miami and worked on some new ones. He proved to be a diligent investigator. Among the most common crimes to be investigated were credit card fraud, burglaries, and hijackings. Though credit cards were not as prevalent as they are today, there were some retailers that used them extensively for catalog customers. Chief among them was Sears Roebuck, based in Chicago and a major customer of UPS.

When someone ordered products from the Sears catalog and charged them to a stolen credit card, UPS and Sears were active in helping the police to apprehend the criminals. Frequently, Dick would follow a delivery truck to a suspect's home, waiting for the driver to secure a signature accepting delivery, and then would step in and arrest the person. Often, someone would accompany him from Sears' security department and, for the bigger ones, the Chicago Police Department. He became friendly with a number of Chicago cops who worked part-time at UPS and began to think about a career as police officer, but he wouldn't be just any police officer. As he would later tell an FBI agent in Mexico, he was contemptuous of cops who accepted petty graft: Dick Cain would never settle for chump change.

When he returned to Chicago, it wasn't long before he sought out an old family friend, Sam Giancana. It was also during this time he became a "made" member of the Chicago mob.

He participated in arranging numerous burglaries in UPS warehouses and the hijacking of UPS trucks. Once, he left his keys with a mob associate while he attended a UPS dinner with his boss, providing himself an airtight alibi. In time, his apparent diligence and crack investigative work were rewarded with promotion to Chief of Security.

This was the type of double-dealing upon which Dick Cain would build his future. As long as he delivered by solving cases, and no one was able to analyze the cases he didn't solve, he could pull it off. UPS became the proving ground for the Dick Cain style of police work.

In 1954, his wife gave birth to a daughter—his firstborn child. They both hoped it would help the marriage, but the reality was that Dick had moved on mentally to a life that had no room for a family. They would come for visits to Bay City and, while we embraced them as family, Dick couldn't get that far.

In the fall of 1955, Dick enrolled at the Keeler Institute of Polygraph to learn how to operate a polygraph machine, a lie detector. Mr. Leonarde Keeler had developed a unique approach to interpreting the results of a polygraph exam and felt his technique increased the reliability of polygraph tests. Years later I interviewed the new owner of Keeler and asked him to retrieve their file on Dick Cain, the student. The file didn't reveal much, he had never completed an application for enrollment, but one curious revelation was that he'd failed a polygraph test given to all new students.

Dick got through the six-week program with little difficulty and was licensed as a certified polygraph operator. He believed the "lie box" would be an invaluable addition to his set of skills, and he felt good about his decision to take the training. Becoming licensed bolstered his confidence enough to apply for a position in the Chicago Police Academy in the late fall. It had been Sam Giancana's idea that Dick attend the Academy. Sam needed an inside guy, a bagman to make the payments he regularly gave to the department. He was told he'd have to work his way up in the ranks as much as possible before that would happen, but he was up to the challenge.

Physically, he was outside the Academy's minimum requirements. He was too short, at five feet seven inches, with eyesight that tested at 20/200. Some well-placed cash saw him grow a full inch and improve his eyesight most miraculously. He wasn't concerned about his ability to keep up with the physical side of the training. He'd grown up fighting on the streets of Chicago, served three years in the army, and continued an exercise regimen after he got out; he could take whatever the police department might throw at him. He struggled with the bookwork, not because it was hard, but because he had been such a terrible student as a young man. He worked hard, though, and fared well. He had the discipline and the intelligence to get through it. He wasn't the genius he wanted everyone to think he was, but he was well above average with an IQ of 125 and could handle any intellectual pursuit he chose.

In May 1956, Dick was sworn in as a member of the Chicago Police Department. He started in the patrol division, but he had his heart set on a better assignment. All it took was a year or so of keeping his nose clean, a little cash and a phone call from his coach, Sam Giancana. The Chicago PD of the 1950s was corrupt to its very core, and in time Dick exploited that fact to find his new home in the detective squad investigating vice.

During this period of major career changes, Dick also initiated some life changes. He got involved with another woman, and when she got pregnant around the same time as his current wife, he faced a dilemma. His wife solved it by packing up and returning to the Virgin Islands with the two girls. His third child was born there and grew up thinking that her father had died.

He married Rosemary Frazier, a sometime model he'd met in a bar while conducting a vice investigation, a few weeks after their twin daughters were born in October 1956. They moved to an apartment just west of the Loop. In June 1958, I last saw Dick Cain. My brother Pat and I spent three weeks there with Dick, Rosemary, and the twins. We were actually the second wave, having been preceded a month earlier by two older siblings, Bill and Mary Ellyn.

Dick drove to Michigan to return two kids and to pick up two more for the return trip. We left the farm in Owosso in the early evening, Dick had a heavy foot, and the darker it got the faster he drove. He was driving a 1958 Mercury Turnpike Cruiser with a massive engine that seemed to cry out for more speed. I checked the speedometer several times and saw it bouncing off 120 miles per hour. Rosemary would watch it too and tell him to slow down. After several of those exchanges, Dick simply turned off the dashboard lights.

The building was adjacent to the Congress Expressway, at 3548 West Congress Parkway, between Kedzie and Hamlin. The Expressway was renamed the Eisenhower Expressway (I-290) in 1964. Dick was also not far from Taylor Street, The Patch, where he had spent his youth and where his mother and father lived during their short, stormy marriage in the thirties. A four-story stone structure, it had a huge stone porch on the front that no one ever used, probably because it was fifty feet from the freeway. All the traffic in and out of the building came through the back, off the alley. Each apartment had a large back porch allowing access to the stairs and the backyard. The yard had no grass, which was just as well because no one would have mowed it. There were remnants of a swing set, leaning hard to one side, and a smallish wooden frame that likely was once a sandbox. By now, though, even the cats ignored it. The only evidence of plant life in the yard was a single dandelion growing in one corner, the one that got the most sun. There was a one-car garage in the corner of the lot, which Dick rented to park his car. The big Mercury was a tight squeeze, but he made it fit. The back of the building faced West Van Buren Street and beyond that was West Fifth Avenue and the commercial district. Around the corner was Garfield Park, one of the city's largest public parks. Just west of their building was a big church, at the corner of South Central Park Avenue and West Congress Parkway.

Dick and Rosemary lived on the second floor. The back porch had a washing machine and a clothesline that hooked to a telephone pole across the yard. The pulley on the line allowed Rosemary to hang her clothes in spite of her being twenty feet in the air. Nobody had dryers in this neighborhood; lots of folks didn't even have washing machines. Frequently, one of Rosemary's friends would come over to wash clothes and then drive home with a basket of wet laundry to hang at home. The back porch was all wood and seemed an afterthought compared to the beauty and ruggedness of the stone building, though most of the apartments in this part of town were built in the same style. The buildings were old, and the porches had a kind of sway to them, like an old horse.

Inside the porch was the kitchen. There were white wooden cabinets, which looked old, but were a perfect match for the old and mismatched dishes they housed. The kitchen was small but seemed adequate for Rosemary's needs: she had no intention of doing any more cooking than was required. Adjacent to the kitchen was a small dining room. The furniture was better than a dinette set, but not quite what one would expect for formal dining, except for the China cabinet, a beautiful antique piece with a curved glass front, that dominated the room. It was from this cabinet that Rosemary reverentially removed and cradled a bottle of Chianti and poured a glass for my brother and me.

I was eleven; my brother Pat was twelve. Back home, our family drank beer. On holidays they drank Seagrams 7 with 7 Up, seven-and-seven they called it. We had tasted beer before, my brother and I, and a little whiskey, but this was something else. My father had talked about "dago red" while he was married to Dick's mother, Lydia. He spat out the words, like he was swearing. When Rosemary offered the wine, I expected I would finally know what my father hated about the Italians. As an altar boy, I had sneaked an occasional slug of sacramental wine, but the priests had clearly never been introduced to Chianti, a wine that could have made the priesthood seem attractive even to me, and to this day a good Chianti is my favorite wine.

Down the hall were two bedrooms and a bathroom. The twins, Kim and Karla, shared a room, which was across the hall from the master bedroom. Then the hallway opened up into a living room and what they called a front room, with windows overlooking the street below and the Congress Expressway. Actually they called it a "FRUN-troom"—the first Chicago dialect I remember recognizing.

The furniture was unremarkable, but life in that little apartment was remarkable indeed. Dick was a vice cop and played the role to the hilt. He loved being a cop; he loved playing the part, a tough guy with a license (his badge) to be tough. He worked nights because that's when the vices are practiced; that's when they live. He would get home at eight or so in the morning, and we would talk some before he went to bed.

The twins, Kim and Karla, were nearly two by this time and were precocious. It was a house rule that they not bother their father while he was sleeping, and they tried their best. One day while they were playing in his room, Karla reached up beyond her sight line to the top of the dresser and searched blindly with her hand, looking for something to play with. Her hand fell on something interesting, and she pulled it to the edge of the dresser slowly. She tried to pick it up, but couldn't manage it, so she just pulled it out past the edge of the dresser. When it cleared the edge, she couldn't control it, and it pulled her little hand downward most abruptly and crashed onto her sister's head. Karla had found the blackjack that Dick had removed from his pocket before he'd gone to bed. The blow to Kim's head knocked her unconscious and scared them all half to death. Kim recovered with a headache, and Dick learned his pistol wasn't the only thing he had to put on the high shelf in the closet when he went to sleep.

Dick enjoyed telling us stories about how he conquered the bad guys. He never told us about corruption, so we didn't know it existed. I wondered sometimes, when I would see him ignoring traffic laws, how he justified that. It was as though the laws were for the other people, not him. Several times, in my presence, the police stopped Dick for speeding or parking illegally, but nobody ever gave him a ticket. He laughed at the laws, and I remember wondering if he felt that way about all laws. He parked illegally one time near his apartment to run into a liquor store to buy some booze. My brother and I waited in the car and, while Dick was shopping, a Chicago cop walked up with his ticket book and spoke to us. He noticed the decal on the window indicating Dick was a member of the police department, but since he'd already started a conversation with us he asked, "Is your daddy a policeman?"

"Oh, no." we told him, "our brother is a policeman."

"What's his name?" we were asked.

"Richard Cain" we both replied, each trying to be the first to get it out.

The nice cop just scratched his head and wandered back to his squad car.

Once there was an incident in the neighborhood involving a stolen car. We heard a car crash into the side of the building, adjacent to the alley. When we looked out the window, the driver had already made good his escape. Dick called the district to report it, but told them he did not want the case. In spite of my hearing only one side of the conversation, I could tell they were surprised at his indifference. Apparently, the cops were rewarded in some way for taking a case of this kind. He wasn't interested, though, couldn't be bothered.

Neighborhoods in a city like Chicago are unlike what I knew from my little hometown in Michigan. They're like cities unto themselves. There's a shopping district, parks, churches, and taverns. When we'd go out to explore, I was surprised some people knew who we were. I thought a big city brought anonymity; not so in the neighborhood, and certainly not if you're Dick Cain's little brother.

We went to a crowded beach one day. Most people didn't go in the water—Lake Michigan is cold, but the beach is warm. I went into the water for ten or fifteen seconds, and then I understood. I was surprised Dick brought his gun to the beach, so he explained to me about a policeman always being on duty. I was impressed. I thought he was very dedicated to his job.

Rosemary was an interesting character in her own right. She seemed almost indifferent to the twins, though she loved them in her own way. She came from a family where love and respect were not among the family values that were taught or practiced. She was obsessed over the appearance of their apartment, though. Years later, when I first heard the term "obsessive-compulsive," I thought immediately of Rosemary. She cleaned constantly and ironed everything, including Dick's underwear. Rosemary drank more coffee than anyone I've ever known, four or five pots a day. She tried to entertain my brother and me and, if she got tired of having us around, she'd put us in a cab to a movie theater downtown, reminding us to tip the cabbie.

Dick took us to the movies once, but he had a hard time sitting through it. It was *The Vikings*, starring Kirk Douglas and Tony Curtis. He left four or five times to make phone calls. At least that's what he told us. I doubt Dick ever sat very long to do anything. Years later, *Chicago Tribune* columnist Jack Mabley told me he thought Dick was a compulsive adventurer and that Dick was never truly happy unless his life was in danger. Clearly, an afternoon at a movie theater with two pre-teen siblings fell short of that standard.

He told us a story that day about raiding a crap game on the South Side. The game was held in an abandoned warehouse and there was apparently a lot of money in play. The cops made a lot of noise coming into the warehouse and the gamblers started to scramble out windows and doors to get away. One of the players was huge, over three hundred pounds, and got stuck in a window trying to make his way to the fire escape. Dick taunted the guy as he scooped up the money left on the floor and stuck his tommy gun in his face. "You dumb bastard," he said, "don't you even know how big you are?" It was a long time after that I realized Dick was mad at the guy because his blocking the window prevented some of the others from escaping, which meant they had to actually arrest them when all they'd really wanted was their money.

Soon it was time for us to return to Michigan. We actually left early due to the unexpected death of a cousin back home. The days and nights in Chicago were indelibly etched in my mind. I treasured the time I was given with Dick and his family. There was, of course, no way to know what a storm lay on the horizon for all of them. It was the next year, 1959, when Dick's life began to change dramatically. He retreated from us, from the Cains, avoiding almost all contact with the Irish side of his family.

CHAPTER

5

As a rookie at the Chicago Police Department, Dick went on uniformed patrol duty but, within a year or so, he had managed his way into the detective bureau. No doubt some money changed hands in the process. The dichotomy of Dick Cain's life was irrevocably set into motion during this time. He made a series of decisions that put him at odds with his family, the police department, the mob, and even himself.

He had been encouraged by Sam Giancana to join the Chicago Police Department, to be their man on the inside. A cop on the Outfit's payroll was not unheard of in the Chicago of the 1950s, but there were never enough of them to suit Sam Giancana, boss of the Chicago mob at the time. Dick was to be one of a very small number that reported directly to him.

Giancana matched Dick's $9,000-a-year city salary, plus bonuses. Dick set out to be the best cop he could be, given the constraints of his commitment to the Outfit. Once he was assigned to the detective bureau, Dick was Giancana's bagman the first week or so of each month, delivering envelopes up and down the chain of command. Captains and above would generally get a personal visit with a very subtle pass of the envelope. Patrolmen, Sergeants, and Lieutenants generally had to come and fetch their share, perhaps at a neighborhood bar. Not everyone wanted this dirty money and if you declined it, that was okay, as long as you kept your mouth shut about others taking it. Corruption was the order of the day, but that's not to say they were all corrupt. Many Chicago cops were, and are, straight, honest cops. The tragedy was that they could do little to stop the corruption that swirled around them.

The amounts paid varied by rank and responsibility, and generally insured a clear line of communication as much as anything. The payments were not intended to protect an Outfit guy from a speeding ticket: if you got stopped for speeding, you were on your own. Rather, the goal was to ensure a certain level of access when a real problem developed. If the Outfit wanted an arrest record lost, they knew whether the guy who had the file was on the take, and they'd call him and say, "You know all that money you've been taking from us for the past five years? Well, now it's time to earn it." If the police were planning a raid on an Outfit operation, they would expect an advance call with time and place.

In the case of non-Outfit operations, like a wire room or a bookie, those guys were on their own and would have to get pretty creative sometimes to protect themselves. One West Side operation rented two apartments in one building, one on the fourth floor, one on the second. In the fourth-floor apartment, they'd installed several phone lines, and surreptitiously run the wires to the second-floor unit. Then they'd installed a burglar alarm in the upper unit, to alert the guys down below in the event of a raid. It actually happened one day that the cops busted into that fourth-floor apartment with a warrant based on over-active telephone records. While they scratched their heads at seeing the place empty, the guys on two scooped up their records and their cash and made good their escape. It took days for the cops to figure out what happened, and by then, of course, the trail was cold.

After Dick delivered the payments in those first few days of the month, he was free to do regular police work. By all accounts, he was a good cop when he was dealing with non-mob-related activities. He made some good busts and built a reputation for being a crack investigator and for being tough on the bad guys, though he had a rather twisted notion of what exactly constituted a bad guy.

When he landed an assignment with the vice squad, he found his home. He was assigned a partner, Gerald Shallow, who had three years experience on the job. They started making waves right away. Whorehouses, gambling dens, pornographers, and abortionists were their primary targets. The press commonly attended big raids; posed photographs ran in all the Chicago papers. Dick cultivated relationships with the press, the closest of which was with Jack Mabley, then with the *Chicago American*. Dick loved seeing his name in the papers; having a picture was icing on the cake. Mabley considered him a good source, but didn't enter the relationship blindly. Early in their time together, Mabley checked Dick out through his FBI sources and got back a clean report.

Mabley told me once about spending an evening with Dick. Dick showed him where the cops in a particular district were collecting their monthly payments. They watched for several hours as detectives and patrolmen alike would walk into a hotel on Ohio Street to pick up the money. Mabley went to the police commissioner with the story and shut the place down, but acknowledged that they likely just moved. I'm still mystified at why Dick would show this to Mabley, except as a ploy to get some of his competition out of the way.

Dick was a showman. He'd carry a Thompson sub-machine gun to break up a floating crap game. He once arrested the operators of a crooked carnival (this was probably where he met Bill Witsman) and filled his trunk with stuffed animals. The next day he picked up Jack Mabley, and they delivered the toys to an orphanage. It was a small gesture, but one that meant a great deal to Mabley. No doubt a calculated move on Dick's part, rather than an example of his generosity, but he made the effort nonetheless.

His relationship with Mabley would be one of the few that endured the coming firestorm. They worked together, shared leads, and helped one another. Mabley gave Dick credit for the stories he was fed, unless he was asked not to. On the flip side though, Dick helped Mabley to achieve some of his goals. Jack was a crusading columnist who hated vice and corruption. He and Dick worked closely in building a case against a crooked judge and eventually got him sent to prison. It was Mabley's finest hour, and he never hesitated to acknowledge Dick's contribution to it. "It was a ball," Mabley told me, and it is from this period that Dick had a series of stranger-than-fiction adventures.

In 1958, at 5:30 on a bitterly cold Chicago morning, Dick and his partner, Gerry Shallow, were about to end their shift when they came across a dead body in an alley in the Loop.

White male, late fifties, medium build, and clearly a homeless person, he probably drank too much, passed out, and froze to death overnight. Dick and Gerry cussed each other for finding this guy, because now they would be required to work three or four hours of overtime filling out the forms, finding and notifying next of kin, supervising transport of the body to the morgue, and so forth. It wouldn't have been so bad if they'd found him at the beginning of their shift, at least then they'd have spent the night indoors.

"There has to be a better way," Shallow whined. "We'll never get off on time, and I've got a court appearance at two o'clock."

It's lost in history just which one of them first offered the suggestion, but they agreed if they could report this guy as a murder victim, then they could turn it over to homicide and let the murder cops deal with the paperwork. That way, they could finish their part in about thirty minutes and still get off work on time. After some deliberation about their options, they concluded they couldn't shoot the guy because someone would surely hear the shot. The clear solution was a knife wound to the chest.

"I'll go get a knife," Dick volunteered. Returning to the squad car, where they always kept a stash of knives that had been confiscated from suspects, he selected a sturdy-looking pocketknife and returned to the alley.

Easy enough, they both thought. Dick opened the knife and plunged it into the man's chest. If the word "sproing" was not yet in our vocabulary on that day, both he and Shallow could have coined it. That's the noise the knife made when it was refused entry into the corpse's frozen chest, frozen so solidly it was virtually impenetrable.

Frustrated but undaunted, Dick removed the man's shoe and used it to hammer the knife into what they hoped would pass as a fatal wound. "You sonofabitch, you've got a lotta nerve dying on my shift," Dick grumbled. The shoe didn't work as well as they'd hoped. Maybe if Dick held the knife and Gerry stomped it with his heel, they might have better luck. By the time they gave up, they might as well have shot the guy, for all of their cursing and yelling woke up more neighbors than a single gunshot ever would have.

Gerry yelled at Dick, "God dammit, Cain, you should have let me shoot the fucker!"

"No, I don't think so," Dick replied. "With our luck the bullet would have bounced off the stiff and taken out one of us instead. That really would have been difficult to explain. ("Sorry chief, we lost a cop tonight, shot by a dead man.")

Feeling defeated, they finally called in to headquarters that they had discovered a body, apparently dead of exposure. They waited for a supervisor, and then they waited for the coroner's hearse, and finally they waited to process the paperwork.

About ten o'clock that morning, while they were filling out forms, they received a phone call from the coroner's office. Did they have any idea about the chipped flesh in the man's chest? They looked at each other and said they had no earthly idea how that could have happened. Shallow suggested, "Maybe he'd been mishandled at the morgue."

It was well past lunchtime when they left the precinct. They met for a drink and, while re-hashing the day's events, concluded even if they had gotten the knife in, the fact the corpse was frozen solid would have prevented his bleeding. Even a civilian would have known the guy was dead long before the knife wound appeared. They had a good laugh over it, though, and called it a day.

Cops don't like not being in control of a situation. Later that same winter, they were serving a search warrant on a suspected drug dealer. A large black woman, Bertha Jackson, was not very cooperative when the police arrived—her dog, Pinky, even less so. Pinky was a German shepherd and fully prepared to eat some cops that night. At gunpoint, Bertha was persuaded to put Pinky in a closet, but that didn't stop Pinky from barking. In fact, it most assuredly made the barking worse. If you've ever heard a German shepherd bark, imagine an agitated German shepherd, locked in a closet.

Trying to ignore the noise, Cain and Shallow conducted a thorough search of the woman's apartment. When the search turned up nothing, Dick sat in a chair across from Bertha and suggested to Bertha she'd better cooperate and tell them where the drugs were hidden, to save herself and her teenage son, who was watching the proceedings nervously. She steadfastly refused, denying any knowledge of drugs in her apartment. Dick believed his information was solid and there must be drugs hidden somewhere.

Now thirty minutes into the search, Dick was certain Pinky had not stopped barking, even to take a breath. The incessant noise emanating from the closet had left him with a headache and a short temper. He finally stood up, threw his hands in the air as he drew his revolver and said to the suspect, "Excuse me, Bertha, while I go shoot that fucking dog." This was intended not as a threat, but as a statement of fact. The dog had just been barking so loudly and so long Dick couldn't stand it any longer.

"Oh, no," she cried, "don't shoot Pinky. I'll tell you where they is, I'll tell you, just don't shoot Pinky." With that, she gave up the secret hiding place, which held about a quarter kilo of heroin. She was arrested, and Pinky was sent to the pound, where he no doubt met with a serious fate.

He made them all wait for Animal Control to get the dog; no way was Pinky getting in his car, even if it was a city-owned car. He was very particular about his own car, too. Dick loved his 1958 Mercury Turnpike Cruiser. It had the biggest engine that could be got in a Mercury, 430 cubic inches and 360 horsepower with a four-barrel carburetor. His car could easily do 120 miles per hour and frequently did. It was a prized possession. Another of his favorites was his Thompson sub-machine gun, a .45 caliber, fully-automatic death machine made popular by the mob in the twenties and the military in World War II. He kept it in the trunk of his car, usually taking it out only for big busts he'd invited the press to attend. He went to retrieve the gun one day and was mortified to see it was gone. The only person who'd recently had access to the trunk was the mechanic who serviced his car.

Dick went to the service station and beat the poor guy silly. He then explained the reason for the beating and offered to give him some more. The mechanic pleaded innocence and before Dick could hit him again, he quickly explained that anyone could have stolen the gun. A design flaw in that model Mercury allowed the trunk to open with a good solid blow to the face of the lock. He demonstrated, with the heel of his hand, how it was done; just a quick pop to the trunk lock, and it opened without so much as a mark to show what had happened. Dick walked away scratching his head and hoping he would never have to confront the thief.

Not long after that, he'd acquired a new Tommy gun and, in February 1959, Dick and his partner arrested a sixty-eight-year-old prostitute named Grace Van Scoyk, using the gun to great effect in scaring the hell out of her. They confiscated more than $100,000 in cash, stored in grocery bags in closets throughout her apartment. This woman had an arrest record dating back to 1915 that included more than fifty arrests for prostitution. Cain and Shallow had developed the case based on information provided to them by the FBI, who suspected her of having been involved in a kidnapping. They provided the police with a list of serial numbers from cash paid out in ransom. It must have taken hours just to count the money, not to mention checking serial numbers on four or five grocery bags full of bills. This proved to be a dead end, and they concluded she had simply accumulated the money from her years of hard work. She was charged with possession of pornographic materials, and her file was turned over to the Internal Revenue Service for possible prosecution on income tax evasion.

She had offered to pay a substantial amount of cash to the two cops if they'd let her walk, but they refused. Not so much because they were such noble cops, but because too many people knew they had been there. This detail didn't stop them, though, from milking the "honest cop" moniker that followed them for a time. She later complained that some $60,000 had disappeared from her safe deposit box and that Dick had taken her key. Her story was that she'd asked for help in finding an attorney. Dick had given her the business card of an attorney and explained that he'd expect a cash payment to represent her, so she gave Dick a key to her safe deposit box so that he could retrieve the necessary retainer on her behalf. The charges were impossible to verify, though, and the whole matter was eventually dropped.

One of the leads they picked up from Grace Van Scoyk had to do with the Cloverbar at 172 North Clark Street, for some time a well-known hangout for prostitutes in Chicago's Loop. When Dick and Gerry Shallow led a raid that closed it, the bar's liquor license was revoked. During their trial the owners produced a photo of Dick with one of their prostitutes, claiming he was in civilian clothes and clearly going beyond the scope of his job. Dick maintained the photo had been altered to remove his partner, who had been with him, and they were indeed on official business at the time and, of course they were in civilian clothes, that's the way detectives dress. No negative could be produced to disprove his suggestion, so nobody pursued charges.

After a string of flashy raids like the Cloverbar, Dick and Gerry were reassigned from the Sex Bureau in mid-1959 because they were shaking up vice in the Loop and had received many threats, some even from inside the department.

Many of his arrests were big news in Chicago. Considering Chicago takes its mob stories with a grain of salt, he was able to disassociate himself from the mob in his official role. Inside the department they seemed to know Dick Cain was Sam Giancana's bagman. On the outside, and in the press, he was respected for his aggressive police work.

Dick always carried a standard police-issue snub-nosed .38. Shallow preferred a miniature cannon known as a .357 magnum. Shallow frequently teased Dick about the peashooter he carried. Once they were dispatched to "un-pole" a pole sitter who refused to come down. Climbing a flagpole and staying there was a popular form of protest in those days and sometimes included a platform that was attached to the top of the pole, providing the protester with a more comfortable place to sit for a long period. Dick tried for twenty minutes to reason with the guy to just come down. When that failed, Shallow drew his weapon, took aim, and said, "Come on down here you son of a bitch, or I'll blow your head off." Not wanting to challenge the officer's respect for the law, the pole sitter returned to earth.

In a more serious lesson about the quality of heavy artillery, the duo had arranged to arrest one Harry Figel, a known pervert who had molested several children and corrupted numerous older boys and young men, drawing them into a life of crime. Figel would attempt to get unsuspecting men to participate in a homosexual act with members of his gang and then would take on the role of a shocked uncle to the boy. He would confront the target and express outrage and threaten to beat them bloody. Eventually, he would get around to claiming he would be mollified if the guy would give him a sum of money. Frequently, he would beat them up anyway. Figel was considered by many who knew him to be both sadistic and manipulative.

Responding to a tip from a concerned citizen, Dick had arrested a member of Figel's gang and gotten him to cooperate. The gang member was to identify Dick to Figel as a target. Figel would play the role of an enraged uncle and demand to be paid not to injure Dick. They had agreed to meet early on a Sunday morning behind the old Greyhound bus terminal in the Loop to discuss the matter. In the alley off Lake Street, between Dearborn and Clark, Dick approached Harry Figel, trying to seem frightened.

When Figel had spoken the incriminating words, Dick produced a badge and announced he was under arrest. Figel objected and produced a small automatic pistol, which he began shooting off with abandon. Dick dove for cover and returned fire, wondering where his partner was. Exposing himself for only brief seconds to shoot, Dick was certain he had hit Figel at least once, but couldn't help but notice he was still returning fire. All of a sudden, he heard his tardy partner across the alley. Shallow confirmed Dick had indeed shot Figel three times and laughed out loud at his inability to stop anything with those candy-assed bullets.

That said, Shallow turned on Figel and, after taking careful aim, blew his head off with one shot. He turned to Dick and said, "That, Mr. Cain, is how you fight crime."

That's how Dick told the story.

According to the official record Figel's injuries included four gunshot wounds: "1 Thru & thru lower right forearm; 1 entrance upper left back, exiting left side of neck; 1 entrance upper left back exiting center of chest; 1 gunshot wound upper left side of skull (no exit)."

They were put on restricted duty after the shooting, which was a routine procedure following an officer-involved shooting that resulted in the death of a civilian. Allegations abounded, especially from Figel's family, that he was murdered, that Cain and Shallow had set him up for a hit. The original meeting place, they said, was miles away from that alley. Clearly, they alleged, he had been taken there to be killed. Four days after the Figel shooting the acting chief of detectives wrote to the commissioner of police requesting that detectives Cain and Shallow be considered for the Mayor's Youth Award. Here's what he said:

> During the course of numerous investigations over a long period of time in which homosexuals were involved from conversation with these people it became apparent that they themselves were being victimized. The name of the individual involved was Harry Figel who was the ringleader of a group of young men who plied on the weaknesses & immoral characteristics of homosexuals by extorting money from them.
>
> Detectives Richard Cain and Gerald Shallow were assigned to direct their activities towards Figel and his gang. After a week of background investigation, the investigating officers had determined that Harry Figel had an extensive criminal record for robbery, con-game, extortion and contributing to the delinquency. He had served sentences to Joliet penitentiary, House of Corrections and the New York penitentiary. He was known among his associates as a ruthless sadist, who enjoyed inflicting pain upon both his victims and his young hustlers. He was alleged to have from 15 to 20 fruit hustlers working for him in the Loop area, Wilson-Broadway area and South Side areas. His method of operation

was for one of his gang to make contact with a homosexual and Figel was notified as to where the gang-member and the homosexual would be at a given time. Figel would then appear and claim to be either a police officer or the uncle of the young gang-member. He would then extort money or jewelry from the homosexual or assault and rob him and then later split the proceeds with the gang member or "hustler."

An immediate canvass of establishments suspected to be frequented by Figel and his associates was begun by the investigators. At the Greyhound Bus station, 64 W. Randolph street, one of the young "hustlers" was located and kept under surveillance for a period of four days and then the officers identified themselves to him and after assuring him that his identity would be kept confidential because of the expressed fear the young man had of Figel, his cooperation was obtained to establish a contact with Figel.

Detective Cain was to pose as a homosexual and by pre-arrangement with the young gang-member at 2:00 A.M. on March 22, '59 Detective Cain was waiting at a public phone booth in the Greyhound Bus depot. The informant was to contact Figel and then call Detective Cain who was supposed to be a homosexual "roped" in by the informant. If at the time of the phone call, Figel was with the informant he would cue Detective Cain by calling him "Baby." At about 2:05 A.M. the phone rang and when Cain answered the informant on the other end of the line said, "Is that you, BABY?" Detective Cain answered in the affirmative and an appointment was made to meet at the Lake street entrance to the Bus station at 5:15 A.M. supposedly for Detective Cain and the "hustler" to meet to go to a hotel together. By the use of the word "baby," Cain of course knew that Harry Figel would be there, supposedly unexpected by Cain.

At 5:15 A.M. Detective Cain was standing in the pre-arranged spot while his partner, Detective Shallow, maintained surveillance from an advantageous position across the street. At about 5:20 A.M. Harry Figel came up to Detective Cain, poked a finger into Cain's chest and said, "you're the son of a bitch that's been fooling around with my nephew John, I want to talk to you!" With that he took Detective Cain by the arm and walked him around the corner, through a parking lot and into the alley in the rear of 64 W. Randolph St. Detective Shallow moved from his vantage point and followed. In the alley, Figel then said, "Now I'm going to take care of you" and drew back his arm in a striking position. Detective Cain protested and asked if this whole thing couldn't be "straightened out." Figel then answered, "well, we can straighten it out right now for one hundred dollars." Detective Cain then counted out $100 in marked money and held it out towards Figel. As Figel reached for the money, Cain also displayed his star, announcing his office and proclaiming Figel under arrest. Figel then looked and saw Detective Shallow hurrying towards them and with that he quickly stepped back, drew a pistol from his pocket and fired twice at both Cain and Shallow. After this overt display of viciousness, the Detectives then withdrew their pistols from their holsters and returned the fire. Figel bolted and ran down the alley while the officers continued firing, Figel then turned around raised his pistol again, pointed at the officers and fell to the ground fatally wounded. The gun used by Figel was .25 cal Colt automatic. He was pronounced dead on arrival at St. Luke's hospital.

The actions of the two investigators truly displays exemplary action and bravery. Through their actions and complete thoroughness, they brought to a conclusion the sadistic career of a malicious felon who victimized people whose morals were not normal and used this condition to threaten and force them to pay him money. A "racket" that he had been successfully conducting for quite some time. In View of these facts, it is therefore respectfully requested, if the Commissioner of Police so approves, that the actions of Detective Richard Cain and Gerald Shallow, be brought to the attention of the Committee for consideration of an award from the Mayor's Youth Foundation and as a department gesture in recognition of praiseworthy duty they be given a Creditable Mention.

The family threatened a lawsuit. The FBI investigated.

Figel's lawyer Edward L. Kelly, produced a witness, Thomas Francis O'Donnell, who claimed to have certain knowledge Figel had been murdered. O'Donnell's story was that he had been with Figel earlier that night and that he and Figel had been standing on the corner of Sixty-third and Ashland when a "1957 Ford, central detective bureau car" pulled up with three men in it. He identified the men as Dick, Gerry Shallow, and Sergeant Thomas Mulvey, their boss from the Sex Bureau.

On August 26, Kelly wrote the following letter to United States Attorney Robert Tieken on the matter:

Dear Mr. Tieken:

Pursuant to your telephone conversation of August 17th with Mr. Rosenberg, I am incorporating most of my notes and investigation in this letter to you.

On March 22, 1959 at 5:15 A.M. Harry Figel was shot and killed by
Chicago police officers Richard Cain and Gerald Shallow. I attended the
inquest at the County morgue on March 30, representing the Figel
family. I informed Coroner McCarron, the Cook County Coroner, who
conducted the inquest, that I had a witness that saw Cain and Shallow at
63rd and Ashland at 4:30 A.M. the same morning that Harry Figel
ended up dead downtown. The Coroner immediately began berating me
and attempting to conceal the facts of Figel's death. I felt as though I was
on trial myself.

Figel was killed in a "T" alley in back of the Greyhound Bus Station
at 64 West Randolph Street. Figel actually was in the company of
Thomas O'Donnell of 3520 West 59th Street . . . until 4:30 A.M. at 63rd
and Ashland. O'Donnell and Figel were drinking heavily and were intox-
icated. Most of their drinking was done in a tavern east of Ashland
Avenue on the North side of 63rd Street. They went into a tavern West
of Ashland on the North side of the street next to Webbers Restaurant,
and purchased a bottle at about 4:00 A.M. O'Donnell said that a woman
named Lill waited on him. I talked to Lill myself. First she said that she
was on duty that evening but that she did not wait on O'Donnell and
Figel. I brought O'Donnell back to this tavern later and she stated at that
time that she didn't know O'Donnell or Figel and that she did not work
on the evening in question. O'Donnell told me that after they finished
consuming the bottle they stood on the corner of 63rd and Ashland.
O'Donnell saw a 1957 Ford, central detective bureau car pull up with
three men it. He can almost positively identify Cain and Shallow as being
two of the men. He positively identifies Sgt. Thomas Mulvey of the sex
bureau as being there.

Figel was beaten and threatened by two unidentified police officers
a week before his demise. He never had an opportunity to inform me of
this personally although he told me on two separate occasions that the
police were extorting portions of his ill-gotten gains from him. Figel told
one of his accomplices that he was beaten and he showed them the
bruises, two of them were O'Donnell and Jerry Wavra who used to live
at the Norwood Hotel at 6400 Normal Avenue. I don't know Wavra's
address however I can obtain him for you. Helmut Fiebieger, . . . was
with Figel and O'Donnell at 2:30 A.M. He seems to have informed the
police as to Figel's whereabouts. Fiebieger was arrested by Cain and
Shallow about two months before Figel was killed. He was arrested
along with Joseph Hagen . . . three weeks before the killing and seems
to have gotten quite friendly with Sgt. Mulvey. Information has reached

me that Fiebieger received five hundred dollars to keep his mouth closed about the Figel incident. Mulvey was under the impression that Harry was earning about one thousand dollars a day, extorting money from homosexuals.

Harry Figel had not been in Chicago's loop for about two years, he stated to me that he would never go into the loop because he was fearful of arrest. Cain and Shallow testified at the inquest that an unnamed informant had made a date for Harry to come downtown at 5:00 A.M., that they met him and gave him marked money. He pulled out a pistol and started shooting, and that they shot in self defense. The transcript at the inquest seems to coincide for the most part with my court reporter's notes; however there are I think, very important discrepancies . . .

The pistol Harry Figel allegedly carried was a twenty-five-caliber Colt automatic, No. 15271. To my knowledge and I knew Harry Figel for approximately six months, he never carried a gun. Harry Figel not only did not carry a gun but from my knowledge of his operations he also told all the members of his gang never to carry a gun. I believe that if you open an investigation of this matter Figel's gang members will also give you this information. Harry Figel had a long record of arrest, however not for carrying guns or cases where guns were used. Figel told me a month before he was killed that the police were shaking him down and that they told him to pay up or leave town. Figel actually left town for a period of time and went to Detroit, Michigan, to give the police a chance to take their mind off of him.

After the first inquest hearing, a reporter from the Chicago Daily News named Jack Lavin telephoned me and asked if I would object to having Thomas O'Donnell take a lie detector test. I agreed, and the test was given on March 31, 1959 at the office of L. Keeler . . . The test was administered by Mr. Harrellson and another man. I cautioned Mr. Harrellson before the test began against asking questions outside the scope of interest in the Figel matter. Mr. Harrellson agreed to this. The test results were negative, according to Harrellson. Harrellson said that O'Donnell could not have been with Figel the evening prior to the shooting or a few hours before the shooting. Harrellson stated that O'Donnell had "a guilty reaction" when he had replied that the had not committed a murder. With the results given me by Mr. Harrellson I decided that the prudent thing for me was to withdraw from the matter.

I apologized to the police officers personally and telephoned Sgt. Thomas Mulvey and made a date to meet him at police headquarters. Over coffee, we, Sgt. Mulvey and myself, in a very friendly manner discussed the probability that Thomas O'Donnell was a liar. I questioned Sgt. Mulvey if he had traced the pistol that Harry Figel supposedly had. Sgt. Mulvey replied that he had checked it to a burglary on the north side of Chicago. Sgt. Mulvey never said that it had been recovered. I received the very distinct and strong impression that Sgt. Mulvey and the other police officers were very tense, I would even say nervous, and that they were all covering for each other.

At the second inquest, Sgt. Mulvey told the coroner that he had traced the pistol to a hardware store in St. Louis, Missouri, in 1909 and the trail had ended there. The coroner's second hearing developed into a whitewashing session and a verdict of justifiable homicide was returned.

Attorney Edward Rosenberg and myself took O'Donnell to the office of Marvin Ziporyn, M.D. . . . O'Donnell was placed under sodium amytal, and was then questioned concerning the evening and early morning before Harry Figel was shot. The answers O'Donnell gave are available for your use on magnetic tape. O'Donnell, in the opinion of the doctor, Mr. Rosenberg and myself, told the truth about being with Harry Figel the night before and the early morning before Harry Figel was shot and of seeing the police car. Harry Figel was arrested with William Oswald . . . about a month before he was shot. They were taken to the Central Sex Bureau and slapped around by Sgt. Mulvey. Frank Hackel was the arresting officer, he is from the 15th police district at 61st and Racine Street.

At three thirty Sunday afternoon, March 22, 1959 Cain and Shallow went to Webbers Restaurant at 63rd and Ashland Avenue in search of Thomas O'Donnell. Because of this obvious attempt to get O'Donnell I hid him in my basement until after the second inquest. Cain's testimony at the inquest was absolutely fantastic. Cain said that he gave Harry Figel some marked money; that Figel pulled out a pistol and shot at Cain, at a close range, without hitting Cain, and then Cain shot and killed Harry Figel. Figel was taken, after the shooting to St. Luke's Hospital and was dead on arrival.

The coroner's physician Doctor Wagoner performed a post-mortem on Harry Figel. Doctor Wagoner found that Figel was shot directly through the top of his head, in the back and left shoulder, and twice directly in the back. The bullet what went in through the top of Harry Figel's head came out his mouth. How anyone was able to stand above Harry Figel and shoot in the top of his skull is beyond me unless of course Figel was on his knees begging for mercy, as he had done the time before when he was pistol-whipped by two police officers.

Shallow changed his testimony while testifying at the inquest. Rather than relate all of the discrepancies, I suppose I have to have the transcript prepared by Mr. Wolfson and the official transcript does not reflect what we were saying.

Richard Cain gave his address as 1533 West 77th Street, Chicago when he lived actually at the Midwest Hotel, 6. N. Hamlin St., Chicago. He was born in Owosso, Michigan on October 4, 1924. He is married to a former miss Frazier who now lives at 3548 W. Congress St. He previously lived at 2224 West 22nd Terrace, Miami, Florida. He was some sort of police officer in Florida and seems to have made a very hasty departure. My contact tells me that he was in on the Dade County gambling operations. From 1942 to 1948 he was in the U.S. Army Intelligence and was discharged as a warrant officer. His mother Lydia still lives at 1533 West 77th Street and Mrs. Vincenza Scully, 7658 South Laflin Street appears to be his grandmother. Cain appeared in articles in the Chicago Daily News on April 1, 1959, April 10, 1959 . . .

Cain either owns interest in or owns the Accurate Laboratories at 2400 W. Madison St. Cain is also a friend of Mr. Harrellson of the Keeler Laboratories, the gentleman who gave O'Donnell the test. From 1949 to 1953 Cain was the chief special agent of the United Parcel Service in Chicago. According to my informant Cain is or was under top security investigation by the Chicago Police Department because he had access to a set of Brinks' keys for eight days, it is believed that the keys were duplicated and were later used in a series of Brinks robberies in the Chicago area.

The pistol that Harry Figel supposedly had I traced to J.T.W. Babcock . . . Evanston. Mr. Babcock gave the pistol to Mrs. Willard Herzberg, she gave it to her husband. Mr. Herzberg owns the Monetary Hill bindery, . . . I discovered this lead from a police department registration card which showed that Babcock had the pistol repaired at Marshall Fields Department store in 1945. The pistol was burglarized from Herzberg's office on March 15, 1959, approximately one week before Harry Figel was killed. Herzberg reported the theft of the pistol to the Sheffield Avenue precinct but did not have a record of its number. Hertzberg never gave the police the pistol number, so that the burglar, whoever he was and I would be the only person who knew that the pistol in question was actually taken in a burglary as Sgt. Mulvey informed me but did not inform the coroner.

Mr. Hertzberg told me the pistol would not fire because the slide would not move because the barrel was split. When I examined the pistol at the inquest it was in firing order.

Richard Cain purchased a .25 caliber from Scaramuzzo and Sons, Gunsmiths, 801 South Halstead Street, about a week before the killing. The gun was a .25 caliber Colt automatic. Cain had it shipped to Mr. Frank Kane in a Chicago suburb, I believe Park Forest, by United Parcel Service. Cain then telephoned his brother-in-law (I believe his name is Frazier) who works for United Parcel Service, Cain advised his brother-in-law that he would pick up the package. Cain's brother-in-law became suspicious and unwrapped the package and copied down the serial number of the pistol. The brother-in-law contacted me through another party to find out the number that was on the pistol, I told the other party and he told the brother-in-law and then I received word that it was not the same gun. For numerous reasons this information to me was obviously false and I believe the guns were one and the same.

Cain's brother-in-law informed the Chicago police about the keys to the Brinks safes, and it is safe to assume about the pistol. The investigation into Cain's activities was conducted by Captain Patrick Deeley who was then chief of Detectives, it was common knowledge among the police that Cain was Deeley's protégé.

Cain and Shallow picked up Jerry Wavra about a month after Harry Figel was killed and took Wavra to the same place where Figel was shot and told Wavra if he didn't leave town he would receive the same thing that Figel got. Wavra states that Cain and Shallow beat him up at that time.

I do not know Cain's brother-in-law, nor would I want the source of my information disclosed so this matter will have be handled rather discreetly. For obvious reasons I have made no attempt to examine the records of Scaramuzzo and Sons or to subpoena Cain's brother-in-law.

Cain, Shallow, Sgt. Mulvey and Captain Deeley have all been removed form the Central Detective bureau since this event, and since the reported event at about the same time that Figel was shot that a business man was extorted for thirty thousand dollars by the police during a sex offense investigation. Cain and Shallow have since sued me for slander (Superior Court of Cook County Case No. 59 S 2736) for my accusations at the inquest.

My informant advised me that Cain's expenses greatly exceed his income, Cain supports his present wife, his former wife, and children, rents at a hotel and maintains two apartments. My informant also advised me that Cain appears to be engaged in various activities of prostitution and extortion.

I realize this a rather sketchy outline of my investigation and that at first glance you would possibly think that I need some outside help in my slander suit; this is not only not necessary but would be much too late to do my civil action any good. As a matter of law I believe that I have a legal defense to this suit, which of course you can check.

If after your examination of this letter you would like to discuss this matter with me personally or have me discuss it with any of your representatives I will gladly do so. I believe I can also produce a few witnesses that may be of great interest to your office concerning financial activities of the Chicago Police Department Sex Bureau.

Very Truly Yours

Edward L. Kelly

Kelly was most assuredly a frustrated man. Practicing law by this time for less than a year, he appears to have been trying to do the right thing. He knew that his clients were scum, but it's not a lawyer's job to judge his clients. A close review of the file would tend to make one feel he may have been right, this may have happened just the way he said it did. Unfortunately for him, nobody cared. Not the cops, not the FBI, not the U.S. Attorney's office. The newspaper cared for a while, until they put Kelly's star witness on the lie-box, then they lost interest too. Figel was thirty-seven years old when he died, he had been arrested at least fourteen times, had spent time in Sing Sing, the Cook County Jail, and the Illinois State Penitentiary at Joliet, mostly for robbery. There just wasn't much sympathy for the loss of Harry Figel.

Kelly's letter was dated August 26, 1959. On September 3, 1959 the U.S. Attorney referred it to the FBI and requested a preliminary investigation. The FBI sat on it for a couple of hours before recommending that the matter be dropped "in view of the slander suit filed by Detectives Cain and Shallow in the amount of $775,000 against Attorney Kelly."

As an aside, there is also a reference in the file indicating that the House Select Committee on Assassinations had copied it in 1978 for review of Richard Cain in regard to the Kennedy assassination. It must have left them all scratching their heads.

At the request of Jack Lavin, the Pulitzer Prize–winning reporter from the *Chicago Daily News*, O'Donnell was given a lie detector test at the Keeler Institute. He failed on no less than twelve questions. The polygraph operator branded the "witness" a cop-hater who fabricated his story to get the cops in trouble.

Several weeks later, the incident was dropped. The family, through their lawyer, apologized to Dick and his partner, the FBI cleared them of any wrongdoing, and the whole issue was over, technically. In later years, though, whenever someone wanted to write something negative about Dick, they always wrote about that time in 1959 when he killed a man under mysterious circumstances and was accused of murdering him. It seemed to give credence to the things being written, though he had been cleared and actually nominated for a commendation for the Figel shooting.

In 1959, political correctness was two words rarely linked in a single sentence so, looking beyond the obvious language issues common in those days, like the reference to "fruits" and the presumption that homosexuals are people of "low moral character," it's clear that Dick's superiors at the police department approved of the outcome of this investigation. Harry Figel was certainly mourned by his family, and rightly so, but his death doesn't exactly evoke a sense of moral outrage. It was what the cops call a righteous shooting, but it annoyed Dick that this event would dog him for the rest of his life.

Dick was always conscious of the PR value of certain types of arrests. While with the vice detail, he raided hundreds of houses of prostitution and often did it with a reporter by his side. Dick's notes reveal an interesting trail of evidence in the quest to control behavior in the Windy City. Hattie was a hooker who lived at 6016 Champlain; when you called her, you'd say that Andy the truck driver gave you her number, or "a lawyer friend of yours." Gertrude had a massage parlor called, curiously enough, Gertrude's Health Studio. She provided "residential service" to the major hotels. If you went into the studio, you would ask for a massage, "then ask for extra treatment, like before when Ramona or 'crippled Betty' took care of you." If you wanted sex with a working girl in the Loop, you would be a "friend of Johnnie's"; or Milton sent you, from the Sherman House; or you were a "friend of Ellen from Detroit." If "Big Mike" sent you, you were okay.

He had pages and pages of names and numbers and codes. Grace, Dixie, Mitzie, Bessie, Boots, and Fran, and even Delight. He'd call to see who they'd been doing lately. He didn't really care about arresting them, though he sometimes did, just to make sure everyone understood who was in charge. He saw them as fonts of knowledge; the things they could tell him could be invaluable later on. He kept his notes, and after he died his mother kept them, eventually to be passed to me. They don't include any narrative, but they tell a story just the same. Names and numbers and codes.

Another side of Dick's life as a vice cop is that he had a close relationship with an unusual cross section of humanity. He had become quite close to a madam from the North Side who regularly shared information with the police and the FBI. Their interest was not in the legality of her lifestyle, but rather in her impressive customer list of politicians and business leaders. She shared it with them in return for a certain amount of protection. Each year at Thanksgiving, she hosted a dinner for her friends in the FBI and the Vice Squad. The hookers were all dressed as waitresses and served the meal to their guests.

Dick called Jack Mabley one year and invited him to this dinner. They went to an apartment in the Loop and were greeted by a group of beautiful women Dick knew to be prostitutes, but who were clearly not interested in working on this day. When they entered the apartment, Dick introduced Jack to the women and to the two FBI agents who had arrived earlier. The agents were paranoid at Mabley's presence and angry with Dick for bringing a reporter to such an event until Dick assured them he wasn't there to write a story. Mabley was a stand-up guy and he never did write about that dinner until some time after Dick's death. He was quite clear, though, about the fact that both his wife and his employer were aware of his presence, his wife even held up dinner for him that night; so he had two turkey dinners.

Shortly after Dick was pulled from the Sex Bureau, a request came from the U.S. Attorney's Office for some investigatory help. Dick was available and was assigned to help young Assistant U.S. Attorney Richard B. Ogilvie with an income tax case against former mob boss Anthony "Tony Batters" Accardo. Cain and Ogilvie hit it off right away. They seemed to have compatible goals and Ogilvie was quickly impressed by the results of this aggressive young cop's work. From Ogilvie's perspective, Dick was tough, assertive, and clearly had a solid network of informants. Maybe he rode a little close to the edge, but that's how you get things done in this business. What he saw were results, and ultimately that was all Ogilvie was after.

What he didn't see was the culmination of years of deceit beginning to pay off for Sam Giancana. Ogilvie was amazed at the amount of information Dick was able to "dig up" on Accardo. He was impressed with the network of contacts Cain had developed in just a few short years on the police force. The part Ogilvie didn't figure out, until many years later, was that Dick's primary source was none other than Sam Giancana. The case against Accardo for income tax evasion was solid and actually resulted in a conviction, though it was overturned on appeal.

Dick's job, from Ogilvie's perspective, was to get details about Accardo's activities that would help to support a conviction. From Giancana's perspective, Dick's job was to provide enough information to convince Ogilvie that he was a crack investigator and along the way to introduce a couple of flaws in the case to ensure that it would be overturned. Nobody expected Accardo would simply beat the rap, but they had the foresight to look down the road.

Before the case could be retried, three of their most important witnesses were murdered. Dick had fed information to Ogilvie that was intended to throw him off track, without jeopardizing his own tenuous position. His value to the Outfit was in directing them to the witnesses and eventually to the jurors involved in the case.

Working with Ogilvie represented an important step for Dick. It gave him a tremendous amount of credibility on the force and opened the door to countless new and valuable contacts. Even though he was known to be Giancana's bagman, the reality was that the Chicago Police Department of that time didn't necessarily see that as a negative. After all, he was the man spreading the money around inside the department.

In an interesting twist of fate, the Accardo case was one the U.S. Attorney's Office was working on very closely with the FBI. One of the lead agents representing the Bureau was Bill Roemer. In a nearly unprecedented breach of bureau procedure, Roemer, with the blessing of his superiors, had chosen to share with Ogilvie the existence of a listening device the FBI had installed at Tony Accardo's headquarters. In those days the FBI didn't share anything with anybody, not even the Justice Department. They made an exception with Ogilvie because everyone thought him to be above reproach, and there was information coming at him from the bug, so he had to know what was valid for use at trial and what was not.

To his credit, it appears that Ogilvie chose not to share that tidbit with his own investigator, Dick Cain. To do so would have undermined what was fast becoming the Bureau's best tool against the mob in Chicago, a tool they relied on for many years beyond 1959.

In the Accardo case, the bug played a particularly significant role. The transcripts from the bug clearly show how Accardo and his top guys strategized about how to fix the trial. They acquired a copy of the jury pool, most likely from Dick, and studied it intently for any obvious signs of a friend. They'd pass the list around the room and ask if anyone recognized a name on the list. One of the guys recognized an address as being near his cousin's gas station. If the juror was a customer, he'd have his cousin approach her.

Eventually, they found a couple of friends in the pool, making it likely at least one of them would be selected to sit on the jury. What they didn't know, couldn't have known, was that the FBI was listening to their conversations. Being careful not to compromise the bug, Roemer explained the situation to Ogilvie. It was now important that this information be shared at a higher level, but with extreme care. Roemer obtained the approval of his bosses to delicately explain this predicament to Judge Julius Hoffman, who was hearing the case against Accardo.

On the day jury selection was to begin, Judge Hoffman announced it was necessary to change the jury pool due to some administrative screw up in the clerk's office. They were presented with a new pool and, of course, no time to "work" it. Accardo lost his edge, but had no clue as to why the change was made.

Later, Richard Ogilvie would base his judgement of Dick Cain on his work on this case. Dick had a sense that Ogilvie was a man with a future and went out of his way to maintain contact with Ogilvie in the coming years.

In January 1960, Dick and Gerry Shallow took a leave of absence from the Chicago PD, ostensibly to take a vacation. They had been under a lot of heat in recent months with the Figel shooting and a string of major vice raids. They told their superiors they needed a break.

In reality they had accepted a contract offer from Paul Newey, chief investigator for Illinois State's Attorney Ben Adamowski, to spy on Mayor Richard Daley's commissioner of investigations, Irwin Cohen, who Dick would later refer to as Mayor Daley's bagman.

Many people in the state's attorney's office (Adamowski was a Republican) were suspicious of why Daley (a Democrat) felt a need for an investigator who answered only to him. Since he was not a member of the police department, Cohen didn't have arrest powers; his function was intelligence gathering, generally aimed at political rivals of the mayor. He was paid a salary of $20,000 per year, plus an operating budget of $100,000. Both Cohen and Daley had refused numerous attempts to force them to reveal how this money was spent. In those days a mayor like Richard Daley could get by with refusing such information, and he did.

The state's attorney's office wanted to know what Cohen was up to and whether any laws were being broken. Also, Adamowski had reason to believe the Democratic machine would use Cohen to undermine his political position. So they hired Dick Cain to spy on the spy, and he rented an office across the hall from Cohen, indicating on the lease that he would run a private investigations firm.

He and Paul Newey had developed a code for contacting one another that revealed an interesting bond they shared. It seems that Newey's wife originally hailed from Owosso, Michigan. When Dick called Newey's office, he would identify himself as Charlie Owosso, and likewise, when Newey called him he would use the same code.

After just a week or so with his equipment in place, they installed a camera in the transom of Dick's office, aimed at the door to Cohen's office, to photograph everyone who came and went. Someone spotted the camera almost immediately. The Chicago PD was called in to conduct a thorough investigation. They found the telephone equipment had been tampered with and evidence that Dick had attempted to gain access to the equipment room. Given Dick's well-known talent for installing wiretaps, it didn't take a rocket scientist to link Dick Cain to all this paraphernalia. When confronted, Dick was quick to deny, but was troubled by the realization that when his leave of absence was up, he would have to return to Mayor Daley's police force and an almost certain indictment.

Following an investigation that lasted nearly four months, it was agreed Gerry Shallow would give up the story, and Cain would take the fall. Shallow cooperated in the investigation and kept his job with the police department, and Dick Cain resigned, with the agreement that neither he nor Shallow would be indicted. Adamowski continued to deny the allegations of his involvement, but no one really listened. Paul Newey later confirmed this version of the story to me.

Several weeks after his resignation, with a police department hit squad after him, Dick called Newey, who still maintained publicly he had not hired Dick. Frightened and feeling helpless, Dick explained there had already been two attempts on his life and he needed help in dealing with this threat.

Newey met him early the next morning at a motel where he was holed up and handed over fifteen hundred dollars in cash with the admonition Dick should leave Chicago for a time and see how things might cool down. Newey tried to intercede with the police department, but was unsurprisingly stonewalled.

During this period of exile, Dick returned to the Cain family farm in Owosso, Michigan. Because of the time he had spent at the farm in his youth, he had a very close relationship with his paternal grandmother. Margaret Cain loved Richard and would have faced his enemies herself if she could have. Dick and Gerry Shallow spent a couple of weeks at the farm, waiting for an all clear from "Charlie Owosso."

It was in Owosso that Dick's double life took on a bizarre twist. At the farm, Dick was an Irishman as green as the Emerald Isles. There was no talk of Italian heritage and no mention of *omerta*. There was "Danny Boy" and "Galway Bay." He made the transition as smoothly as a native son, singing for his beloved grandmother at her command, singing with a voice every Irishman dreams of. Had any of his "paisans" seen him in Owosso, they would not have believed their eyes.

She had heard some of the stories about his life in Chicago, but believed none of it. She was once visited by a pair of FBI agents seeking background information about Dick, and assumed their goal could only be to hurt him, so she not only refused to help them, she ordered them off her property.

Dick always tried to cultivate relationships that he thought would be of long-term benefit. The FBI was one of the organizations he thought might help, but he didn't know what they knew about him. In March 1960, one of their bugs, most likely Little Al at Celano's Tailor Shop, overheard the following conversation between Frankie Ferraro and Sam Giancana: "Tonight Mabley, the newspaper guy, and two coppers go boom boom at Jean's Log Cabin." It was assumed that "boom boom" meant they were all going to be killed. Ferraro went on to say that Sam should advise Frank Pape, a police captain in the central district, to "keep the heat down," meaning he wanted the cops to make themselves scarce. In an FBI memorandum from Alex Rosen, deputy director for investigations, to D. J. Parsons, deputy director for domestic intelligence, it was stated that

"SAC Lopez [special agent in charge of the Chicago office of the FBI] rec-
ommends that we call the editor of the *Chicago Daily News* [the paper
Mabley wrote for at the time], one Collins . . . and without evaluating the
information, advise him that we have received information through a
source that the people in Lyons and Cicero apparently know that Mabley
will be out there tonight. Lopez stated if anything should happen to
Mabley and we are sitting on this information, he would feel it was our
responsibility to advise the *Chicago Daily News* of it beforehand just to
alert them."

They acknowledged that Dick and his partner, Gerry Shallow, were the
two coppers in question. It was well known that Dick frequently took
Mabley to some of the seedier places around Chicago to give him a taste
of the world of vice.

Rosen, acting as the conscience of the FBI, went on to say, "I do not
agree with Lopez. I see no obligation on the part of the Bureau to advise
the newspaper concerning the activities of one of its employees and I do
not feel that we can imply that some harm is intended for Mabley, because
we would be reading this into the language when actually no statement has
been made that harm is to be brought to Mabley or anyone else. If you
approve I will advise Lopez that we feel he should not take any further
action, except to remain alert to developments." A hand-written note on
the memo indicates that Parsons did approve and Lopez had been advised.

"Tonight Mabley and two coppers go boom boom at Jean's Log
Cabin." If you think about it, there's no implied threat there, and who
could blame the FBI for putting the existence of Little Al ahead of the lives
of three human beings? Little Al was important. Fortunately, nobody actually went boom boom that night but, rest assured that if they had, the
memo quoted above would have been shredded quicker than you can say
Hoover's FBI.

Some of Dick's troubles during this time had been triggered by allegations from his wife, Rosemary, that he had come home with large amounts
of cash. Rosemary called Dick's boss at the police department and later
granted an interview with a newspaper reporter, who naturally loved the
story. She later admitted the charges were untrue, but she had inflicted
irreparable harm to Dick and to his relationships in the department.
Nobody really believed her when she recanted. It was simply assumed that
she had been convinced that her health was at risk. At one point she was

interviewed by a police detective and, two days later, was assaulted outside her home by two men who suggested she "not talk so much." Dick apparently wasn't involved in the assault, but it certainly originated with his "colleagues." He and Rosemary were separated more often than not and frequently fought when they were together. Her statements to the police were probably true, but were ultimately motivated by a desire to hurt Dick and not out of any sense of moral outrage, a circumstance that was pretty obvious to everyone involved.

Jack Mabley counseled Dick on the importance of keeping an intact family and suggested that Dick should try to reconcile with Rosemary, if only for the sake of their twin daughters, Kimberly and Karla. Jack helped Dick find a house to rent in suburban Glenview, telling them both the suburbs would help them to behave more like a family.

It must have been near the middle of January 1959 when a long black limousine made a midnight appearance in front of Dick Cain's Glenview, Illinois, home. Six men emerged from the car and disappeared into the garage. The limo sped off as unobtrusively as it had arrived, under cover of darkness.

It was time for Glenview to work its charm on the six men from the limo. They stayed in the garage, though, and ate their meals there, except for one. One of the men was invited to the kitchen for meals. It was done out of respect for the man and did not reflect any disrespect for the five men left in the garage. When he spoke, he spoke only to Dick and always in Spanish. He was polite to Rosemary and the twins, but avoided engaging them directly in conversation.

After several weeks, another limo arrived and took the men away in the middle of the night. They were very grateful to their host and left a handsome thank-you gift.

Years later, when the twins were teenagers, they were having dinner with their father. "Daddy, do you remember when we were in the house in Glenview?" Karla asked. "Some men came to the house and stayed in the garage for a time. One of them ate with us in the kitchen. Who was that man?"

"Fulgencio Batista," he replied, "the former president of Cuba."

"Oh," was all they managed to say. They knew who Batista was, but they didn't grasp the significance of his presence in their house, and Dick didn't offer any more information.

The twins were nearly four at this time and spoke fondly of that brief time in their childhood when they had a semblance of normalcy in their lives. Dick's Outfit friends loved it out there, too. They felt like they were in the country, no worries about who might be watching them. They didn't flinch at loud noises; they left their guns in the car. One in particular, William "Action" Jackson, was like a kid when he was in Glenview. A syndicate loan collector by trade, he loved children and would take the twins out in the back yard and roll around with them for hours. The girls called him Uncle Act. Dick thought it was hilarious to watch this huge man, over three hundred pounds, a fiercely intimidating man, rolling in the grass with the girls in a seven-hundred-dollar suit.

Uncle Act represented the fringe element of mob activity. He was well-connected, most likely a made guy, but his job was as a juice collector. Sometimes he had to get rough with his clients but, for the most part, his was just a job. He was, by all accounts, a nice guy. Action Jackson was murdered by Sam DeStefano after a brutal three days of torture while DeStefano tried to get him to admit he was a government informant. He never did admit to it—because it wasn't so. The whole incident grew out of a misunderstanding when Uncle Act made a careless statement in the presence of a bartender who passed it on to DeStefano.

Following his resignation from the Chicago Police Department in May 1960, Dick landed a contract to assist in the investigation of police corruption in the city of Springfield, Missouri. His primary role was to administer polygraph tests to members of the police department. His report to the city council, filed in early August of 1960, resulted in the firing of thirteen police officers, including the chief of police.

Dick's partner in the investigation was really the lead person on the contract, but Dick assumed a very public presence and called a press conference to announce his acceptance of the job, taking full credit for landing the contract. Years later, a Chicago police detective, working in the criminal investigation division, called the guy who had landed the contract and asked what prompted him to hire Dick Cain for such a high-profile job. It seems he needed a polygraph operator, and the only one he knew had turned the job down because it didn't pay well enough. At a hundred dollars a day, Dick Cain jumped at the opportunity. Dick's partner said he fought with Dick during the entire investigation because Dick wanted to meet with the press daily and keep them apprised of the progress in the case. He felt they should be invisible until after they turned over their report to the city council. He said he would never hire Dick Cain again for this kind of a job.

On his return from the job in Missouri, Dick began to refocus his efforts on building the business at Accurate Laboratories. His office was located in room 308 of 166 West Washington Street in the heart of the Loop. His business card indicated what he considered to be their specialties: "Investigations, Guard Services, Undercover Operatives and Polygraph Examinations." His strong suits were wiretaps and polygraph.

He befriended Chris Gugas, the founder of the National Board of Polygraph Examiners, in an effort to add more credibility to his own credentials. Building on the polygraph side of the business he landed a contract with Playboy Enterprises to administer polygraph tests to the Playboy bunnies. Hugh Hefner, it seems, was very rigid about the rule that his bunnies could not date or otherwise have contact with the customers of the club. Dick's primary contact at the club was Vic Lownes, a trusted confidant of Hefner who several years later moved to London to manage the first Playboy Club Casino.

CHAPTER

6

Fulgencio Batista was a sergeant in the Cuban army in 1933 when the dictator Gerardo Machado was overthrown. A few months later, Batista led a military revolt, elevated himself from sergeant to the rank of lieutenant colonel, and declared the military in his control. He aligned himself early with the communists and was instrumental in having the Communist Party legalized in 1938 in order to get himself elected to office. He was eventually run out of the country, only to return after being elected to the Senate in 1950, while living in Ft. Lauderdale, Florida. On March 10, 1952, Batista led a coup and installed himself as head of state.

Despite his communist leanings, Batista was instrumental in expanding Cuba's tourism industry. He was the quintessential corrupt government leader. He developed alliances with Sam Giancana, Meyer Lansky, Santos Trafficante, and most of the others who controlled Havana's casinos, and he encouraged them to share the profits. Giancana and Lansky were more than happy to spread some money around and became—functionally—full partners with the Cuban government. According to testimony given to Congress in 1957, Batista shared in all slot-machine profits to the tune of fifty percent. This was money paid directly to him, not to the government of Cuba.

It was the 1952 coup, just months before Cuba's first scheduled free elections, that sent a young lawyer named Fidel Castro into the mountains with a rifle. Castro despised Batista for his communist leanings and dictatorial ways. He went to work immediately on the revolution that would end with Batista's departure from Cuba. Castro's revolution was known as the 26th of July Movement, named to commemorate the attack on the Moncada barracks on July 26, 1953, in Santiago. The attack was actually a dismal failure, but it became a rallying point as Castro promised to return the country to the people.

Fidel, his brother Raul, and the Argentinean Che Guevera set up training camps in Mexico to prepare for their return to Cuba. They returned in 1956, sailing from Tuxpan in Veracruz, and were nearly crushed but managed to survive long enough to escape to the hills and eventually recruit additional fighters.

Castro enjoyed widespread support in the United States, not only from Cuban-Americans, but also from the American government, which saw its role as saving Cuba from communism. Castro came often to the United States to raise money and buy guns. He had made many friends in the United States through his contacts in the Cuban community and others as a result of his attempts to garner support for his cause. From 1952 through January 1, 1959, Castro led a small band of insurgents that grew to a respectable army as local support increased. The fighting took years, and the toll on the Cuban people was high, but through perseverance and dedication, Castro's army was victorious.

The mob had long considered Cuba to be the best of all possible worlds. The tropical climate made it an ideal place for tourism. Tourism provided an ideal platform on which to build their business. The casinos and hotels in Havana were among the best in the world. It was a playground unmatched anywhere. Everybody made money. The casinos paid taxes, of course, but they also paid millions of dollars in bribes up and down the ladder of the Cuban government. They provided thousands of jobs and enjoyed a period of unprecedented success for many years.

But all that changed when, in the early morning hours of January 1, 1959, Batista fled the country. With Batista's ouster, everything was different. Castro set about to establish control and eventually to close the casinos. He ran the mobsters out of the country and saw to it they left without their cash. In fact they were not allowed to take anything out of the country; at the airport they were stripped of all jewelry and money before they were allowed to board the plane. Several casino operators were put in prison without charges or trial and kept there until they divulged where their spoils were hidden. He wasn't asking for ransom; he only wanted the money that was in Cuba and therefore belonged to the Cuban people—all of it. Once Castro had the money, he allowed them to leave.

Members of the American Mafia had been active participants in the government of Cuba. Batista had embraced the mob. He took their money and saw to it the laws looked favorably on their casinos, in contrast to the way things were in Las Vegas where they were constantly trying to hide their interests from regulators by using "front men" as owners and taking their cut by skimming cash in the counting rooms. In Cuba, they were recognized and respected. They still used front men, to insulate them from scrutiny, but it was pretty much out in the open.

Until the Anastasia murder in the barbershop of the Park Sheraton Hotel in New York City—a huge event that had people talking everywhere. The New York Police Department feared that it would trigger another long running war between the families. Apparently the families had the same fear. They called for a meeting of the "commission." Mostly informal up until now, the commission was made up of the heads of the mob families from around the country. There's no evidence they had ever met as a group before, but there hadn't been such a crisis before.

In January 1958, the FBI prepared a report for Alex Rosen, assistant to the director of the FBI, which carried the heading: "Gambling Activities in Cuba." They acknowledged the pressures that developed after the murder of Albert Anastasia on October 25, 1957, and the Apalachin, New York, commission meeting, which was convened to find a solution to the issue of wars between the families. The meeting was disrupted by the New York State Police on November 14, 1957. It was becoming painfully obvious to the bureau that they could no longer deny the existence of an organized crime element in this country.

The FBI's report speculated that Santos Trafficante was a suspect in Anastasia's murder. He was known to have arrived the day before. He had dinner with Anastasia that night and shared a suite with him. The next day, Trafficante returned to Florida and Anastasia was killed.

Trafficante had come to New York to talk about who was going to get the lease for the casino in the new Hilton hotel being built in Havana. There was tight competition for the lease; Las Vegas was after it, with a group headed by Moe Dalitz and Morris Kleinman, formerly of Cleveland, and Abner "Longie" Zwillman of Newark, New Jersey, all of whom had an interest in the Desert Inn at Las Vegas. Trafficante also had a desire to secure this lease for himself and Sam Giancana, to add to the Sans Souci which they already controlled. Trafficante knew that Meyer Lansky, who ran the Nacional, would be going after it as well, and that was why he had made the trip to New York. Lansky told Anastasia in no uncertain terms that he was to stay out of Cuba. Now it was Trafficante's turn—they talked about who would control it, how the proceeds would be shared and, of course, who would be the "front men." Everyone recognized they couldn't have their own names appear on any of these documents; they needed clear names and those people would be handsomely compensated, but they wouldn't really own anything.

The NYPD advised the FBI they were considering the possibility that Albert Anastasia was killed because of a turf war involving the casinos in Cuba. They pointed out that, sometime before Anastasia was killed, there was a dinner meeting attended by Anastasia, four unnamed Cubans, Trafficante, and John W. Hauser, executive vice president of the Hilton hotel chain. The Hilton folks eventually backed away from the negotiations completely and washed their hands of the casino. The owners of the building, the retirement fund of the Caterer's Union, would have full responsibility for the casino and Hilton would only provide the basics like cleaning and cocktail services.

Trafficante and his boss, Sam Giancana, both attended the Apalachin conference, which was a watershed event within the ranks of organized crime. Not only were they "outed" as a real criminal organization, they were targeted by the feds for the first time since Prohibition. Trafficante had been captured by the New York State Police, but he was the only one they caught who refused to accurately identify himself. He had identification with him that showed him to be Luis Santos—a real person, who had died thirteen months earlier in Cuba. Corporal Vincent Vasisko of the New York State Police positively identified a photo of Trafficante as being the man who had identified himself as Luis Santos.

Following Apalachin, the mob guys tried to resume business as usual. For the FBI, business would never be the same again.

As time marched on, and the FBI observed, a newspaper account in Cuba tipped them off to the fact that two former FBI agents had been hired by the new Havana Hilton to screen applicants for the casino. Agents from FBI headquarters in Washington contacted George McSwain and

Downey Rice to request their assistance in investigating gambling operations in Cuba. McSwain and Rice had a difference of opinion about their allegiance to their former employer. When approached by an agent of the Washington Field Office, Rice advised the agent that he considered his investigations to be privileged information and he refused to share. Former agent McSwain, on the other hand, was more accommodating and made available the entirety of Mr. Rice's background investigations on a "confidential" basis, of course.

Rice's report, no longer confidential, claimed that Trafficante went to New York to personally deliver a letter to Albert Anastasia, written on Sans Souci letterhead, no doubt by Trafficante himself. The letter advised that Anastasia was to be prepared to entertain a group of Cubans who were coming to New York to meet their new partners. The NYPD found the letter in the suite at the Warwick hotel that Anastasia had shared with Santos Trafficante. The Cubans were led by Roberto Mendosa, a personal friend of President Batista and, ultimately, the man who signed the lease; they were found to have been registered at the Warwick for October 17–25, 1957.

Mendosa was picked up on December 20, 1957 and interviewed by District Attorney Hogan in New York City. Mendosa said that Trafficante was never in on the deal for the Hilton. It was eventually awarded to Mendosa, his brother Mario, a Havana attorney with solid political connections, a New York law firm with ties to Meyer Lansky, and a Nevada state senator named Kenneth Johnson.

Back when Batista took control of the government of Cuba he promised free elections at a future date. When the elections were scheduled for June 1958, Andres Rivero Aguero was Cuban prime minister and frequently mentioned as the likely candidate to succeed Batista. Aguero's "assistant," a man named Suarez Rivas, approached Jake Lansky, Meyer's brother, and told him that "for a contribution of $3,000 a month from each of the casinos controlled by them, Meyer Lansky could be assured of encountering no difficulty with the Cuban government." Jake Lansky told Rivas to take a hike. He felt they were sufficiently well-connected that they didn't need to start lining the pockets of potential candidates for the presidency.

Naturally, all of that became moot a short time later when Batista beat his hasty retreat to a garage in Glenview, Illinois.

Giancana had extensive business interests in Havana, most notably the casino at the Sans Souci, which provided millions of dollars in cash flow to the mob. He was seething with anger over the realization that not only had this well gone dry, but Castro had also confiscated millions of dollars of his money. He hated Castro for taking it from him. He could not comprehend how such a thing could have happened. Giancana was convinced that he would eventually return to reclaim what was taken from him, but in the meantime he could only feel anger at the terrible losses he'd endured.

When he left Cuba, Batista struggled to find a country that would grant him asylum; he needed to buy some time. It's very often difficult for an exiled leader to find a home, but having a large stash of available cash was certainly a big help. He would bide his time and hope to find a friendly country that would allow him and his family to live in peace.

This was when he called his friends, asked for a place to stay, and wound up in Dick's garage. Eventually Spain agreed to allow him a permanent visa, and it was there, in Guadalmina, that he lived until his death on August 6, 1973. His legacy was certainly marred by the level of corruption that he allowed to endure in Cuba, but the fact remains that Cuba had a vibrant economy under Batista's reign. Sugar exports were substantial and the growing cigar industry was becoming a major factor. Tourism was a huge part of the national economy and, again, today is a key part of the new Cuban economy, though nearly forty years of neglect have left Cuba with an uphill battle.

The U.S. government was frustrated, too. Under the admittedly corrupt Batista years, Cuba had a viable free press, which included many newspapers and television stations. They had more radio stations in the pre-Revolutionary days than did the United Kingdom. Education was available to a higher percentage of the population than in most other Latin American countries. They were good trading partners and, while few people were comfortable with Batista's communist leanings, one could make the case that there was more freedom than in many other communist-led countries.

Now that Castro had won he slowly showed he was openly embracing his communist comrades, and clearly a communist Cuba under Castro would be vastly different from a communist Cuba under the old Batista government. Castro closed the casinos and, over time, he nationalized the cigar industry as well as many other elements of Cuba's economic base.

Nineteen-sixty seemed to drag on for Dick. He'd been forced to resign his position with the police department in May and was trying to establish himself as a private investigator. But by August, it was clear Cuba would be lost to communism unless something drastic happened. Dick redoubled his efforts to stay involved in the Cuban community around Chicago.

Richard Bissell, the CIA's deputy director for plans (the covert branch), approached Sheffield Edwards, Director of security for the CIA, with the outrageous plan to ask Edwards to establish contact with mobsters who had been active in Cuba and recruit them to participate in an assassination plan. In September, Edwards contacted Robert Mahue, a former FBI agent who was then a private investigator and whose principal client was Howard Hughes. He told Mahue about their plans and asked him to help establish a link between the CIA and the Mafia. Mahue knew Johnny Roselli, the mob's guy in Los Angeles. When Mahue first told him of the plan, Roselli said he'd be interested, but he couldn't make such a move without including his boss, Sam Giancana.

With the benefit of hindsight, it's clear that this was a bluff on Roselli's part. He technically worked for Giancana, but was also a longtime associate of Santos Trafficante, the mob boss in Florida, and he could have worked it with Trafficante alone. He took a calculated risk in bringing in Giancana. The CIA didn't flinch, so it became Sam's project.

Giancana relished the idea of being able to do something beneficial for the government. His world revolved around doing favors and expecting favors in return. He wouldn't make any exceptions to accommodate the CIA, and it amused him that the CIA had come to him for help. This project had the added benefit of giving him the opportunity to strike out at Castro. As Sam would later say, "That rotten bastard, he stole millions of dollars from us. I can't wait to kill the fucker."

The CIA point man for the project, James P. O'Connell, had been introduced to Roselli as an employee of Mahue, representing a private client. It didn't take long for Roselli to see through that, and he told O'Connell he was sure that O'Connell was "a government man—CIA." But he also told O'Connell that he didn't want him to confirm it, he said that "as a loyal American, he would do whatever he could and would never divulge the operation."

Roselli did tell Giancana, though, and, ever the cynic, Sam insisted he meet with someone who was making the decision, not just Robert Mahue or O'Connell. Mahue was a cutout, a person who gave the CIA plausible deniability. Sam liked to use cutouts too, but he wasn't about to be victimized by one. He wanted to make sure the government knew who would carry out this plan. A meeting was arranged for Giancana to meet with Sheffield Edwards. During the week of September 25, 1960, Sam Giancana, Johnny Roselli, and Robert Mahue met in Miami to discuss the contract offer from the CIA.

Back in Washington, Sheffield Edwards briefed Allen Dulles, the director of the CIA, describing the plan as an "intelligence operation," careful not to mention the word "assassination." Bissell, who was there for the briefing, later said that while the explicit goals of the operation were not spelled out, there was enough of it on the table that Dulles "certainly knew the nature of the plan." Following that meeting, Bissell committed $150,000 to Edwards, who eventually paid most of it to Giancana.

When the CIA gave Sam Giancana the contract to hit Fidel Castro, Dick Cain was a logical person for Sam to turn to; he was fluent in Spanish and knew his way around Cuba. The CIA was hoping for a traditional mob—hit-speeding cars, blazing guns, all of that. Sam was opposed to that because it was unlikely an assassin could safely get out of the country. This was a golden opportunity for Dick; it had all the elements of an activity that could hold his interest: it was dangerous, it involved espionage, and it was potentially lucrative.

Eventually, it was agreed poison would be the vehicle. Mahue reported back to Edwards that Giancana had agreed to take on the contract, but the CIA was to provide the deadly dose. The CIA labs decided the most effective and hard-to-trace poison would be botulin, which could be delivered in a pill the size of a saccharin tablet.

When the pills were delivered to Sheffield Edwards, he dropped one into a glass of water and waited for it to dissolve. The pill not only didn't dissolve, it didn't even disintegrate. It just sank to the bottom of the glass like a little round brick. Edwards sent the pills back to the lab, where they were tested on guinea pigs. Inexplicably, the guinea pigs didn't die and didn't even get sick. After several more tests, they realized that guinea pigs had a tremendous resistance to botulism, so they tested it again, on a monkey this time, and found it to be quite effective. The poison pill was then delivered by O'Connell to Giancana and Roselli.

There was talk of trying to recruit a Cuban national for the job, someone who could inconspicuously place him or herself in the presidential palace to set up the hit. Through Johnny Roselli and Santos Trafficante, the conspirators contacted at least one Cuban college professor who later couldn't go through with the plan, because he lost the job that had given him access to Castro.

Immediately following that meeting between Edwards and Giancana, Dick Cain filed a passport application in Chicago, stating on the application he was going to visit Central and South America and the Caribbean, and he was leaving from Miami on October 15, 1960.

In late October, Dick was in Miami, interviewing Cuban refugees and preparing reports he shared with CIA station chief William Lohmann back in Chicago. Lohmann, in turn, generally passed them to the Cuba desk at CIA Headquarters and to the State Department. He nearly always qualified each report by explaining Dick Cain was not an "approved" source and that he might be a loose cannon.

Dick had contacted the CIA station chief prior to his departure for Miami. He told them he'd be on assignment for *Life Magazine*, and he expected to be making several trips inside Cuba. The CIA was leery of this guy Cain, whom they referred to as "our own private Dick," but told him they would be happy to hear what he had to say. Even if they had trusted him, they would likely have never asked him for specific information. To do so would have been a breach of security and would have tipped their hand to an "outsider" about their goals.

His first report, dated October 28, 1960, is indicative of his attempts to direct the content and style of his reports to the interest of the readers he wanted most to impress—the CIA.

Miami Beach, Florida
Friday, October 28, 1960

Chicago Operative #3719
Chicago Investigator C-101 Reports:

The vast airfield of San Antonio de los Banos was built by the United States during World War Two. From this Cuban position, our Air Force patrolled the Gulf and Caribbean area, the approaches to the Panama Canal, and allied supply lines. At the cessation of hostilities, the airfield was given to our ally, Cuba.

It is now being used as an F.A.R. (Air Force—Rebel) field.

Last June, several Czechoslovakian Communist pilots arrived at the field, and, in their enthusiasm, were in the air, flying Cuban airplanes twenty minutes later.

Immediately, the majority of the Cuban Pilots stationed at San Antonio de Los Banos revolted. These pilots had fought for Castro and, feeling betrayed by orders to obey the commands of the Czechs, bolted the airfield, heading for the counter-revolutionary forces in the mountains.

They were hunted down and shot on the spot, without even the dubious benefit of Military courts-martial. The few who temporarily escaped were later captured and are now serving sentences of 20 to 30 years at hard labor in the coal mines at Sierra Maestra.

The Cuban Rebel Air Force of San Antonio de los Banos is now comprised exclusively of Czech (or Russian masquerading as Czech) pilots.

To Judge Raul Delgado, communist influence in Cuban affairs was no longer a matter of rumor or conjecture. It was a fact. He had witnessed it first hand.

On August 8, 1960, less than two months after East European Communists took control of the San Antonio airfield, Judge Delgado and his wife Ophelia, escaped to Miami. This is the new face of Cuba.

Then, a second report, filed the same day:

> Miami Beach, Florida
> Friday, October 28, 1960

Chicago Operative #3719-3
Chicago Investigator C-101 Reports:

The new face of Cuba is very evident in refugee filled Dade County, Florida. Cubans are performing every imaginable occupation—doing anything in order to eat, and simultaneously playing havoc with the Miami labor market.

I had a long talk with two unemployed Cubans. I met them casually while they were seeking employment. Although their story had an unmistakable ring of truth, I did a little checking later, and everything I found supported them.

Ramiro Fernandez Moris is 53 years old. He was born in Cuba, as was his wife, Alicia, and his son. In 1934, he graduated from the

University of Havana Law School, then in 1936 competed against 120 law graduates for the position of Municipal Judge.

For many years, Cuba has assumed the attitude that a good politician does not necessarily make a good judge. Therefore, once each year, or whenever a vacancy is open, 120 lawyers can compete in written examinations for a judgeship. Prior to Castro, therefore, every Cuban judge was scholastically superior to the 120 other lawyers who applied for the position. To further eliminate politics from the judiciary, once a judge was sworn in, he retained that position unless impeached for wrongdoing.

So in 1936, Ramiro Moris was made a judge in the Havana Municipal Court, and in that position he remained through the regimes of Martin, Prio, Batista and Castro. He saw the presidents in Cuba come and go, some through democratic elections, others via revolution. Yet, during the parade of presidents, Cuban law generally remained status quo. Although an Army sergeant named Batista could overthrow a President, he had not the stomach to take on Cuban law, which is incidentally modeled on American jurisprudence.

Until Castro. The first breach between the Municipal Court and the Revolutionary Government of Cuba was brought about by the formulation of the Military Tribunal. In the United States, a citizen cannot be tried by a Military Tribunal, because as a citizen, he is not subject to the less Constitutional laws of the military, which are necessary to maintain discipline.

The same prevailed in Cuba before the advent of Castro. However, Castro tried, and executed, over 600 citizens in Military Tribunals. In the majority of cases, the Military judges in these tribunals had no legal background whatsoever. The process of appeal was made a mockery.

The next breach between Castro and the Municipal Court judges occurred over the Communist influence in the Cuban Supreme Court. Irresponsible precedents were set. States Judge Moris: 'Justice came to be justice for Communism only.'

Two months ago, after examining his conscience, after looking back on 24 years on the Municipal bench, after examining his possessions and his small farm in the province, Judge Moris applied for a visitors permit for himself and his family at the American Embassy in Havana. On arrival in Miami, he sent his resignation to the Cuban Supreme Court. Had he resigned in Cuba, Judge Moris feels he would have been imprisoned. Other judges in Cuba are cognizant of police surveillance.

Judge Moris is presently seeking a position of law clerk in a Miami law firm. He hopes some day to practice before a free and democratic Florida bar.

That is, if he is unable to return to a free and democratic Cuba.

The other Cuban I talked to is Raul Delgado. His career is quite similar to Judge Moris', with one exception. Raul Delgado also attended the University of Havana Law School; was also admitted as a Municipal Judge after an examination in 1934. But he was assigned as a municipal judge in the small town of San Antonio de los Banos.

Judge Delgado, as did most other Municipal Court judges, experienced the rift between the Castro Government and Cuban law. But in addition to this, Judge Delgado saw something. In his little upcountry community, he witnessed an event that I am sure we Americans have not heard the last of.

He saw European Communist troops in Cuba.

The reports were embellished, if not in content then certainly in attitude. Dick was in his glory. This was where he wanted to be—telling the government of the United States the things he had learned, the things he wanted them to know, and reported in the fashion of the cheap spy novels popular at the time. There was no mention in the reports of the conditions at the mob-run casinos in downtown Havana; that information was for another report, one that would be made in person to Sam Giancana. Giancana was hopeful that with Castro out of the picture, they could reopen the casinos, and he could begin to reclaim his losses.

Dick had tested the waters with those first two reports and became convinced the CIA wanted him to continue to keep them apprised of the situation. Certainly, good intelligence was at a premium during these dark days for Cuba; they seemed appreciative of his help, even if they took his editorializing with a grain of salt.

His next report was dated October 29th:

Miami's Bayfront Park was lonely and windy last night, as I sat and talked into the morning with two Cuban counterrevolutionary Intelligence officers. My ego will not allow me to believe that anything other than the wind from Biscayne Bay caused the hair to rise on the nape of my neck, and made me shiver while I heard the latest news from Cuba.

Earlier I had watched the lumbering Pan American plane land at Miami's International Airport, and was introduced to the two agents after they had disembarked and completed telling the usual lies to Customs and Immigration. But they had been too busy to talk at that time. Their superiors were awaiting a report in the big house on NE 17th Street and Biscayne Blvd., hence the meet in Bayfront Park.

As we smoked and talked, I noted the serious attitude of chagrin on the part of the Agents. I later learned that they had previously been doing the same type of work for Castro while Batista ruled Cuba.

The news? Well, they had definitely established the rumors were true regarding Russian MIG planes being in Cuba. Although well guarded, he had seen five MIG's parked off the runway at San Julian Base, near the town of Guane, in Pinar Del Rio Province. The MIG nearest them bore the numerals 1017.

They also established (although not as candidly with me) that last month, a Russian ship unloaded, in the dead of night, a minimum of nine medium heavy tanks. They say minimum of nine because they have located the whereabouts of this many. All civilians had been ordered out of Havana Harbor on the nights the tanks were unloaded. The agents have had no experience in the identification of tanks, in contrast to aircraft, and, therefore, cannot tell whether they are Russian tanks or not.

I wonder if Russian ships are now hauling cargo for aggressive imperialist-intervening America?

The agents also stated they had been busy in Cuba investigating domestic matters. They learned that on last Thursday afternoon on a Cubana Airlines flight from Havana to Miami, Maj. Raul Castro, Commander of Cuban Armed Forces, and a company of soldiers boarded the plane prior to takeoff and forcibly removed his, and Fidel's sister, Rita, and her five children.

She and her children were attempting to escape to the United States.

The party was taken to a building at 17 y O Ave., in Havana.

One wonders what atrocities are now being performed on this poor woman by her brothers and their communist masters.

Her crime was to almost disrupt the extensive communistic propaganda program being conducted throughout Latin American countries by Red agents based in Cuba.

Isn't there a Bible quotation about "a house divided?"

One of the counterrevolutionary agents told me how he used to obtain arms and ammunition in Chicago when he was working for Castro and the 26th of July movement. This man, whose code name is Pancho Villa, would meet another agent every Friday in the Adler Planetarium in Chicago. He would obtain, usually, 7500 rounds of .45 caliber ammunition from this other agent, which would be packed in two suitcases. Separating, Pancho Villa would drive to the Del Prado

Hotel where he would park his car and, carrying the two suitcases, go in the front door of the Del Prado and out the side door to a cab, and finally to Midway and New York. In New York, the ammunition would be placed in a locker at the airport and the locker key mailed to a predetermined address where other agents would transmit the ammo to Castro in the mountains of Cuba.

"'To think," said Pancho Villa, "that here I am, an American citizen, and I was to risk my citizenship to help my mother country—and for what? For communists? No. So now I risk a little more than my citizenship—this time for freedom.

On October 31st Dick reports:

Juan and his aunt. His story is an often-told one, as far as the agents were concerned; I had never heard of such a thing.

Jaun, a remarkable clean, sloe-eyed little boy with white, even teeth, and a attitude that was polite to the extreme, told me, in this halting English, that he attends elementary school in Havana. When school started again after the summer vacation, he found there were no more textbooks handed out to the students. He was told he could select his own subject so as to freely develop his own character and future. Juan knows nothing of these things, so he selected the same curriculum his best friend did. The previous year, Catholic nuns had taught Juan, as he is Catholic, and, states Juan, he was happy. This year, there were no nuns. But the men and women teachers placed there by the Castro Revolutionary Government were nice enough. One could play all day if he wanted. There were so few rules. It was nice. Easy.

Then one day, the principal called a meeting in the Assembly Hall of Juan's school. All of the students, amounting to about 600, attended.

Mr. Principal is a very nice man. Very kind. Understanding.

According to counterrevolutionary sources, this gentleman is a Cuban who was educated in Spain and Russia, and returned to Cuba only after the advent of Castro.

Well, the principal asked all the students who pray to God to please raise their hands. Almost all hands raised.

Next, all the students who like toys, raise their hands. This time, all hands raised.

Then students, tonight you must pray to God to bring you toys. Pray very hard. Tell him you want lots of toys. Tell God it's very important that you get new toys.

The students, ranging in age from 5 to 12, were then dismissed.

The next day, just before lunch hour, a meeting of all students was again called for in the Assembly Hall.

"How many students obtained all the new toys they prayed for last night?" asked Mr. Kind, Understanding Principal. "Raise your hands."

Not a hand was lifted.

Well then—we find that the lies you innocent children have been taught in the past—they do not really work, no?

Now then—let us get to the Truth. Tonight, go home and pray to Fidel. Let us see which is the strongest—a story book God, or Fidel.

A meeting was not called in the Assembly Hall the next day. It was not necessary. Half of the children had brought the new toys they found on their doorstep to school with them.

During the night, Fidel Castro's 'milicianos' had placed several thousand dollars worth of toys on the front steps of the students' homes.

I have seen little children dead, diseased, and dying, beyond medical help in the Far East; I've seen "pore white" kids suffering from malnutrition in the south, and I've seen colored babies living in filth and squalor on Chicago's South side. But I have never felt sorrier for a child anywhere than I feel for this little Cuban boy.

His difficulty is not a misfortune of environment, hatred or war. His was no awful, accidental twist of fate.

The mind of little Juan was attacked deliberately and with malice aforethought. His mentality; his religious traditions; his background; and his future were attacked by means of a cheap Carny trick—but in accordance with the principles of enlistment in the Communist Party.

As Juan departed the Democratic Revolutionary Front headquarters, holding his aunt's hand, I saw her hesitate before a picture of Jesus on the Cross. Her lips moved in silent words as she continued on.

"Por Dios," she had said. For God.

These reports provided some insights for the CIA, but not a great deal in terms of facts. Indications of the presence of East European troops, MIGs, and the tanks may have been helpful, but they could have learned of those things from other sources. In fact, U2 flights over Cuba had already identified the presence of Russian aircraft. Dick knew that. That's probably why he threw in the story of poor Juan Sanchez, to tug at their strings just a tad, to show he could be a spy with a heart.

When Dick worked for William Buenz in Miami in the early fifties, he placed a number of wiretaps on the phones of Cuban dissidents both in Miami and in Cuba. Buenz's client was Fulgencio Batista, soon to become the president of Cuba. That Batista was a communist did not concern Dick at the time. Years later, after Batista had been run out of the country, Dick did some work for Constantine Kangles, an attorney who represented the interests of Fidel Castro in the United Sates. Kangles was involved with Castro's 26th of July Movement. Initially the work for Kangles involved installing wiretaps in the Chicago area to monitor anti-Castro activity. Dick handled that work and along the way he developed a series of informants within the Cuban exile community.

The May 1967 Inspector General's report on the CIA-Mafia plots reveal the CIA as being in a pressure cooker. They qualified their explanations by saying, "We cannot overemphasize the extent to which responsible Agency officers felt themselves subject to the Kennedy administration's severe pressures to do something about Castro and his regime. The fruitless and, in retrospect, often unrealistic plotting should be viewed in that light."

The report goes on to say, "CIA twice (first in early 1961 and again in early 1962) supplied lethal pills to U.S. gambling syndicate members working in behalf of CIA on a plot to assassinate Fidel Castro. The 1961 plot aborted and the pills were recovered. Those furnished in April 1962 were passed by the gambling syndicate representatives to a Cuban exile leader in Florida, who in turn had them sent to Cuba about May 1962."

On May 7, 1962, Attorney General Robert Kennedy was briefed on the CIA-Mafia plots to assassinate Fidel Castro. Clearly they had failed and in light of the fact that this phase of the plot had originally developed during the Eisenhower administration, Kennedy didn't feel particularly responsible for it. He did, however feel that as attorney general he should have been briefed on the plan sooner than he had. He admonished the CIA to remember that the next time they sought to assassinate a head of state.

Paul Newey introduced Dick to William Lohmann, CIA station chief in Chicago. Newey was the state's attorney investigator who had hired Dick to spy on Mayor Daley's Irwin Cohen and as an ex-OSS/CIA officer he carefully maintained contact with his former colleagues. The day after Dick got his passport (it didn't take six to eight weeks in those days), he contacted Lohmann and told him he was going to Cuba and would be airlifted into the Sierra Maestra Mountains. He offered to share what he learned with Lohmann. Lohmann agreed to accept whatever he chose to share, but he should in no way interpret that as a sanction; Dick was on his own as far as the CIA was concerned. They did not approve of his actions and would deny knowing him if anyone asked.

Dick was excited about the prospect of this contract because it validated his perception of himself as an intelligence operative, a spy. Dick never accepted the notion that he was a mobster or a crooked cop. His criminal activities were not born of a criminal nature; rather, they were rooted in his sense of adventure and his need for risk-taking.

Dick called his father, John Cain, to wish him well for the Christmas holidays. When they reached the inevitable "what have you been up to" part of the conversation, Dick told him he had been to Cuba on a secret mission for the government to assassinate Fidel Castro and that, while he hadn't succeeded, he had gotten so far as to be in Castro's office. He and a Cuban woman, whose identity is unknown, traveled as a couple. Flying under cover of darkness, they made numerous trips into Cuba to try and hatch a plan. On one such trip Dick made it to Castro's office, but was unable to locate a suitable way to plant the botulin tablets to ensure they would be ingested by Castro. While exiting the grounds that day, his female partner was captured, and he only narrowly escaped himself. She was quickly and quietly tried and executed. Dick was shaken by the experience and felt he had done everything possible to make the plan work. They had been up against incredible security, and he doubted he could safely get that close again. He felt defeated and reluctantly left the island.

This story came to me primarily by way of the Cain family version of the wiretap, an extension phone. When Dick called our house in Bay City to talk to J. B., my sister Mary Ellyn happened to pick up the upstairs extension at the same time my father picked up downstairs. She heard them talking and recognized Dick's voice right away. Being careful not to reveal her presence, which would have triggered a firm "hang up the phone" from dad, she listened in on the entire conversation.

It was unlike Dick to share this kind of information, but in his never-ending quest to earn his father's respect and his love, Dick must have thought his father would approve of his "working for the government" on such an important mission. He was wrong. John was angry and asked why Dick was involved in that kind of stuff. It was stupid, John maintained, as well as dangerous. And so, once again, Dick was thwarted in his efforts to regain his father's approval. He'd get over it: he didn't need the old man anyway.

When Dick returned to Miami, he met with Giancana at the Riviera Hotel. They agreed it was too risky to make further attempts on Castro with their own people. Dick would try to recruit a Cuban for the job, but the project had ceased to inspire either man. Sam and Johnny Roselli continued to string the CIA along about continued attempts, but there were none. Eventually the CIA recovered its pills from Giancana and halted this phase of their plan.

It was clear, though, that Dick had actually been inside Cuba, so the CIA began to take Dick more seriously and asked the FBI to conduct a background investigation. One of the first things the FBI did was to track him down in Miami. On November 2, 1960, they met with Dick in the lobby of his hotel and talked for some time. Their report back to the CIA indicated they believed Dick to be who and what he said he was, and his information was accurate but unremarkable.

On December 8, Dick called Bill Lohmann and told him he had been unable to get into Cuba. The only logical reason for Dick to make a statement like that would be to cover up the fact he actually had been to Cuba.

Along the way Dick met up with Tony Varona, head of the Cuban Revolutionary Council. Varona had earlier been president of the Cuban senate and an active participant in the overthrow of Batista. Eventually, he broke with Castro and in 1961 left Cuba permanently. He worked on plans for the Bay of Pigs invasion and was an active go-between with the Mafia and the Cuban exile community in Miami and Chicago. He met with Meyer Lansky to solicit funds for weapons and training, Lansky pushed him toward Sam Giancana and the Chicago Outfit where he found comfort, solace, and a quarter of million dollars. He and Giancana spoke often about how they could kill Fidel, but ultimately they never pulled it off.

The following month, things started to heat up. On January 3, 1961, President Eisenhower severed diplomatic relations with Cuba. It was one of his final official acts, just prior to the inauguration of John F. Kennedy.

On January 28, 1961, Dick was observed by the FBI attending a meeting of the Freedom of the Press Committee in Chicago. This was a known communist front organization. The bureau was surprised that he would be at a meeting of this sort because at the time they only knew him as a former cop who had gotten himself in trouble. His presence was, no doubt, associated with his work with Tony Varona, who as one of Castro's closest confidants, had been disillusioned by Castro's turn toward communism.

Dick had nurtured his contacts in the Cuban community. He'd listened to Giancana rant and rave about how much money he lost when Castro closed the casinos. He knew that if he was able to get in tight with the Cubans and participate in their recovery of Cuba, then he would be a big man indeed in the eyes of Sam Giancana and the rest of the organized crime bosses. So he attended rallies and meetings and he tried to get to know the leaders on both sides; the Communists and the groups on the Right.

In February, Dick reported to the CIA that Castro was building Soviet-style concentration camps in Cuba. He included diagrams. The CIA was convinced at this point he was actually traveling in and out of Cuba, but they still kept their distance. They didn't discourage his sharing of information, but they were careful never to ask specific questions so as not to reveal too much about their interests. Though their interest was probably piqued when his next report advised he had met with his old attorney friend, Constantine Kangles, in Miami on March 12. Kangles represented Castro's interests in the United States and was en route to Havana to urge Castro to stop his anti-U.S. tactics and to make peace with the Americans. Kangles was beginning to fear Castro's vulnerability to the communists. By this time there were Russian advisers in evidence at all high-level meetings. While it would be some time before Castro would openly embrace the communists, it was clear he was heading that way.

A few weeks later, the disastrous Bay of Pigs invasion would seal the fate of Castro's relations with the U.S.

On April 14, 1961, a small fleet of aging B-26 bombers piloted by Cuban exiles and CIA officers attacked a series of air bases near the Bay of Pigs. Their goal was to disable the Cuban Air Force so that when the invasion force captured the airport the rebels could fly in relief supplies and additional personnel. There was to have been a second wave of bombers, but Kennedy had pulled the plug on the operation.

On April 17, more than 1,400 Cuban exiles invaded Cuban shores at the Bahia de Cochinos, the Bay of Pigs. Castro's army was waiting for the invaders. They waited, dug in at the beach, and prayed with their heads turned skyward, looking for the a miracle that might have saved them, could have saved their country. There were 114 Cubans killed that day, 1,189 taken prisoner. Within weeks, Castro's army had arrested 200,000 dissidents and housed them in the concentration camps Dick had seen two months earlier. In addition to the Cuban tragedy, there were dozens of American CIA officers involved in the landing who were shot down, killed, or captured. Some of these American heroes are still not accounted for today.

Kennedy couldn't have committed U.S. troops for an invasion without causing a deeper divide with Russia, but there were CIA officers left out in the cold. Even though it was probably caused by brinkmanship within the agency, Kennedy never regained the respect of the CIA, certainly not of the field personnel who lost friends and colleagues that day. The fallout from this disastrous event has given rise to speculation among some conspiracy theorists that the CIA was involved in JFK's assassination as retaliation for his abandonment at the Bay of Pigs. It makes good theatre, but there isn't really any credible evidence to support their involvement at any level. The CIA may not have mourned Kennedy's passing, but they didn't participate in it.

By May 1961, the Cubans in Miami and elsewhere in the U.S. were in a frenzy to reclaim their country. Dick continued to try to capitalize on the situation, offering his services to all comers, working every contact from Miami and Chicago. On May 17, Jose Ignacio Rasco came to Miami from Cuba and engaged Dick as a bodyguard. Rasco's Christian Democratic Party was concerned about Castro's embrace of communism, and Rasco wanted to see for himself how his countrymen were handling things in the U.S., to take their pulse. Rasco, one of Castro's closest personal friends, was an important adviser until Castro openly embraced his communist benefactors and Rasco broke off contact with him.

Eventually, Dick sensed that opportunities were drying up as far as Cuba was concerned, so he started to broaden his search. One contact he'd made in Miami was with a Frenchman, Pierre Kroupensky. A public relations expert on the outside and a schemer on the inside, Kroupensky and Dick quickly became friends. Kroupensky had been promised a contract from the government of Panama to conduct a nationwide survey of Panamanian attitudes about democracy vs. communism. Kroupensky would handle the survey. Dick's job would be to infiltrate youth groups and other organizations to get a sense of their attitudes and to identify communist recruitment efforts.

Dick's pending contract with Kroupensky was just the impetus he needed to get out of the country and declare himself an international free agent in espionage. He would move to Mexico and set up a base of operations, but would seek work throughout the world. A fresh start would give him the freedom to become self-reliant at last.

CHAPTER

7

In anticipation of his move to Mexico, Dick returned to Chicago to tie up loose ends, raise some operating capital, and prepare for a life as an expatriate. When he told his mother of his decision, she was crestfallen. As a child, Dick had been the bane of her existence. But now that he was an adult, she felt closer to him than she ever thought possible, especially since 1952, when she had gone to Florida to hide her darkest secret. They had become more than mother and son; they had become friends.

He reviewed his "friends" list, the people he wanted to stay in touch with. He used to send calendars each fall as a way to keep his name in front of people; it's a telling list, including Tony Verona, Constantine Kangles, Richard Ogilvie, Jack Mabley, Vic Lownes of *Playboy*, Sam Robards (the police chief of Springfield, Missouri), Captain Pat Deeley of the Chicago PD, and a host of reporters and columnists.

In early July 1961, he headed to Mexico to set up a base of operations for an investigative agency. He had been planning for months and had a checklist of skills. He would sell his polygraph skills in any way that he could. He would install wiretaps for anyone with the money to pay him. He also knew that once he started earning a living, new opportunities that he hadn't considered before might present themselves. He kept telling himself that things would be okay, that he could make it.

He knew that he would miss Chicago, but was concerned that there were actually people there who wanted him dead and, for now at least, he could allow them time to settle down. He'd saved some money, and went with enough cash to hold him over for several months, but he knew he'd have to start earning right away if he was going to make it work.

He felt he had developed some solid contacts during the Cuba job and if he was going to capitalize on those contacts at all, he was going to have to do that right away, too. He had to move slowly at first, though, because he was in clear violation of Mexican immigration laws by trying to run a business.

It was also important, for many reasons, to maintain his best contacts in Chicago. Dick polished his letter-writing skills during this time. He wrote to his mother, he wrote to Dick Ogilvie and to Bill Witsman, a carnival barker he'd arrested and befriended. Gerry Shallow, his old partner with the Chicago PD would, he knew, be an important friend later. He wrote to all of the people he considered most important in his life. He wrote to the twins, though he suspected Rosemary was throwing the letters away. He was probably right. As it turned out, Rosemary was seeing Bill Witsman at the time, and even though he was well over his marriage to her, he wasn't very keen on the idea of her going out with his friends.

This was the "grand experiment," and Dick was scared half out of his wits. He had an idea he could be successful, but he knew he was taking a risk. He had no assurances he would have any work. Many of the people he'd met during what he called "Project Cuba" had ties to Mexico. He planned to exploit those relationships to the fullest. He would also have to develop new ones, contacts that would be his own, that weren't tied to others with the inherent obligations.

Mexico City was, at that time, one of the largest cities in North America, with a population of about five million people. Mexico City is a federal district, much like Washington, D.C., and is ruled by federal law. Built on a geological fault, the city was still rebuilding in 1961 from a major earthquake that had occurred in 1957, inflicting extensive damage. Much of the earthquake damage had been along El Paseo de la Reforma, a beautiful street that runs through the middle of the business district.

About every three blocks on El Paseo de la Reforma was a glorieta. Glorietas (The English have a similar traffic cruelty called a roundabout) are circular intersections which interrupt the street periodically, providing a forced pause in the midst of bustling traffic, as well as an ideal place to lose a tail. The FBI had been alerted to his arrival and was following Dick because of his extensive contacts in the Cuban community. They just wanted to know what he was up to, they didn't necessarily think he was doing anything wrong. He was not, at this time in his life, considered to be an organized crime figure. He was more an anti-communist loose cannon.

"I pick up a tail about once every three days," Dick wrote back home. "I think I'm driving them slightly crazy. After one fellow loses me in those wonderful intersecting circles that are spread all over the place, he has been going to a particular cantina to call in. Yesterday, after he got through with the call, he turned around to find me waiting to use the phone with a 20 centavos piece in my hand. He promptly lost me in traffic again. He couldn't admit to his boss that he was so stupid he let me get the phone number he reported in on."

Generally, the FBI's foreign activity is restricted to surveillance of persons and organizations that are suspected of being involved in U.S. domestic criminal activity. FBI agents in foreign countries are called Legal Attaches (LEGATs). Officially, they advise embassy staff members on matters related to U.S. law. It's the CIA that concerns itself about foreign countries, and when Dick showed up at the American embassy asking to speak with a CIA representative, they quickly updated everyone's file on Richard Cain, communicating with Chicago and Washington. Curiously, their report back to headquarters indicated that Dick never actually stated a purpose for his visit. He just wanted to meet them.

Staying in touch with Richard Ogilvie was of paramount concern to Dick throughout his stay in Mexico. They corresponded regularly and when Dick couldn't write or didn't have anything to say, he had his mother call, sometimes just to say hi. He knew that Oglivie had political aspirations that could be helpful to him in the future.

Later, people would wonder how Richard Ogilvie had been fooled by Dick Cain. Ogilvie saw Dick as a good cop who made a lot of good vice arrests. What Ogilvie didn't see was the direction Dick got from outside the department on which vice arrests to make. He raided non-mob whorehouses and, occasionally, mob-involved operations where it seemed necessary to send a message to the operators. He put some bad guys behind bars, but he was more selective about his definition of a "bad guy" than he was supposed to be.

Ogilvie saw a cop who understood the criminal mind and got results. He recognized that Dick was close to the edge, but Ogilvie convinced himself that, if necessary, he could control Cain. What Dick saw in

Ogilvie was the future. Ogilvie was brilliant in the law, his political savvy was extraordinary, and he appeared to be scrupulously ethical. If that were true, Dick Cain saw an opportunity to hitch himself to a star that could be manipulated.

He wrote Ogilvie regularly, sometimes offering advice on matters such as whom to trust or not trust within the police establishment. Ogilvie discarded as much advice as he heeded, but he respected Dick's input and nearly always responded to the letters from Mexico. In late December 1961, Ogilvie wrote to Dick, encouraging him to return to Chicago. In that letter, Ogilvie talked about the upcoming campaign for sheriff, which he hoped to enter. He implied there might be a spot for Dick in the department.

Dick sent information to help Ogilvie discredit his competition for the Republican nomination. Behind the scenes, he began to plant a seed with the First Ward Democratic machine that they might well want to throw their support behind Ogilvie, because Dick thought he could work their relationship to the benefit of the mob. He passed this information to Pat Marcy. Marcy was the man who controlled the First Ward Democratic machine and he clearly bought into the concept since the Democratic candidate was going to be impossible to handle.

Dick's first billable engagement in Mexico City was for Sears-Roebuck. He tried to sell them on using the polygraph to screen their employees, but they wouldn't bite. They did want his expertise in conducting investigations though, and he was glad to have the business.

He'd gotten some interest in polygraph training from several police agencies he'd contacted. Not enough though to do any direct work at one agency. He was going to have to arrange a class on his own and sell each seat individually. He did just that and scheduled his first class for December 1961.

Before that, though, he followed up on his engagement with Pierre Kroupensky by scheduling a trip to Washington, D.C., in September 1961. They were to meet with the Panamanians to set out a game plan for execution of their contract. He was excited about this job, but moderately concerned he was not getting an advance, and he would soon be near the end of his financial cushion. It was naïve of him to take on a job like this without up-front money, but he was desperate, or nearly so. When he returned from Washington, Dick immediately began loading up the tools he would need and boarded a plane to Panama City.

On September 25, Dick arrived in Panama and began the task of infiltrating local communist organizations in and around Panama City. His contract with Kroupensky called for him to recruit up to five locals to help so that his coverage area would be increased. Their goal was to identify the level of communist recruitment activity, to determine whether their message was being embraced or tolerated, and to get the names of leaders of identified cells.

He took an apartment there and buried himself in work for about six weeks. Dick complained that the phone service in Panama was underpowered, and therefore difficult to tap. The technical issue was that there was barely enough electrical current in the lines to carry the voices of the callers, and that adding a third unauthorized circuit to the conversation made them difficult to hear and harder to record. He returned to Mexico with an uneasy feeling about collecting for the work he'd done and worse yet, Pierre shared his fears. Dick wrote, "I'm living on about 25 pesos a day [$2.00 at that time] and working on getting a job every day, but it seems hopeless, and soon I'll be down to the transportation money and will have to return. How I hate to fail so completely."

Time was his enemy, so he began organizing the upcoming class that had been approved by the Federal Police with space provided by the University of Mexico City. It was to be a thirteen-week course, and now he had everything riding on the success of this class. He would be well paid but, more importantly, this class would give him a much-needed psychological lift.

I've been pretty busy with my class. I've got 30 students representing every law enforcement agency in Mexico, from the equivalent of the FBI on down to the local police, and I'm writing a 15-minute movie script for the local police on Arrest, Search and Seizure. Also, I'm a doctor of Police Science, issued as an honorarium by the University of Mexico City, at the instigation of the Secret Service, to give me more respect in my classes. So the class calls me Doctor, Professor, or Maestro. I have to laugh about it, but really, it would have been nice to have graduated from high school. I have an invitation to teach in the month of April at the U of M's [University of Mexico City] Police Science School, and May at the Univ. of Moralia. And in March, when the class is through, I've been invited as guest of the government of Yucatan to lecture the judges and prosecutors there for a week on how to use the lie box in court.

These letters home were a critical part of his emotional stability in these days and months. Being able to spell out his schedule to Lydia helped him to organize his future plans, and it was probably the closest he ever got to therapy.

He began to socialize at a higher level and spent Christmas Eve at the home of the general of police of Mexico City. The Mexico City Police Department was more than ten thousand strong, and this was a very important contact for Dick. He relished the accomplishment.

He began writing articles for police-related magazines. They didn't pay much, but they did improve and increase his exposure to his target audience. Some of the writing was original, but most was probably plagiarized from the Chicago Police Department magazine, newsletters, and daily bulletins his mother sent him every few weeks. Lydia was a district secretary and had access to many publications, and Dick had no remorse about stealing the words of others.

By January 1962, Dick had filed suit against the government of Panama, the first part of the process of accepting the loss. Revenue from the polygraph class allowed him to open an office, hire a secretary (whom he seems to have later married), and begin to feel a small taste of success. He met the chief justice of Mexico, who agreed to help Dick in setting precedent to have polygraph tests accepted into evidence in Mexican courts.

He used this newfound clout to get an extension on his visa. Americans were automatically granted a six-month visa, but anything beyond that required permission from the government. He also initiated the four-year process of declaring dual citizenship.

He explained the current state of affairs in a letter to his mother:

As far as my immigration and working papers are concerned, I'm technical Advisor to the Policia Judicial del Procuradoria. The Procurador has the job that is the Mexican equivalent of Bobby Kennedy's [Attorney General], and his Policia Judicial is the equivalent of the FBI. Actually, I receive a salary from him that amounts to about 200 dollars a month, but the only time he'll make me work (he sez) is on cases involving Americans, or when the newspaper heat is so bad he needs the air cleared by a 'renowned police authority' (?).

I'm taking my [polygraph] class to the Govt. nuthouse for practice running loco's next Friday. The head psychiatrist has read some of my work (?) on psychopathic personality cases with the polygraph, and has asked me to give the staff a talk in March. That makes four speaking engagements in March, in Spanish. It seems so silly when people call me Doctor. But as you say, my charm does come through in the end. I don't laugh anymore.

Am doing the same old thing for the Cubanos here. I always feel like a blushing virgin when someone tells me they need me—all they want to really do is rape me for assistance.

The "same old thing" was training Cuban expats in the use of weapons for what they all believed would be the second invasion of Cuba. Many of the Cubans he'd met the year before had fled Cuba and come to Mexico to plan for the invasion. Dick would meet with them at several training camps they had managed to set up. He would help with small arms training and, if he found capable trainees, he would share some of his wiretap knowledge. He also made the point with them that his polygraph skills would be helpful, after they had returned to power, in weeding out the Castro sympathizers. He wanted to be with them when they took Cuba back.

On March 11, 1962, the following article appeared in the Yucatan newspaper *Diario del Sureste:*

After attending the Course in Techniques of Interrogations and application of the polygraph favored by the Banco de Mexico. It began in the city from 4th of December of last year to the 28th of February. Mr. Ernesto Abreu Gomez, chief of the Department of Registration and Identification of the Attorney General of the State, returned to the city by way of car.

In a brief talk with Mr. Abreu Gomez, he told us that the bank was invited to send an official to take advantage of the course being given, and he was granted the honor of attending.

He added that the course was headed by Prof. Richard S. Cain, Doctor of Psychology of the University of Loyola, Chicago, Ill. US, ex-member of the Service of Intelligence of the North American Army; ex-Lieutenant of Detectives for the Police in Chicago and graduate of the Keeler Institute of Chicago.

He later expressed that the courses developed with all regularity and efficiency and the class had a total of 23 students. Among them members of the Judicial Police of Mexico D.F., Secretary of Farms, Police Headquarters of Mexico, D.F. Dept. of Investigations of Banco de

Mexico, the University Nacional Autonoma de Mexicon and himself, sent by the Executive of our state.

The course consisted of the following: Physiology, Physiologic aspects, Elements of Psychiatrist, Medical aspects, Hypnosis, types of lie detectors, Criminal Interrogation, Exams with the Polygraph machine, Legal aspects, General Practice, Interpretation of Graphics, reports and files.

Finally Mr. Abreu Gomez informed us the closing of the classes was in the auditorium of the General Attorney at Law of Mexico, D.F. and presided by attorney Fernando Roman Lugo who personally gave the diplomas to all the graduates. During this ceremony, Dr. Alfonso Millan, professor the Technical Institute of Police dictated a very brief and interesting conference about Criminal Law and Dr. Alfonso Qurioz Cuadron, chief of the Dept of Special Investigations of Banco de Mexico, S. S. had some very good words to say about the course that had just ended.

Before saying goodbye, at our request Mr. Abreu Gomez put before us the diploma he had received.

The article included a photograph of the graduating class surrounding Dr. Cain.

Dick sent a copy to his mother, explaining that, "unfortunately, I can't let myself believe my own public relations—and it's been rather tough sledding pulling up from absolutely nothing after Operation Panama, but thank heaven things are showing a little progress."

In April he started another two-month polygraph class for the police of the state of Mexico. A small class, only three students, but it was good work and would surely lead to more. He began marketing a larger class, set to begin in June, and he attended a trade show for grocers and made a presentation on the effectiveness of the polygraph and felt there was a genuine possibility of landing some lucrative contracts. He also organized the first Polygraph Examiners Association in Mexico, joking to friends "first you teach them, then regiment them."

He had communication with Panamanian President Roberto Chiari, acknowledging payment for his work in Panama would be impossible. Chiari did, however, promise to make it up through recommendations he be hired by businesses in Panama that owed him favors. Dick doubted anything would ever come of the promise and simply accepted that he'd lost out.

He tried to stay upbeat in his communications back home to Lydia, telling her:

> I was appointed Asesor Tecnico (Technical Advisor) to the Policia Fiscal de Hacienda (a combination IRS-Border Patrol-Narcotics of the Treasury Dept.). They gave me an office there and are buying a new polygraph. Main thing is I've got government police ID, which is almost impossible to get here for a foreigner. This is also the only agency that is charged with the investigation of Communism in Mexico. My official partner-chauffeur killed a prisoner (Red) last year while transporting him to the shithouse. Tried to escape?
>
> Am starting a wiretap job tonight. The telephone power here is less than in Chicago, and I had to do a lot of experimenting over the weekend to get the damn equipment working so some conversation can get through. (want to intercept, not interfere).
>
> Am in the usual financial jam. Business has been very slow due to the Semana Santa (Easter Week) at which time everyone here gets a week vacation—so there was no work, and consequently, no money.
>
> I've been asked to edit a new magazine to deal with police & investigative subjects. Have arranged to get local photos of crimes, etc. but I could use any more clippings you may notice in papers in regard to stories about police procedures, important cases, etc. I translated and used that clipping about hair ID you sent me, and it looks good in Spanish, especially with an accompanying photo of hair, and will use an old clipping (edited and changed to fit a mag story) about electronic eavesdropping devices also. Really, I'll be stealing a lot of material, because there is no money to pay reporters, writers, etc but if it goes over the first few issues, things could change. So if you see anything interesting in the papers, I'd appreciate you clipping it for me.
>
> I've been invited to go to Caracas for the revolution. Declined.

By May 1962, Dick was working steadily with his teaching and private polygraph work, investigations, and wiretaps. He wasn't getting rich, but he was less desperate.

Among the clippings Lydia sent him was Jack Mabley's column about the Chicago Stadium Corp. He replied right away:

> I got a kick out of Mabley rapping the Chgo Stadium Corp. I had a tap on their phones once, and let Mabley hear a few conversations. He's hated them ever since.

> I starred in a movie made yesterday. About scientific criminal investigation. The name of it is *Mente Y De Crimen* (*Crime and the Mind*) it's 2 hrs long and is classed as a documentary. Will be shown before UNESCO in Sept in Paris as part of a scientific film prize. The whole thing is the story of a scientific investigation into a rape murder suspect, and most of the scientific things fail, because of the bad evidence, etc. etc, but the circumstances really make the lead actor look guilty. Then I come on with a lie test, (and the side of the film simultaneously shows a running graph with reactions) and, because of the reactions, it really looks to the audience like he's guilty, but then, it's very dramatically mentioned that he's innocent and an explanation is given regarding reactions. The cop who got all the bad evidence is the guilty one.

Dick's ability to generate publicity kept him afloat during these times and enhanced his credibility in the circles he was attempting to work in. That he was described as an "eminent psychologist" and "Dr. Cain" is testimony to his complete lack of interest in honesty or integrity. Rather, his focus was on succeeding in this pursuit at any cost.

Also by May 1962, it was apparent Ogilvie would be elected sheriff of Cook County, and Dick wanted to do everything he could to encourage, help, and be remembered by Ogilvie. Dick had worked hard to cultivate Ogilvie, because Ogilvie had a reputation of being incorruptible. To get in tight with Ogilvie would be a significant coup and would elevate his status in the mob beyond where it had been when he was with the police department.

In June 1962, Dick was deported from Mexico, no doubt related to an incident in which he delivered a severe beating to an impertinent parking attendant and arrested him, using his Mexican police credentials. The kid was later beaten some more in jail by one of Dick's former students. A few weeks later, Dick was arrested and charged with carrying a loaded revolver, possession of brass knuckles, possessing Mexican treasury department credentials and violating his visa by working as a private investigator and for the Mexican government. He had also been working on tapping the phones at the Czechoslovakian embassy and had been found out by the FBI. They put him on a plane to San Antonio where he knew virtually no one. He was broke and broken, but he'd been in worse straits. He made his way to Houston and took a job with a personnel screening firm, administering polygraph tests and training company personnel in the use of the polygraph.

He didn't enjoy any part of being in Texas. His one goal was to earn as much as he could as fast as he could and get the hell out of there. By mid-August he had put away some cash and was ready for his return to Chicago. The elections were just around the corner. Dick wanted to get there in time to do some work for the campaign that would solidify his relationship with Ogilvie.

He left Houston on September 1, traveling by bus, taking three days to get to home.

He knew returning to Chicago carried some risk, but he also knew opportunities awaited him. He stopped at a pay phone along the way and made two appointments for his first day back: lunch with Sam Giancana and dinner with Dick Ogilvie.

CHAPTER

8

The office of sheriff of Cook County has a dubious history at best. It's been a political office since the first sheriff was elected in 1831. Since then, only one sheriff has come to the job with a law enforcement background, and he may well have been the worst of the lot. When Richard Ogilvie was blessed with the Republican Party nomination to run for sheriff, he was determined to approach the job with an open mind and a clear conscience. He wouldn't campaign as a reformer, but he certainly had some ideas about changes he would make.

Ogilvie's opponent in 1962 was Roswell Spencer, a man with impeccable credentials for this job. Spencer was a former FBI agent and former chief investigator for the Cook County state's attorney. At any other point in history Spencer, in previously safe Democrat-land, would likely have crushed Ogilvie, but in 1962 the citizens of Cook County were angry with the current Democrat, Sheriff Frank Sain. They were angry with the Democratic Party for having put yet another do-nothing sheriff in charge. Not that Ogilvie was a bad choice. He was clearly qualified as well. A former federal prosecutor with a reputation for being tough on the mob, he brought his own strengths to the race.

Ogilvie had successfully prosecuted Tony Accardo in a high-profile case. It was his only major conviction, and it was overturned on appeal, but he clung to the victory anyway. He vowed to take personal charge of the makeup of the Cook County Sheriff's Police Department. In its history of more than 130 years, this job had served up more consistent corruption than perhaps any other elective office in the state. Ogilvie said he was going to change that. He appeared to be honest, and people believed in him.

As political contests go, this one was pretty boring. Both men took the high road. There was to be no mudslinging in this race. Truth be told, both Ogilvie and Spencer were so squeaky clean they'd have had to make up stories in order to get dirty. They both played it straight and, in the end, Spencer was defeated by the record of his predecessor.

Following Ogilvie's election as sheriff of Cook County, it was time to deliver on his campaign promises. He had told the voters he would crack down on vice in Cook County, and he devised a plan to accomplish that by introducing an elite new arm of the Cook County Sheriff's Police, named the Special Investigations Unit (SIU). Ogilvie announced his plan to name Richard Cain its chief.

Word spread fast about his intention to hire Dick Cain as chief of special investigations. Ogilvie was surprised at the reaction to his plan. Several people, including Bob Fuesel, then an investigator with the criminal division of the Internal Revenue Service, and later executive director of the Chicago Crime Commission, approached Sheriff Ogilvie with words of caution about Dick: "Bad news, mob-connected." The allegations were wide-ranging and damning. Worse yet, Fuesel was only the first in a string of naysayers. The list eventually included FBI agent Bill Roemer who knew for a fact that Dick was at least connected, if not a made guy. But Roemer wouldn't tell all he knew, partly to protect his source (Little Al) and partly because Ogilvie's decision to appoint Dick would have given the FBI pause regarding Ogilvie's own loyalties. Hell, even Harrellson at the Keeler Institute called Ogilvie to give an anti-Cain speech.

But no one could point to a single criminal act with which to associate Dick. Ogilvie asked them all to give him concrete reasons, but all he got was innuendo and unsupported allegations. All true of course, but none that had been proven in court, and Ogilvie interpreted this to mean they each had other agendas. Ogilvie recalled how effective Dick had been during the Accardo trial, and that trumped all.

Dick had returned from Mexico just weeks before the election and, although he worked during the final weeks of the campaign, his newcomer status prevented him from having much of an impact. More importantly, it prevented his enemies from having much time to educate Ogilvie about the true nature of his trusted friend's character. Ultimately it didn't matter, since Ogilvie saw only that Dick was working hard and that they had won the election.

Ogilvie remembered that during the Accardo case Dick had regularly developed considerable intelligence on the mob. Acknowledging that Cain had mob ties was, to Ogilvie, simply a matter of tipping his hat to good police work. A network of informants provided Cain with the information, nothing more sinister than that. Ogilvie agreed Dick was a bit of loose cannon, but felt confident in his own ability to control him. Further, Dick had stayed in close contact with Ogilvie after leaving the Chicago PD, sending him copies of some of his reports from Miami and Cuba. These appear to have had the desired effect.

Ogilvie regularly passed this information to the FBI, indicating he believed it had merit. Years later, when Ogilvie ran for governor of Illinois, his opponent went to great lengths to taint Ogilvie with the "Mark of Cain." Ogilvie's opposition in the governor's race published a four-page flyer with the banner headline MYTH OF OGILVIE—MARK OF CAIN in which they claimed that in Ogilvie's career as a federal prosecutor he tried only five cases, and his only conviction of a mob figure was later overturned. In his campaign for sheriff they said he'd promised to "chase the crooks out of the sheriff's office and run the gangsters ragged."

I have no reason to believe that Richard Ogilvie ever knowingly committed a crime. But there comes a time when you have to ask yourself "what was he thinking?" I don't know everyone Ogilvie spoke with about Dick, but to a man, all of the ones I do know were consistent in their negative recommendation.

I'm pretty sure anyone who was supportive of the idea of appointing Dick Cain was either married to him or a crook. So, was Ogilvie simply a pragmatist who made a trade to get the support of the Outfit's political machine? Or was he a willing conspirator? I don't know the answer, but the facts certainly beg the question.

Bob Cooley, former mob lawyer and author of *When Corruption Was King*, told me that Ogilvie could not have been elected without the blessing of the First Ward Democratic Committee, (i.e., Pat Marcy). That doesn't mean they had an arm's-length deal, it just means that for some reason he was given the nod.

CHAPTER
9

Despite all of the negative information others claimed to know about Richard Cain, Ogilvie decided to cast it all aside and name Dick chief of the Special Investigations Unit. He was thirty-one years old.

All of the non-uniformed members of the Cook County Sheriff's Police reported to him. In most big cities, the sheriff's department doesn't have much of a presence, but Cook County was always exceptional. They had the traditional uniformed cops who delivered subpoenas and managed the jail, but the county police also had huge unincorporated areas for which they provided both traffic enforcement and criminal investigations. They had the authority to investigate crimes within incorporated areas if certain conditions were met, but the conditions were vague and generally gave them carte blanche.

Dick's specialty was vice, and the charter of the Special Investigations Unit was to attack vice in Cook County. The conversation between Dick Cain and Sam Giancana must have been momentous. What a dream job. As a mobbed-up cop, a mobbed-up chief of SIU, he was in a position to virtually control vice in Cook County. No one would operate so much as a craps game without paying tribute to the Outfit. If they refused, he would send in the Cook County Sheriff's Police. For those who cooperated, he gave advance warning of an impending raid so they could minimize their losses. Avoiding raids altogether would have been too obvious.

Sam Giancana, the current boss of organized crime in Chicago, paid Dick five thousand dollars a month, several times his county salary, and

Tony Accardo kicked in some more. This money insured the mob against attack by the sheriff's department. If an investigation turned up a prostitution ring, a gambling operation, or other misdeeds, Dick always checked to see if it was an Outfit-sponsored business before executing any raids. If it was an Outfit-related group, or "in the book," Dick would either quash the investigation or coordinate the raid in such a way as to ensure that whatever charges came out of an arrest would be dropped before trial. One of the most pervasive complaints about the Ogilvie era was that it was filled with splashy raids but few successful prosecutions.

John D'Arco was the alderman from Chicago's infamous First Ward, the district that includes Chicago's Loop, or downtown area. In the aldermanic system employed by the City of Chicago, there are fifty seats on the council—one for each of fifty wards. The alderman has a great deal of influence over what goes on in his ward and is able to help his friends and punish his enemies. John D'Arco was no different.

An old pro, D'Arco had mob ties that went back a long way. He had grown up with Sam Giancana in The Patch, and they still met regularly to share their thoughts on running the First Ward. Giancana's opinion probably carried more weight than D'Arco's.

Pat Marcy was the "fixer" in the First Ward political arena. As secretary to the First Ward Democratic Committee, Marcy was another extremely influential person. Though not in an elected position, he was truly the man who pulled John D'Arco's strings. His real name was Pasqualino Marchone. Like Dick Cain, Pat Marcy was not who he appeared to be.

Even though John D'Arco had grown up with Sam Giancana and essentially answered to Sam, D'Arco was still an outsider as far as the Outfit was concerned. In mob parlance, D'Arco was known as a connected guy. Pat Marcy was a made guy, an initiated member. Made guys work first and foremost for the Outfit. If they do their jobs well, they are rewarded with money and influence; if they don't, they might be killed. Connected guys are rarely killed for bungling an assignment, only for egregious offenses such as snitching or trying to muscle in on a made guy. Even though Giancana and D'Arco were personal friends, Marcy had more status within the mob and was, therefore, the point man. Also, D'Arco, an elected official, had to appear to hold the interests of his constituents uppermost; Marcy had no such limitations.

Dick removing a policy wheel during one of many gambling raids

Dick Cain in his office at the Sheriff's Department

Dick's police academy class—1956

Dick with second wife Rosemary and the twins, Kim and Karla

Dick's Chicago Police Department ID photo—1962

Dick at the home of a friend in Switzerland in 1973, a month before his death

Dick with Senator Barry Goldwater and Dick Ogilvie
during the 1964 presidential campaign

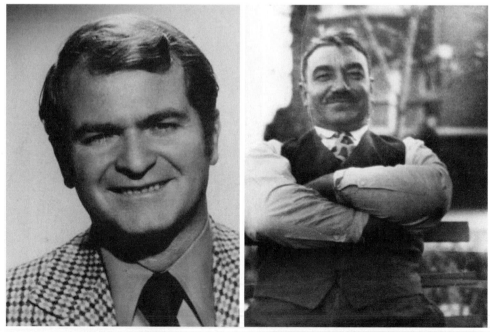

Dick's passport photo—1972

Dick's maternal grandfather, Ole Scully,
a short time before his murder by the
Black Hand in 1928

John Cain and Al Scully at Hot Springs,
Arkansas, March, 1932

Lydia and Richard, July, 1932

John Cain (circa 1930)

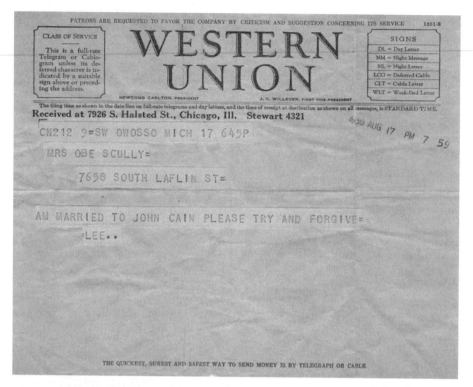

Lydia's telegram to
Vincenza, August, 1930

Lydia (circa 1983)

John Cain with his mother at the farm, 1936

Richard with his uncle, Lawrence Cain, 1936

Richard as a teenager

Dick's Chicago Police Department ID photo—1956

It's probably worth noting here that a made guy in Chicago is a little different than a made guy in New York. In New York there is a solemn ceremony where all the guys get together to welcome a newly made member. He takes an oath, he spills some blood, and he swears to uphold the rules of *omerta*. In Chicago, it's a matter of the boss or some other senior person declaring "you're with us now." It's very informal. This lack of formality probably derives from the fact that Chicago's Outfit does not have Sicilian roots like most of the rest of the country. That's probably also why they don't refer to themselves as Mafia, since the Mafia, as it exists in New York, can be traced directly back to Sicily.

D'Arco had the position of alderman, but Marcy had Sam Giancana's ear. Marcy was the link between the Chicago Outfit and city politics. D'Arco did what Pat Marcy told him to do, believing Marcy's words were Sam Giancana's words.

Dick's association with Marcy pre-dated his assignment to the police department, and they had worked closely together during Dick's time with the PD. Marcy knew how valuable Dick had been in the past and could be in the future, and the two men spoke regularly.

From the bug planted by the FBI in the First Ward Democratic Committee offices, the FBI listened in on conversations such as the one where Dick called and asked Pat Marcy to find out whether a business in Cicero, which had fifty phone lines, was actually a mob gambling operation. Through a series of conversations with various mobsters, it was learned this was a legitimate business with an active telemarketing department, so Dick closed his investigation. The interesting point here is the first part of his investigation was to clear it through Marcy.

Pat Marcy not only pulled John D'Arco's strings, he was said to have been the de facto manager of the City of Chicago. If you wanted to get a job with the city, whether as a police officer or a garbage truck driver, Pat Marcy could make that happen. If you wanted a promotion or a transfer you'd want to talk to Pat Marcy before you talked with your supervisor, then you could explain it as a fait accompli. If you wanted a liquor license . . . well, you get the idea. His power in the city was not rooted in his position or his leadership ability; it was rooted in cash. He knew who to pay and how to extract his quid pro quo. He was a very visible, approachable guy and, if you had a problem with the mob, he was the guy to talk to.

People wonder how this incredible corruption could have existed under the watchful eye of Mayor Richard Daley. Truth be told, Daley was known for maintaining Chicago's status as the city that works. The system may well have been corrupt to its very core, but it worked and even the voters accepted that as evidenced by their oft-repeated re-election of the mayor, or Da Mare, as they called him in Chicago. He was a pragmatist who cared more *that* it worked than about *how* it worked.

The stated mission of the Special Investigations Unit was to crack down on vice in Chicago and Cook County. Dick recruited some interesting talent to get the job done, including his old friend Bill Witsman, a former carnival barker and professional wrestler with zero previous police experience. He was hired as a sergeant and frequently worked as Ogilvie's chauffeur, no doubt using the opportunity to keep his boss apprised of the sheriff's activities.

Another hire was James Malcotte, a twenty-two-year-old rookie from the Chicago Police Department who had been in the army. After a month-long orientation and for reasons known only to the Chicago PD, Malcotte's first assignment was go to work at the phone company to learn about wiretaps. They didn't tell the phone company that, though. He became an installer. After five months with the phone company, he was installing phones in a business one day when the owner asked if he'd like to interview for another job. He answered yes, without really knowing what he might be opening himself up for. He called the number the guy had given him and wound up talking with Dick Cain. They arranged to meet later that week in Dick's office.

When Dick offered him a job, he finally admitted that he already had a job with the police department. Dick picked up the phone right then and called the police commissioner and arranged for him to take an indefinite leave of absence.

James Donnelly, a twenty-year veteran of the Chicago PD, would ensure good communication between the departments, and ensure that Dick was up to date on who to trust and who not to trust. For all of its corruption, the Chicago PD had a lot of cops who were straight shooters, who wanted nothing to do with payoffs. They wanted to be good cops, and they were. The crooked cops just had to know who they were, so they could steer clear of them.

The rest of the crew came from a variety of backgrounds, but their most important quality would be their commitment to Dick Cain. Mornings at the SIU generally started with a squad meeting during which Dick would tell the guys what their goals were for the day. He generally had some specific arrests in mind, bookies to raid, and brothels to bust. Then he'd retire to his office with a cold Coke—he never drank coffee— and begin chain-smoking Dunhill cigarettes.

Dick was an accomplished hypnotist, and during one of these morning sessions one of the members of the team asked him for help in giving up smoking. Dick agreed, but insisted they start immediately and seated him in a comfortable chair. Hypnosis generally begins with the hypnotist saying some soothing words—"you'll feel a great sense of peace"—and then putting the subject in a deep sleep while manipulating a visual distraction like a swinging pocket watch. In Dick's squad room it was probably a pen; the purpose of the distraction was simply to give the subject some animate object to focus on. So he told his subject, "Your eyes are getting heavy; when I count to three and snap my fingers you will close your eyes and you will be in a deep sleep. One . . . Two . . . Three." Then he snapped his fingers and the guy stared at him as if to say, "What the hell was that all about?" Just then, they heard a crash at the back of the room. One of the detectives had decided to stick around to watch—he was fascinated by the very idea that someone could be hypnotized. It didn't take on the guy sitting safely in the armchair, but the guy in the back of the room who had just hung around to watch went into a deep sleep when Dick snapped his fingers. Unfortunately for him, he was leaning on the corner of a desk at the time and simply keeled over and hit the floor. That was the last time Dick attempted hypnosis with an audience.

In the spring of 1963, the Special Investigations Unit began investigating a series of restaurant bombings that had been going on for nearly three years. They were usually after-hours bombings that destroyed the business. There seemed to be a pattern that linked most of the bombings, which generally involved the use of dynamite or a firebomb.

On January 25, 1963, Dick picked up Joey Aiuppa, allegedly to question him about the bombings. Aiuppa was in a leadership position at the time, and a peer of Tony Accardo, but Sam Giancana was the man in charge. Dick may well have gone after him just to mess with him, and assert his own position. He took him to the sheriff's office, where Ogilvie questioned him personally.

Some of the bombings were against mob-owned restaurants. These could have been motivated by rivalry, or by an attempt to collect insurance money.

Dick received information that a restaurant in Lisle was going to be hit by a well-known arsonist, so he and Lieutenant James Donnelly and Sergeant Jim Malcotte went up to spend the night there waiting for something to happen. After the restaurant closed and all the employees left, Dick and Donnelly helped themselves to a couple of glasses of scotch and took up positions at the bar. They directed Malcotte to position himself up front near a big plate glass window and they waited for something to happen. The mind can play tricks on you when you're sitting through a long stakeout. Malcotte was a little nervous to begin with, and speculated to himself that they may have put him where they did in order to make him a target. Imagine the great press they'd get if one of their own should lose his life in a bombing. The more he speculated, the more frightened and uncomfortable he became. Donnelly was sitting at the bar cradling a Thompson sub-machine gun, right hand on the trigger, left hand playing with the selector switch. "Click," single shot. "Click," full automatic. "Click, click, click." It seemed to Malcotte that the noise got louder and echoed through the building as the night dragged on. "Click . . . click . . . click."

The bad guys never showed.

In the early sixties, before Roe v. Wade, abortion was illegal. There were basically two types of abortionists in those days: physicians who saw it as a part of patient care and back-alley abortionists who preyed on women in need. Often the latter worked without training, sterilization, or anything like the proper equipment. The Special Investigations Unit frequently targeted abortionists, not so much as criminals but as lucrative targets who would pay a lot of money, in cash. The SIU hardly bothered with the back-alley coat hanger abortionists; they focused on the physicians. After all, that's where the money was. This was never about upholding the law; it was all about the money, and the SIU became a crime wave of official larceny.

In one such case Dick recruited one of his cousins, who was pregnant, to set up the target. She made an appointment and, on the day of her scheduled abortion, she nervously allowed the doctor to prep her. She was in the stirrups and in a near panic when Dick and his team rushed in at the last second. Once she composed herself she gave Dick hell for coming in so late.

A doctor on the North Side was said to have a lucrative abortion practice and the team was expecting a big score, since they usually kept all the money they recovered on these raids. Vanity, however, ruined the day as Dick invited a reporter and photographer to join them. He liked seeing his name in the papers and pictures were even better. On this day they raided the doctor's home. Expecting to find the cash in his home office, Dick and Bill Witsman took that room to search and sent the reporters to a back bedroom with one of the deputies. The deputy led the way into the bedroom and began a search. Cops are never very neat when they search a suspect's home, and they tend to be downright theatrical when the press is with them. The deputy opened a closet and found it stacked high with shoeboxes. He grabbed several of the boxes and tossed them across the room with dramatic flourish. The instant they left his hands he knew he had made a mistake. The boxes opened in mid-flight and scattered their contents about the room. In all, there was $545,000 in the stack of shoeboxes. Since the press was there, they had to turn it all in. The deputy told me it would have been their biggest payday ever.

On another occasion, a doctor who worked out of a motel room was interrupted while he was about to perform an abortion. They had gotten a passkey from the manager and entered the room with the woman in the last stages of preparation. They waited while she dressed and left the room, then Dick and Witsman took the doctor into the bathroom and beat him senseless. The curious thing about the bust was that they didn't arrest him. The doctor and the chief and the sergeant had come to some accommodation in the confines of that motel bathroom. One of the deputies was asked to drive the doctor home and, before the doctor left the car, still bloodied from the beating he'd taken, he inexplicably handed the deputy his card and told him to call if he ever needed a doctor. Some time later he did just that, and the doctor who was nearly beaten to death by the cops became a trusted family physician to the deputy and his family for many years thereafter.

Another prime target of the "reformers" was gambling. Bookies were everywhere in Chicago in those days, and still are. But in Dick Cain's

Chicago, you had to pay a tax to make book. Not necessarily to him, but to the Outfit. If you paid a share of your profits to the Outfit on a regular basis, regular being weekly, you were pretty much left alone. Nobody in the sheriff's department really looked at bookmaking as a crime—it was what people did. But if you made book and didn't share, then you'd have a problem. You'd likely get a visit from the Cook County Sheriff's Police, and what they would do is take all your money and split it amongst themselves. They might arrest you too, but not to worry. Since they had taken all your money and wouldn't want that discussed at trial, somehow the charges would get dropped or pleaded out to some insignificant misdemeanor.

It was how the Outfit kept control of such things. They called it a street tax. If you were a criminal and you didn't pay your taxes they wouldn't protect you, and they might even do something far worse than sending the sheriff's department. If you did, then you'd get a pass. Dick usually checked with Pat Marcy before taking down a bookmaker, to see if he was protected. Sometimes, though, the wires got crossed. The SIU raided a bookmaker in the Loop and confiscated $70,000 in cash. The bookie had been paying his tax, and looked to the Chicago Police Department for protection. The day after the raid, Dick got a call from Marcy telling him to return the money. Reluctantly he did so, delivering the cash to the police captain for that district. Years later, the captain admitted to one of the members of the SIU that he had kept the cash himself, telling the bookie he'd been unsuccessful in his efforts to get it back.

It was during this time that the structure of the mob began a metamorphosis of sorts. In the old days there was a boss and underbosses or captains that were given responsibility for a territory. Everybody in the Outfit ultimately reported to the boss. The new face of the Outfit would be a loose confederation of guys who collected a street tax from whomever they could, wherever they could. As it evolved, there would no longer be a boss like in the old days. Tony Accardo was probably the last of the Outfit bosses in Chicago. They probably have Sam Giancana to thank for the change. Sam was a psychopath who couldn't or wouldn't maintain the level of control necessary to keep everything together. He was himself ultimately killed by the guy he trusted most in the Outfit simply because he had rendered himself irrelevant.

To say there was a lot of gambling in Chicago is akin to saying there were once a lot of livestock slaughtered there. A VFW hall in suburban Cook County was a regular supporter of the concept of police protection, and it paid off for them one night when Dick received a tip that a big poker game at the hall was going to be robbed. Dick rounded up two of his deputies and drove out to the club. They dragged a piece of three-quarter inch steel plate up to the top of the stairway which led to the poker room. After securing their armor, they crouched behind it and waited. As if on cue, three bad guys entered the hall, armed with shotguns, and started to make their way up the staircase only to be mowed down by a fusillade of bullets from three Thompson sub-machine guns. The card game went on uninterrupted; no one even came out to see what the commotion was about. Later, when the local city police showed up, they simply turned around and left when they saw that Dick Cain and the SIU were involved.

On balance, there was another VFW hall that hadn't been so generous in its tributes to the Outfit. When the sheriff's department raided them, the players were all asked to identify themselves and then they were sent home. The manager was taken to an isolated corner of the building to be questioned. Lieutenant James Donnelly came equipped with a set of keys that unlocked the slot machines that were on the premises; the guys on the team were all amazed that he seemed to have keys to everything. They didn't confiscate the slots, but they did clean them out. When they returned the premises to the manager he was mystified, since his own keys had never been out of his sight and yet his machines were empty. One of the younger guys on the team got the nickels that night, and he and his wife were up 'til dawn counting them.

Chicago was also home to another interesting business that impacted gamblers. Empire Printing Co. was one of the country's largest manufacturers of marked cards, shaved dice, and loaded dice. Most of their products were shipped to Las Vegas and found their way into the pits at mob-run casinos there. When the Special Investigations Unit raided Empire, their entire inventory was confiscated and, theoretically, destroyed. But they wouldn't have destroyed all that good stuff. It's out there somewhere.

Mah Jongg was the game of choice in Chinatown. Invented by Chinese aristocrats, the game of chance was then introduced to the masses around 1920. In the fall of 1963 the SIU paid a visit to a Chinatown gambling den. They made 114 arrests that night, including all the players and the operators. The cops were confused by the language barrier and, of course, none of the Chinese admitted to speaking English. The obvious solution was to take them all to jail and let somebody else sort things out. While the team was processing those arrests at the scene, a couple of the guys started wandering around in the maze of tunnels that ran under the streets of Chinatown, connecting many of the buildings there. In one of the tunnels, they discovered a safe and tried to open it. There were no safecrackers on the team, so they went after it with a sledgehammer. After an hour-and-a-half of pounding, they realized they were up against a very formidable safe and finally resorted to peeling.

To peel a safe you must literally peel off the face, using a chisel to get between the outer layer and the concrete center. It's tedious work at best and difficult physically. Once the face is removed you can break up the concrete core of the door to reveal the inner locking mechanisms and dismantle them. This, of course took several more hours and, when they got it open, they found only a single piece of jade inside. Well, not just a piece of jade, it was a piece about the size of a large watermelon. Its value today could be in excess of half-a-million dollars. They took it back to the sheriff's department and stored it in Dick's office for several days. They never did know what it was worth and had no idea how or where they could fence a gemstone that large anyway. The unofficial mayor of Chinatown called Mayor Daley and insisted that it be returned, which it eventually was. They were happy to be rid of it.

In time, the 114 men they had arrested for gambling were brought to trial. The defense attorney called the eleven members of the Special Investigations Unit to the stand and asked each one in turn to explain to the court how these men gambled at Mah Jongg. "Detective, please explain to the court the definition of a Pong."

"I don't know."

"Detective, please explain to the court the definition of a Chow."

"I don't know."

"A Kong?"

"I don't know."

None of them had a clue how the game was played, much less how one gambled at it, so when the defense attorneys approached the judge, they said, "Look, these guys stumbled into something they didn't understand

and their solution was to arrest everybody in the room. My clients were simply playing a traditional Chinese game, similar to your dominoes. Your Honor, would you arrest people for playing dominoes? Nobody produced any cash which might suggest there was gambling going on, and these cops can't even define how one would gamble at this game even if there had been cash." After listening to each of the detectives embarrass himself on the stand, the judge dropped all the charges.

Dick also started to use wiretaps as a weapon, a tool to enhance his own position. With a well-trained wiretapper on his staff, he could virtually go after anyone. He once tapped the phone of a sitting judge, in the courthouse. The taps were never done with a court order and never used to build cases; they were used to gather information that could be used to enhance Dick's position in the Outfit. Frequently he'd share some of the recorded conversations with Jack Mabley, then a columnist with *Chicago's American*, to show Mabley how corruption worked in Chicago. He was always careful to share this information about his enemies, not his friends.

He tapped the phone of Cook County State's Attorney Ben Adamowski. Paul Newey, who was Adamowski's chief investigator at the time, was told about the tap years later and insisted it couldn't have been done because he personally swept the office every day. The problem with that is the sweeps were looking for FM devices or recording equipment. The recorder was placed in a trashcan outside the building and the wires were concealed behind a downspout. The deputy responsible for maintaining the tap had to go by on the mornings when the trash was collected, remove the device for a time, and reinstall it after the trashmen had left.

Installing a wiretap can be tricky. Concealment of the wires is only the first step, because it's not much good unless it's attached to a recording device. When they installed a tap on a farmhouse in rural Cook County they had to run five miles of wire to a secure listening post.

Sam DeStefano was one of Dick's early wiretap targets. DeStefano was the personification of pure evil, and Dick wanted to find out what he was doing. DeStefano, a juice loan specialist was feared by all who knew him. When he found it necessary to apply strong collection practices, he was well known for the sadistic pleasure he derived from torturing his victims with an ice pick or a blowtorch. It was during the installation of the

DeStefano wiretap that Dick's tapper met the FBI's tapper and they initially challenged one another, each pretending to be working for the phone company on adjacent telephone poles. Neither bought the other's story, and they nearly drew guns. When it turned out that the county tap was a better connection than the FBI tap, they shared tapes, and that became the basis of a long-lasting relationship.

Dick had a score to settle with DeStefano that dated back to 1961, when DeStefano killed a friend of Dick's, William "Action" Jackson, a juice collector. "Uncle Act," as he was known to Dick's twin daughters, was a big guy who used the intimidation of his imposing size more than actual physical force in his job. Uncle Act worked for Willie "Potatoes" Daddano and, through a misunderstanding, he was suspected of being an FBI informant. DeStefano took him to a meat-packing plant and suspended him from a meat hook for three days while he questioned and tortured him. Action Jackson was not an informant and died because of Mad Sam DeStefano's cruel nature. Dick's daughters remembered him as a wonderfully happy man who played with them in Dick's backyard.

Not long after that, Dick sent his wiretapper to the Florida Keys to tap the phone of a judge's wife. The judge suspected she was being unfaithful, and he asked for Dick's help. While the tap was being monitored, she received a call from a neighbor telling her that her phone conversations were broadcasting on top of the audio for Channel 7, a local television station. She immediately called the police but, by the time they arrived, all evidence of a wiretap had been removed. The deputy sheriff from Cook County was high-tailing it for home. He never figured out what caused the crossover with the TV station, but figured the prudent thing to do was just to get the hell out of there, so he quickly pulled his wires and drove past the approaching police cars as he made his escape.

The several bugs the FBI had planted around Chicago were of inestimable value to the bureau over the years. They were illegal, though, and could not be used to produce evidence in any criminal investigation. Their value then was in developing intelligence about how the Outfit operated. According to former FBI agent William F. Roemer, Jr., in the beginning they were stunned at the size and scope of the mob's activities.

The first bug was installed in 1959 at Celano's tailor shop on Michigan Ave and went active on July 29. Bill Roemer installed the bug, which is really a misnomer; as the microphone was almost the size of a small pineapple, he named it "Little Al" in honor of Al Capone. In the days prior to this time, J. Edgar Hoover, the FBI's crack, cross-dressing director, denied there was such a thing as the Mafia and prevented his agents from doing any meaningful surveillance. It's long been a curiosity to me whether his denial was a form of protection or simply a sign of his incompetence. It's been well documented that he was friendly with, and likely blackmailed by, Frank Costello and Meyer Lansky, who were aware of his homosexual dalliances and who possessed a number of photographs of him in big puffy dresses. Hoover had been photographed at the racetrack with Costello, and Costello once commented, "You can't believe how many races I had to fix for his silly bets."

That Hoover ignored, if not aided, the growth of organized crime from his appointment as director in 1924 through at least the late 1950s is irrefutable. The questions that still linger are, how did he get away with it, and why does the FBI continue to honor this man? It seems clear to me that he was complicit in the entrenchment of the Mafia in this country and yet we name buildings after him.

These bugs in Chicago would seem to follow his pattern of "collecting data" about his enemies, but they also allowed the bureau to acquire confirmation about Dick's ties to the mob. When Dick was part of a conversation he was usually referred to by a nickname, as was the general practice. Dick was known as the "Redhead" inside the Outfit, owing to his reddish-brown hair. He hated the name because it alluded to his Irish heritage, which he tried so hard to hide from them. Interestingly, the FBI never let on, even to Sheriff Ogilvie, what they knew about Dick's mob ties. They were convinced that any discussion would lead to a request for proof of what they knew, and they were determined not to divulge the existence of these bugs to anyone—the lone exception being three years earlier during the Accardo trial. They were, after all, illegal bugs and any request to defend their existence would have resulted in their removal.

Next to the tailor shop, the second most valuable bug was installed in the offices of the First Ward Democratic Committee, Pat Marcy's home base. It was there they first associated Dick with Sam Giancana. Marcy was the conduit through which most people had to go to get to Sam. Likewise, when Sam had instructions for Dick they would frequently pass through Marcy. The transcripts from those bugs reveal a close relationship that began to deteriorate late in 1964 as Dick's troubles mounted inside the sheriff's department. It doesn't appear to have been related to any bad blood, but rather to Dick's own decision to pull back. He even refused Marcy's offer of help during his perjury trial.

Probably the third most valuable bug, and the one they were most protective of, was in the law offices of Mike Brodkin and George Bieber. Indicative of the FBI's concern about this "source" was the following statement, which preceded each report of activity from the bug: "Extreme caution should be exercised in the use of this information. It should not be included in the body of a report even though paraphrased. It should not be used in lead coverage or as the basis for an interview unless specific clearance is obtained from the bureau and from Chicago. This is an extremely delicate and sensitive source which the Chicago office is making every effort to fully protect." The statement appeared at the beginning and end of each report in all caps and underlined. The source was referred to as CG-6753-C and chronicles the day-to-day dealings of a high-level mob lawyer who represented all the big names in town.

CG-6753-C also confirmed to the FBI that Dick Cain was working both sides. They overheard conversations involving Dick and Lieutenant James Donnelly, where Brodkin and Bieber asked directly for information, inside information, which would help them to get their clients out of a jam with the courts. In one instance, Joseph D'Argento and Paul "Peanuts" Panzko were arrested for possession of burglary tools, and they tell Brodkin in detail how they were arrested after stealing a car they "needed" for a burglary they were planning. Brodkin told them "Jimmy Donnelly is getting all the dope on this case."

On March 27, 1963, two Chicago FBI agents visited Dick in his office. They had a laundry list of issues to discuss with him concerning some illegal wiretaps that were being blamed on him. He denied any knowledge of the wiretaps, but did agree there was good reason for him to be a suspect. Then out of left field, they asked if he had attended the February 1961 wedding of Ross Prio's son, Ross, Jr. They engaged him in conversation, and he told them he realized he had a reputation of being involved with the Outfit. He told them the reputation was the result of his intense investigation of the mob, and his frequent visits with mob members were related to his attempts to develop informants.

He said although it was the common belief he was Irish, he was actually Italian and had only a small percentage of Irish blood. He told them his father was Italian and was murdered by the Black Hand. As a result of this, he insisted, he had an intense hatred for the Italian hoodlum element and could hardly stand being civil to them when it was necessary to make contact in an investigation. He said if he were asked whether he had ever shot anyone without justification, he would have to take the Fifth Amendment, but would not be afraid to justify any inquiry concerning his relationship with the Chicago hoodlum element.

Conversations like that must have been both frustrating and hilarious to the FBI agents; frustrating because they couldn't call him on his lies and hilarious because they knew beyond a doubt he was lying.

Dick attempted to maintain his connection with the CIA through his old friend Bill Lohmann, whom he had met prior to his departure to Cuba in 1960. Lohmann represented an important link in what Dick thought would be his next career change. His love of espionage was much stronger than his ties to the mob, so he wanted to legitimize his vision of himself as a spy by one day joining the CIA clandestine services, or KUBARK as they referred to themselves.

On August 19, 1963, Dick had dinner at Adolph's on Rush Street with Lohmann and an associate from the Chicago office of the CIA. The purpose of the meeting was to discuss activities of Cuban Counterrevolutionary groups that were active in Chicago at the time. Dick had developed a network of informants and had even attended a number of their meetings himself. He was actively working with the Cubans, training them for what they hoped would be the next invasion. He drove to dinner and parked in a no-parking zone near the restaurant. A local traffic cop named Philip Tolan recognized Cain's car as one he had ticketed thirty or more times at a bus stop outside the Marina City complex where Dick lived. Tolan ticketed the car and later, when he saw Dick and his friends drive by, Tolan pulled his three-wheeled motorcycle up alongside, pulled Dick over, and asked for identification. To Dick, this was a situation that could be extremely embarrassing. He was in the company of the CIA station chief, whom he felt obliged to protect but, at the same time he couldn't allow himself to be pushed around by a mere patrolman.

Dick flashed his badge, thinking that should be adequate. Tolan asked for a driver's license and Dick refused. He told Tolan he was with the sheriff's department and was driving a sheriff's department car, and that should be the end of it. When Tolan went to his radio to check the license number, Dick drove off. Tolan took up chase and pulled him over again a few blocks later. By this time, several patrol cars responded and showed up on the scene. Lohmann and his partner got out of the car and walked away, grateful to be washing their hands of the encounter.

After no small effort to make the situation go away, Dick drove to the police station. He was relieved of his weapon and placed in the bullpen until ordered released by a deputy superintendent.

For a different spin on the evening, here's the report Lohmann sent to CIA headquarters reporting what happened:

The meeting was arranged by Chief, Chicago Office after a call from [deleted] on the afternoon of 19 August. Subject (Cain) arrived at the Lake Shore Drive Athletic Club shortly after 1800 hours.

Subject is in his middle or late thirties, approximately 5'8" in height and weighing about 150 lbs. Subject, who has gained considerable notoriety in the Chicago press as a tough cop, a polygraph expert and as Chief Investigator for the Cook County Sheriff's Office, could well pass as a graduate of the Harvard Business School; neatly and conservatively dressed, black horn-rimmed glasses, and hair cut short and combed close to the head. Subject speaks well though occasionally lapsing into bad grammar.

Subject is thinking of taking a job as Chief Investigator for the Illinois Crime Commission, which would considerably negate his value to us. In the far future, Subject would like to work overseas, possibly with KUBARK. It was pointed out to him his work with KUBARK now might be of value if he did apply to work with KUBARK in the future.

Subject is married to a Mexican girl, speaks good Spanish and has considerable contact with the Cuban community in Chicago. Subject is, through his position in the Cook County Sheriff's Office, also in contact with the less legal adventures of the Cubans in Chicago. Subject was told generally of our requirements and agreed to help us wherever he could; particularly in noting any rumors of CIA contact in Chicago, providing information on the undercover activities of the Cubans, particularly Paulino Sierra and his contacts; and providing the names of any Cubans who might be useful to us.

After leaving the Lake Shore Drive Athletic Club, Subject, Chief Chicago OO Office, and a third party went in Subject's car to Adolph's Restaurant. Subject illegally parked his car, though Chief Chicago OO warned him he would be ticketed. The group left the restaurant sometime later, got in the car and started to drive away, only to be immediately flagged down by a motorcycle policeman. Subject stopped his car and walked back to the cop, who was probably twenty or thirty feet behind. Subject showed the cop his credentials. The cop, whose predecessor was a headline hunter, has followed in the tradition ticketing the Governor, the Cardinal, etc. Subject's credentials were enough for the cop, who saw another press notice. Consequently, the cop told Subject to pull over into a side street. Subject did, stopped and again went back to the cop. At this time, Chief OO office and [deleted] to avoid any notoriety by osmosis, left the car and walked away. The newspaper article the next day covering the events mentioned that two unknown men were seen to leave Subject's car and walk into the night.

Dick lived in Marina City. Twin circular towers situated on the Chicago River, it was an exclusive place to live and not one he could afford on a cop's salary. One of Dick's neighbors was Murray Humphreys, an old time Chicago mobster whose participation reached back to the days of Al Capone.

In November 1963, an incident took shape involving an alleged wiretap on the phone of Chicago Attorney David Bradshaw. Bradshaw was chairman of the subcommittee of the Illinois State Crime Commission that was in the process of screening applicants for the position of executive director, for which Dick was a candidate. When the tap was detected, Bradshaw notified the Cook County Sheriff's Department of his concern. Richard Cain responded to conduct the investigation personally.

The next day, the FBI overheard the following conversation between Pat Marcy and Anthony Tisci, Sam Giancana's son-in-law:

Marcy said, "Now, let's talk about the Redhead. He wants to kill this Siragusa thing." Siragusa was Dick's competition for the job.

"Do you think he'll be able to?"

"I think he's got it made. He took the shot that will make him anyway. He will be here any fucking day. I told him, 'Now listen, you're sticking your neck a mile out and you're going to get the fucking jacket.' He said, 'No I won't.' I said, 'Listen to what I tell you.' He wanted to cripple this guy."

"You know," continued Marcy, "Cain was the investigator on the complaint from Bradshaw about his fucking wiretap."

"You're kidding me!" roared Tisci. He laughed uncontrollably for several minutes.

On November 6, 1963, *Chicago Tribune* reporter Sandy Smith told Marlin Johnson, the special agent in charge (SAC) of the Chicago office of the FBI, that he was absolutely convinced Cain was responsible for the wiretap.

Agents visited Dick at the sheriff's department to ask him about it. He, of course, denied any involvement. The bureau asked him to keep their conversation confidential, which was the red flag that sent Dick to his reporter friends to tell them the FBI was conducting an investigation.

Charles Siragusa was the leading candidate and eventually got the job, but Dick had thrown his hat in the ring, with the blessing of Sheriff Ogilvie, and thought he had a shot at the job, but only if he could get Siragusa out of the race. Formerly director of the Federal Bureau of Narcotics, Siragusa was the clear front-runner.

Apparently, on November 1, a number of Chicago-area reporters, including Sandy Smith and Jack Mabley, found audiotapes on their desks, which contained a recorded telephone conversation of David Bradshaw, the crime commission lawyer, that was unflattering to Siragusa. The existence of the tapes constituted incontrovertible proof that a wiretap had been in place and clearly contained recorded telephone conversations, so the question was how and by whom?

Bradshaw contacted Sheriff Ogilvie who immediately assigned his chief of investigations to look into the matter. Dick went immediately to the offices of David Bradshaw at 30 North LaSalle Street to see what he could see. He met with Bradshaw and quizzed him at some length about the reasons someone might want to tap his phone. It was a golden opportunity for Dick to size up his competition and he made the most of it.

Dick assured reporters he was investigating the matter with diligence.

Dick wanted that job and undoubtedly spent hours fantasizing about how he'd manage the Outfit's business at the state level. The end of the dream came when his wiretapper came into Dick's office one day to tell him that Siragusa, whose phone had also been tapped, had just received a phone call from Bobby Kennedy, then the attorney general of the United States, congratulating him on being selected for the job.

In February 1964, Scott Cohen, a member of Charles Percy's campaign staff, contacted the FBI. Percy was in a race seeking the Republican nomination for governor of Illinois. Cohen suspected that Dick was involved and he wanted the FBI to conduct an investigation of Richard Cain, suggesting Dick had been granted a leave of absence by Sheriff Richard Ogilvie for the purpose of developing negative information about Percy so as to discredit his campaign. Ogilvie had also been mentioned as a potential candidate and this seemed quite a coincidence to Percy.

The FBI referred Cohen to the phone company and advised the director of security at Illinois Bell, Bernard Eggenberger, that he would be hearing from Charles Percy's people.

Eggenberger wasn't much help, as Dick rarely kept them in the loop about his wiretaps because he never requested a court order to install them. Consequently they had little information about his capabilities.

Not entirely satisfied with the FBI's refusal to investigate, Cohen contacted a friend of his at the CIA and invited him to lunch. Throughout their conversation, Cohen repeatedly brought up Richard Cain, wanting to know if the CIA was aware of his activities and asking what they knew about him and how they felt about him. The CIA predictably did not give up any information. Cohen was told that Cain was regarded as "a controversial individual, an apparently honest policeman, and a product of a rough upbringing with a limited education but still trying to be a decent individual."

Dick had, in fact, been on a leave of absence from the sheriff's department at the time, but indications are he spent some of the time in Spain, visiting his daughter and undoubtedly working on a drug trafficking plan for Giancana, but he was also traveling with Barry Goldwater on the campaign trail.

In 1964, presidential politics were on everyone's mind. The war in Vietnam was beginning to escalate into a major conflict. Lyndon Johnson had not yet revealed his terrible plan to expand our involvement in Vietnam, and Barry Goldwater was considered the hawk in the race. Goldwater came to Chicago early in 1964 to campaign, and Ogilvie asked Dick to join them in a meeting. Goldwater and Ogilvie, it seems, were old friends, and the presidential candidate had asked for supplemental security for the upcoming Republican National Convention.

Goldwater was distrustful of the Secret Service team he had been assigned, fearing they were reporting back to the Johnson camp about his activities. His distrust was not based on anything they'd actually done, rather it was his own paranoia showing but, in any event, he planned to replace them with a team from the Cook County Sheriff's Police, headed by Richard Cain.

Goldwater liked Dick and told him when he was elected president of the United States, he wanted Dick to come to Washington and be his guy at the Secret Service. Dick told him that he would be delighted to move to Washington. A Secret Service job could have worked out to be better than director of the Illinois Crime Commission.

In preparation for the convention, Dick and his team flew to San Francisco a week ahead of the event, which was to be held July 13–16, 1964. Dick wasn't terribly concerned about the candidate's welfare, everything seemed to be going smoothly, so he sent two members of his team to help make sure that Goldwater won the election. What they did was to hit the sewers of San Francisco, looking for the telephone lines that led to the Johnson campaign headquarters.

It took three or four days of crawling in really awful conditions. Each night they would throw away the clothes they had worn that day and replace them with new ones. Eventually, though, they located a bundle of wires that appeared to cover that section of the city. The fifty-thousand-pair bundle was too big to reveal the actual pairs that serviced the Democratic offices, so they did the next best thing: they cut the whole bundle. They were pleased to see that the phone company had thoughtfully installed electrical outlets in the sewers, so they simply used a Skil saw to zip right through the bundle, which was nearly three feet in diameter. When they finished the job and rejoined the candidate at the Cow Palace, they asked Dick what made him think about this particular plan of attack.

"We did it in Chicago a few years back and it worked extremely well. Cut out the whole First Ward, so they couldn't communicate and find out how many votes they needed to conjure up. It may have been the only honest election in Chicago history."

Apparently the phone company in San Francisco didn't want to talk about the disruption of service, so they didn't release any information and just quietly went about repairing the damage.

The FBI had installed a bug in the office of Celano's Custom Tailors on Michigan Avenue, a men's tailor shop run by Jimmy Celano. A room at the back of Celano's was the unofficial headquarters of the Chicago mob. As detailed by Bill Roemer, installing the bug was a difficult and challenging task, given the state of technology in 1959. The "bug" was a World War II–era microphone, roughly the size of a pineapple, nicknamed "Little Al," in deference to Al Capone. Little Al was in place from mid-1959 until July 11, 1965, when the mike just went dead, never to be heard from again. This flow of information was interrupted only once when Murray Humphreys announced he was going to have Dick Cain sweep the office for bugs. By discussing his concerns in the presence of the bug he feared might be there, Humphreys alerted the FBI, giving them enough notice to re-enter the building and disable Little Al for a couple of weeks. After what seemed a reasonable time, Roemer entered the building once again and re-installed Little Al.

The information the FBI acquired from this bug was immensely valuable intelligence, but they could not introduce it in court: only a court-authorized bug could produce admissable evidence. To protect the existence of this and several others installed later, they chose not to seek a court order. They were so protective of this source it was not even disclosed within the bureau to agents not directly involved in organized crime investigations, or what they called the "Top Hoodlum Program." On several occasions they heard plans being made for someone to be hit. In those cases, where they could, they attempted to contact the intended target to offer safe haven. They allowed other crimes to happen just so they could protect this valuable source. No one in the Justice Department knew of the bugs, and no judge was ever told about them, except in one instance when Julius Hoffman had to be told.

When the Zahn Drug Company of Melrose Park, Illinois, was burglarized in 1963, the thieves got away with a $250,000 truckload of prescription drugs. Dick was the lead investigator for the Cook County Sheriff's Police and had not made any arrests on the case. In January 1964, Dick led a raid on the Caravelle Motel in Melrose Park where they recovered $42,000 worth of the missing drugs. The newspapers carried staged photos of Dick standing guard over a pile of boxes, holding his Thompson submachine gun. The press had been invited to attend the raid so they could get a scoop on the story.

One of the reporters who covered the story later returned to the hotel and asked to see the registration card for the room that had been raided.

The name was fake, as one might expect, but he thought he recognized the handwriting as that of Sergeant John Chaconas of the Cook County Sheriff's Police Special Investigations Unit, who reported directly to Dick Cain.

Not long after the reporter filed his story, Dick and three of his detectives were indicted for perjury, accused of lying to a grand jury about their involvement in the raid. The state maintained that the day before the raid, Sergeant Chaconas had rented the motel room where the drugs were recovered. Their offer of proof included the registration form in Chaconas' handwriting and testimony from the desk clerk and a handwriting expert. No arrests were ever made in the burglary, and the rest of the drugs were never recovered. But it was revealed at trial that Dick had contacted Zahn's insurance carrier and offered to sell them the drugs a couple of weeks prior to the incident at the Caravelle Motel. The offer was conveyed to Louis Zahn, owner of the company. While he gave the offer considerable thought, he decided he'd better get some legal advice and so he did what we all would do; he called his nearest lawyer-relative, a brother-in-law. Irony of ironies, his brother-in-law was Daniel Ward, the Cook County state's attorney.

Ward opened an investigation and subpoenaed grand jury testimony from all of the members of the SIU who participated in the raid on the Caravelle Motel. To a man, they all denied having "set up" the raid. The grand jury was unable to determine who actually stole the drugs, but they were convinced, that Cain, Witsman, Chaconas, and Donnelly were lying and indicted them for perjury. Ogilvie defended his men, claiming there was a vendetta in the state's attorney's office that was politically motivated.

In November 1964, FBI wiretaps revealed that Dick went to Peru to investigate a business opportunity on behalf of Sam Giancana. The FBI monitored his movements on the trip and confirmed he had been there, but were unable to determine with whom he met, or the outcome of his meeting or meetings. Later, when Bill Roemer debriefed Dick, they learned that the reason for the trip was to secure a casino permit from the government of Peru. Gambling was actually illegal at the time, but both men had been told that with patience and an up-front payment of $150,000 they could be the first. Dick met with several Peruvian legislators and came to the conclusion there was a great deal of risk associated with their investment. He sent word to Giancana about his misgivings. Giancana agreed and told him to pass on the opportunity and come home.

In December, a court convicted Dick, Bill Witsman, John Chaconas, and James Donnelly of conspiracy to commit perjury by lying to the grand jury about the raid on the Caravelle Motel. Sheriff Ogilvie fired all four of them, no doubt a painful thing for him to have done. Even then.

CHAPTER

10

During Dick's term with the Cook County Sheriff's Police, the United States suffered the assassination of John F. Kennedy. Several years ago an author accused Dick Cain of being the shooter who occupied the sniper's nest in the Texas School Book Depository. On the day that book was published, I received phone calls from FBI Special Agent William F. Roemer, who was by then retired, and G. Robert Blakey, former chief counsel to the House Select Committee on Assassinations (HSCA). The HSCA was created to conduct an investigation into the Kennedy assassination in response to the many people who criticized the Warren Commission's Report. Both men told me, for different reasons, that it was preposterous to think Dick Cain killed the president.

Roemer was from the lone-gunman school and believed that Oswald acted alone in killing JFK. I tried several times to coax him off that perch, but he was steadfast. Like most others who believe Oswald was a lone nut, he had accepted what he had accepted and wasn't interested in any new information.

Blakey was convinced that Kennedy was killed by elements of organized crime, but from New Orleans, not Chicago. In their book *The Plot to Kill the President* (Times Books, 1981), Blakey and Richard N. Billings went to great lengths to explain their persuasive theory about the involvement of Carlos Marcello and elements of the New Orleans mob. Blakey told me, "Michael, I had subpoena powers, I talked to dozens, hundreds of witnesses. Not one of them tried to lay this at your brother's feet."

At the time of the assassination, the FBI had five bugs planted at various locations around Chicago, listening in on daily conversations involving all the major players in the Chicago Outfit. Roemer told me he requested all the tapes from those bugs for six months prior to the assassination of the president and six months after, and listened to every tape just to see if they'd missed something. There was talk of murder and mayhem, crimes of every sort were freely discussed at all levels of the mob, but there was never a single mention of whacking the president of the United States. Certainly this is not conclusive proof of their innocence, but given the absence of *any* real evidence suggesting involvement of the Chicago mob, it's highly unlikely they were.

The mob had few Kennedy fans within its ranks. They were furious with Bobby Kennedy because he turned on them and began aggressive prosecutions of organized crime figures. At thirty-two years of age, Bobby was the youngest attorney general in history. He was idealistic and committed to what he saw as an obligation on his part to fight organized crime.

Many rumors after the 1960 election intimated that Joe Kennedy had made a pact with Sam Giancana to deliver Illinois and West Virginia. Those two states put Kennedy over the top in one of the closest elections in history. Nixon supposedly knew the votes were tainted, but he refused to request a recount. Some have suggested that the GOP had been involved in some voting "shenanigans" itself, so he just accepted it. If true, Giancana would have made the deal with Joe Kennedy on the basis of their common roots in bootlegging, not out of political ideology. That's why the quid pro quo was broken when Bobby started to come after the mob.

In an effort to resolve the question of whether my brother killed the president, I threw myself into the assassination conspiracy community to find out if there was any possibility of truth in the accusation. First, I joined an online discussion group and introduced myself, asking for any known evidence. I attended conferences hosted by the research community, specifically JFK Lancer (jfklancer.com), and was invited to speak at a couple of them. I interviewed, and was interviewed by, many of the leading authors and researchers on the subject of the Kennedy assassination.

I found a tremendously active research community, with limited resources. Initially, I had to find individuals who were willing to talk; then

JFK Lancer became a clearing house of sorts, publishing a researcher directory to facilitate communication among researchers. After the movie *JFK* was released, a renewed interest in the story emboldened Congress to pass the Assassination Records Review Act, which eventually declassified several million documents previously withheld from the public. All the while an unimposing woman in Dallas named Mary Ferrell accumulated a house full of documents herself. Prior to Mary's death in 2004, she transferred her entire collection to what is now known as the Mary Ferrell Foundation, and the foundation is in the process of putting her entire collection online at www.maryferrell.org.

What I learned from all of those sources was that no one could place Dick Cain in Dallas in November 1963 and, while a number of them truly wanted to believe it, most ultimately backed off the theory. I communicated with this group for more than ten years, shared information with them, including files I had uncovered showing Dick's involvement with the Cubans specifically and, in turn, they agreed to advise me whenever Dick's name came up in their research. In the end it seems the entire allegation could be traced to that one particular book. It sounded sexy to think that Dick Cain might have done it so, rather than seek the truth, some people just accepted that he did it and moved on.

Finally, in 2006 I found a long-sought witness. Jim Malcotte worked for Dick at the sheriff's department in 1963. He told me that on November 22, 1963, he was in the grand jury room at the Cook County Courthouse testifying that one Eddie Lee Jones had shot him during an undercover drug buy. While Malcotte was testifying, a sheriff's deputy burst into the room and announced that the president had been shot. Malcotte remembered the event clearly because of the gravity of the news and the fact that it was unprecedented to have testimony interrupted in the grand jury room. Malcotte also remembered that his boss, Dick Cain, was waiting in the hallway to testify after him.

All of us who were old enough at the time remember where we were on that day. I was in class at St. Joseph's High School in Bay City, Michigan. I was in the tenth grade at the time, and distinctly remember that my English teacher, Mrs. Erickson, cried and sent us all home. I didn't really grasp the gravity of the event then, but I certainly remember the events of the day.

To confirm Malcotte's story I contacted the Cook County archivist and learned that because of the secretive nature of grand jury testimony, all their records are destroyed. Finding trial transcripts proved challenging as well because Chicago is home to an unusually large number of men named Eddie Lee Jones and quite a few of them have misbehaved in Cook County. Because of limited access to the county archives, I never found the actual trial Malcotte told me about, and even if I had, it may not confirm the grand jury appearance, but I believe it happened just the way he said it did.

There's a lot of evidence to suggest there may have been a plan in place to kill Kennedy in Chicago several weeks before Dallas, and there is conflicting evidence about what Dick may have known at the time. There is no evidence that I am aware of to indicate he had any knowledge of these plots, but that doesn't prove anything except that I haven't found any proof. I have many of Dick's personal notes and over four hundred letters he wrote over the years to his mother and none of them makes any reference to JFK's murder. It seems to me that if he had any knowledge of it he would have mentioned something in all that correspondence, if only to offer an opinion on the matter.

A CIA memo written around the time of JFK's assassination claims that Dick was "heavily involved" in investigating any Chicago connection to the assassination. There are those who believe his Cuban connections had something to do with that planned attempt, but there's no documented trail to support the belief, only circumstantial evidence and speculation. It's well documented that he was very much involved in the Cuban exile community in Chicago to keep tabs on communist groups and to arm and train the anti-Castro expatriates. There is even some speculation that he a may have attended a meeting where Lee Harvey Oswald made an appearance. It was reported in the Chicago papers that Dick was the person who notified the FBI about where and when Oswald's rifle was purchased. But whether this is true and what it may signify, I simply do not know.

I entered the JFK phase of my research with an open mind, fully acknowledging that Dick was capable of the crime, but in the hope that I could clear him of it—as a brother as well as a writer. I think I have, but I welcome any new evidence and I encourage those researchers who have a serious interest in the subject to continue to probe and explore so that one day we might learn the answers. The speculation won't dissipate just because I believe Dick was not involved. In fact, I very much want the discussion to continue so that someday we can finally know what happened in Dallas on that awful day. The key is to follow the evidence.

CHAPTER

11

In 1961, the FBI was preparing to subpoena Sam Giancana to invite him to talk with a grand jury about mob activity in Chicago. Special Agent Ralph Hill, perhaps the agent in Chicago most knowledgeable about the mob, produced a comprehensive 175-page report on Sam to ensure the justice department was ready for him. Their plan was to grant him immunity from prosecution for his testimony; if it worked they'd have to let him go, but they would be able to cripple the organization with his information.

This was happening at a time when keeping your mouth shut still meant something in the Outfit, so they had no guarantees the plan would work, but they were going to give it a shot anyway.

The report began with a listing of the various aliases Sam was known to have used—twenty-seven in all. They noted that he was born either on June 15, 1908, or June 30, 1908, and that he had been last arrested on April 15, 1957, by the Chicago PD. The charge was listed as "General Principles." His arrest record dated back to 1926.

Sam had married Angeline De Tolve in 1933, and she had died on April 23, 1954, in Florida as a result of two cerebral hemorrhages. He had three daughters, Annette, Bonnie Lou, and Francine. He had two brothers and five sisters.

They interviewed Sam's doctor and the doctor's nurse to learn that Sam had recently undergone surgery for hemorrhoids and had been referred to the doctor under an assumed name, Russell Paige. He was admitted to the hospital for treatment under that name as well. The doctor "commented that Giancana earned the reputation among the hospital staff to be the coldest and most antisocial patient they have ever had and as a result of his attitude toward the hospital staff, he suggested that Giancana leave the hospital early and complete his recuperation at home or elsewhere."

The report went on to name a long list of Giancana's associates, including Tony Accardo, Murray Humphries, Gus Alex, Paul De Lucia (Paul Ricca), Marshall Caifano, Felix Alderisio, Sam Battaglia, Joey Aiuppa, Charles Fishchetti, and twenty-seven others, a real Who's Who of the Chicago Outfit, and the bureau pulled out all the stops.

Each of the associates was detailed, with evidence of their known associations to Giancana. Reports on several of Sam's female associates included dates and places where they had rendezvoused, including Phyllis McGuire and, curiously, Darlene Caifano, then the wife of Marshall Caifano.

Ever the gentleman, Special Agent Hill went on to report on some of the quasi-legitimate businesses the Outfit operated or had influence over, specifically the Villa Venice, operated by Jimmy Meo on Sam's behalf. In describing how prostitutes plied their trade there in the several gondolas that floated in the adjacent canals, Hill wrote, "Prostitutes were brought to the Villa by hustlers and turned their tricks on the gondolas with the male customers. Most of these sexual activities did not follow conventional patterns."

The report gave details about Sam's interest in several Chicago-area motels, as well as the Stardust, the Riviera, and the Desert Inn, all in Las Vegas, including interviews with the "front" men in each of these establishments. In some cases they got blank stares, in some cases belligerence, but in all cases they were completely stonewalled. Sam's name did not appear in the records of any of these companies. But one common thread that seemed to pop up was the name Tony Champagne, Sam's lawyer. Sometimes they'd be told Champagne was the trustee for an unnamed trust, sometimes it was "Fuck you, if want any information talk to Tony Champagne." They seemed to accept that they weren't going to prove anything, but that there was enough circumstantial evidence to tie them all together.

It took some time before they were able to get the justice department's blessing to conduct an investigation; U.S. Attorney Ed Hanrahan had first to convince Attorney General Nicholas Katzenbach that he was in a position to produce indictments and convictions, not just a lot of good press. Finally, in the spring of 1965, he got their approval to proceed and went on a witch hunt the likes of which Chicago had never seen. He served grand jury subpoenas to everybody who was anybody in the Outfit, oftentimes knowing full well they wouldn't talk, but just their presence in the grand jury room would make everyone else nervous about what was being said.

The parade of witnesses, including Dick Cain, provided no new information to the government. Some of them wouldn't even give their name. They'd be kept in the jury room anyway, to give the perception they were talking. When Sam's turn finally came up he held his ground, refusing to answer questions based on his Fifth Amendment right not to incriminate himself.

Then the government finally showed its hand. From the beginning, the plan was to go after Sam; they brought everyone else in for the sole purpose of harassment and to completely unnerve Sam. By the time they got him on the stand, they were ready to spring the trap—they offered Sam Giancana a sweeping immunity that would have forgiven all crimes from his storied past. All the murders, the extortion, the smuggling, all of it. And all they wanted from him was a complete and open discussion about the affairs of the Outfit in Chicago. They figured that if it worked, they'd have to let him go, but they would have so many indictments on the rest of his crew that nobody would even notice.

After briefly conferring with his attorney, and to everyone's surprise, Sam accepted the offer.

The lawyers took over for a time and Sam's lawyer tried to limit the scope of the questioning, knowing full well that Sam would perjure himself within the first few minutes. By the time they got around to questioning him, Sam had reconsidered, realizing that he'd be killed in short order if he actually gave up any of his friends, or even if they thought he might. They asked his name; he answered truthfully. They asked where he lived; he answered truthfully. On the next question, and for every other question after that, he took the Fifth.

The judge explained to Sam that he would be held in contempt. Since he had been granted immunity and had accepted it, he must talk, he must answer the questions. But by then Sam realized the government could do nothing to him that would compare to what his friends would do. He held his ground and refused to talk, so he was bound over to the Cook County Jail for the duration of the grand jury. They were empaneled for eighteen months and had about twelve months to go.

Since he could only be released by coming back to testify, the judge told him, "You have the key to your own cell." Sam wasn't happy, but he did his time. There was a minor scandal when two jailers were caught doing his laundry and were summarily fired. Richard Ogilvie was sheriff at the time and quite sensitive to any charges of pandering to the mob. Eventually, late in May 1966, he was released. Hanrahan had been defeated, and Sam may have gloated in front of his friends, who welcomed him home with a big party, but he knew what a close call he'd had.

The government gave serious consideration to calling him before the next grand jury to put him through it all again, but the boys in Washington called Hanrahan and told him to let it go. "If you can't get the evidence to get an indictment, you're not going to use the grand jury to hide your failings."

During his absence, Sam had become a pariah to the Outfit, and he knew it. More importantly, everyone else knew it. They'd lost elder statesman "Milwaukee" Phil Alderisio during Sam's incarceration. He'd had a heart attack and died when Bill Roemer attempted to arrest him, so they had been rudderless in Sam's absence. Sam knew it was time for him to get away, so after taking a few weeks to get his feet back on the ground, he announced that he was going to live in Mexico, and he left in June 1966. Butch Blasi drove him as far as Texas, where they met up with Dick Cain. Dick drove him the rest of the way to Mexico City, where he'd arranged for an apartment. Soon after, they would move to Cuernavaca.

From their base in Mexico, Sam and Dick underwent the process of building an international presence. Sam's old friend Eddie Jones, from Terre Haute, was still living in Mexico City, where Sam had set him up in business back in the forties. Eddie would periodically smuggle money into Mexico and across the ocean to Switzerland, where he would deposit it for Chicago's mob bosses.

Dick would frequently travel back to Chicago and meet with Butch Blasi, who was looking after Sam's interests in the Chicago area. It was on one of those trips, in December 1967, that he was asked to meet Bill Roemer on the street in front of his hotel. Roemer placed him under arrest and, while they both knew he would immediately post bail, it marked the beginning of a difficult odyssey for Dick.

CHAPTER

12

Corrupt cops lead complicated lives. Many of the things they do seem routine and proper. That's the nature of the beast. On most days it's just a job, chasing down bad guys, making cases.

Dick Cain had no prior knowledge that the Franklin Park Bank was being targeted for robbery by a gang of bumbling thieves in the blue-collar West Chicago suburb of Franklin Park. The robbers came together out of mutual need and perceived skills. It was their incompetence that led mob fixer Willie Daddano to reach out to Dick Cain and ask him to solve an internal problem several weeks after the robbery had taken place.

Most of the robbers had been arrested within four days of the robbery, and some of them believed there was an informant in the gang. After all, how could the G have caught them so quickly? These were not "made" guys. They were connected guys. They knew the mob guys, and when they made a big score, they passed some of it up the line in the form of a street tax. Many of them had regular jobs and went to work every day. They gambled though and, often as not, that habit was the genesis of future scores, future trouble. When they got a hot tip on a game or a horse they were likely to bet big because, after all, that's what gambling is all about; to make the big hit. Well, if the game or the horse didn't work out the way they hoped, there was money to be paid to the bookie. Bookies aren't like loan sharks, they are not interested in carrying any paper, all debts are paid current each week. No exceptions. Except when there's an exception. But for most people, if they owe a bookie and can't pay, they're expected to contact a loan shark to get the money. That keeps the bookie afloat and keeps the loan shark doing what he does best. When you're into a loan shark, you're expected to pay every week. If you can't pay off the principal, you must at least pay the "vig" or vigorish (a Yiddish slang word derived from the Russian word for winnings). The vig is substantial when dealing with a loan shark, and thus the term. Calling it interest would be inappropriate.

Gamblers who lost too much and then borrowed money from loan sharks often saw no way out of their dilemma but to make a "score." That could be anything from a burglary to a hijacking to a bank robbery. They'd kick up some of the proceeds and pay off the shark, so they never really got ahead on their crimes, they only covered their past. When they got into trouble, they turned to the mob for help; that's one of the ways the mob earned their tax. In the Outfit, they're known as "fixers" because, well, they fix things. Here's the story direct from the trial transcript:

On September 17, 1963, Mike LaJoy, Joey D'Argento, Frank DeLegge, Sr., and Larry Fletcher were riding in a car from Detroit to Chicago. They had gone to Detroit a day earlier to deliver some stolen cars. It's common practice in the mob to sell stolen cars to their *compari* in other cities, the distance making it less likely they'll be found out. Local cops everywhere circulate a list each day of stolen cars they're aware of, but the list only includes cars that were reported stolen locally; there is no inter-city sharing of this kind of data on a day-to-day basis. The Feds do publish a national list, but nobody looks at it unless they have a specific suspicion to check out. So if you steal a car in Chicago, you take it to Detroit where nobody is looking for it. It's a decent sideline business, but it doesn't generate enough money to pay off big debts. Usually the cars are sold to chop shops, which dismantle them and sell the parts. The non-traceable parts of a car, those with no VIN numbers, can be sold for two or three times the value of the car in its complete state, and most of the stolen parts can't be traced. Occasionally, cars are loaded into shipping containers and shipped overseas where the lack of a title is a non-issue.

Each of the four men had a couple of grand in his pocket, eager now to place more bets on the weekend. On this trip home, the discussion turned to easy scores, and Frank complained to his pals, "I'm really gettin' heat from this shark about a payment he wanted last month."

"I need a big score," he said, "not this chicken shit couple-a-grand we get for these cars, I need some real money."

They talked about big scores. A truck hijack would be very lucrative, but they took time and you had to have a place to hide the loot until it could be fenced; an eighteen-wheeler is no easy thing to hide. A bank though, that's pretty quick. Instant cash. They agreed they'd like to work together to rob a bank, if they could find the right one. The conversation continued through most of the drive home. When they arrived in Franklin Park in the early morning hours, they drove past the Franklin Park Bank. Joey D'Argento said, "If you guys want to rob a bank, there's a bank we can rob."

Frank said, "I do business at that bank! Besides, you guys ain't got the balls to knock over no bank. I been watchin' you for years. You ain't never pulled no decent jobs."

"We can, too, handle that bank as long as they don't got a guard."

Frank got up later that morning and went to the bank, located at 3044 Rose Avenue, to check it out and find out whether the bank had an armed guard. He wondered if this was really smart. This was his own bank, for Christ's sake. He walked up to a teller window, asked to break a fifty, and looked around to see what he could learn. Even though he'd been banking there for years, he'd never looked at it as a score. It changes your whole perspective, he thought.

Satisfying himself that they had no guard, Frank contacted the others and arranged for a meeting at Sansonetti's Restaurant on Grand Avenue and Mannheim in Franklin Park.

Once all four men arrived, Frank reported he had visited the bank and it had no guard. "Here, let me show you," Frank said, as he began to draw a diagram of the inside of the bank.

D'Argento and Fletcher said they wanted to see for themselves and left the restaurant. After examining the bank for a short time, they returned and D'Argento said, "I think you're right, Frank. We can take that place, but it's going to take some planning. You know, there's train tracks that cut through between the bank and the police department. Just now, when we was leaving the bank, there was a really long freight train come through there. All we gotta do is time the job to be three, four minutes ahead of the train, clear the bank in two minutes then keep the coppers on the wrong side of the tracks and they'll get stuck waitin' for the fuckin' train. It's a beautiful thing."

While they were gone, Frank DeLegge, Jr. had joined LaJoy and his father. Mike LaJoy was a first cousin of Frank, Jr. and had known him all his life; he told the others Frank was okay. "Frank's a stand-up guy," he said. "We can count on him."

Frank, Sr. said, "Yeah, he's my kid and he's with us all the way."

D'Argento and Fletcher reported the bank appeared to be a good target. They had plenty of money, and the bank didn't seem terribly well protected. They knew the area well, and there were good escape routes.

LaJoy said he wanted to visit the bank himself to see if the rest of the guys really were assessing it properly. "Uncle Frank," he said, "could you drive me by the bank so I can have a look?"

Chicago banks in the sixties generally had public telephones in the lobby, an excellent aid to the planning of a bank robbery. LaJoy pretended to use the phone in the lobby and studied the interior of the bank. From this vantage point, he had a good view of the nine tellers' cages. He pretended to talk on the phone for several minutes and then decided he'd better leave before he started to attract attention. He and Frank, Sr. returned to the restaurant. LaJoy told them he was in agreement with the rest of the gang about how easy it would be to knock off the bank. "I'm ready. Let's get this thing planned."

Everyone accepted that the DeLegges couldn't go into the bank, because they might be recognized as customers, so they all agreed that Frank, Sr. would drive the crash car, taking out any pursuing police cars. Frank, Jr. was going to make a call to the police department, maybe an "officer needs help" call to keep the cops across the tracks until the train came through.

Joe looked out the window and saw Frank, Jr.'s plumbing truck. "Hey Frank," he said, "are you a plumber?"

"Yeah," replied Junior, "I'm partners with Angelo Scalini."

"Maybe you could make some lead weights for us, you know, to prop the doors open in case the bank's got electrified doors. I'd hate for those fuckers to lock us in."

"Sure, sure," Frank said, "no problem."

DeLegge, Sr. wanted the robbery to take place the following Friday, September 20, 1963. He explained that a creditor of his had contacted him that morning and was demanding payment. They agreed the following Friday would be a good date for the robbery, feeling the bank would have more money on hand to cash payroll checks at the end of the week.

Before they left the restaurant, LaJoy suggested they should have a "professional" driver. Pat Schang was suggested, but LaJoy said he'd call Johnny the Bug.

Johnny "the Bug" Varelli came by his nickname honestly. Born in an insane asylum where his mother was a patient, no one ever knew whether an inmate or a staff member had raped her, but Johnny, raised in foster homes all his life, had begun to show signs of the schizophrenia that had claimed his mother. His friends had long thought of him as a little "buggy."

The next day, Wednesday, at around 12:30 P.M., D'Argento, DeLegge, Sr., and Fletcher were at Sansonetti's Restaurant again. DeLegge, Sr. reported that he had checked for a train schedule, but there were none available for freight trains. D'Argento mentioned he had observed a freight train going by the Franklin Park Bank at approximately 11:00 the previous morning, and it was probable that one would pass the bank at the same time on Friday.

By Thursday the nineteenth, LaJoy had contacted Varelli about driving the getaway car and Johnny the Bug said he was in. That afternoon, LaJoy and Varelli picked up D'Argento, DeLegge, Sr., and Fletcher and drove around in the vicinity of the bank to plan a getaway route. Varelli told the group he would need to find a location where they could switch into another car following the robbery. They'd have to ditch the work-car as soon as possible after the robbery; it would be way too hot. DeLegge, Sr. offered the use of his house on Dora Street in Franklin Park as a drop-off point. The house had been up for sale for several months, was vacant, and would be convenient for the switch. The gang then proceeded to find the best route between the bank and the Dora Street house.

At one point they pulled into the parking lot of a supermarket to check a map. While they were parked in the lot, a patrol car pulled up behind them, and a policeman approached the car. To the officer's inquiry, DeLegge responded that he was a real estate salesman inspecting some available properties in the area. The officer accepted that, but before leaving he recognized DeLegge and made a point of saying hello.

As the gang was exploring getaway routes, they passed Guy Mendola as he drove by and waved to them. LaJoy said, "Oh shit, now that Lover Boy has seen us together, he'll know it was us knocked off this bank when he hears about it. I think he seen us, John."

"What do you think we should do?" someone asked.

Varelli said, "Well, I heard the guy's a stool pigeon, and I don't trust him. Maybe if we bring him in, he won't be able to rat us out. We won't have to worry about him. Besides, he's a good shooter and if we get into it with the cops, he'll be good to have." And so it was decided "Lover Boy" Mendola would be invited to join the group. "I'll talk with him tonight," LaJoy said.

Before the group broke up for the day, Varelli suggested that Friday was too soon for the robbery and it should be changed to Monday the twenty-third. D'Argento pointed out that one of the reasons for the early date was the pressure being exerted on DeLegge, Sr. for an outstanding debt. DeLegge, Sr. said he could stall his creditors another couple of days, and so it was agreed Monday would be the day.

That night, Mike LaJoy found Mendola at the Owl Restaurant in Franklin Park. He discussed the plan with Mendola, who said he was on board. They went over to Frank, Sr.'s house to make sure everyone had a chance to meet.

DeLegge, Jr. brought in several bars of lead and a melting pot. He and LaJoy went into the basement and melted lead into two coffee cans. Lead melts at 621 degrees Fahrenheit. The heat was so intense the cans sank into the paint on the basement floor, leaving two perfect circles in the paint. These circles later proved pivotal to the prosecution when the FBI tied the circles on the basement floor to the cans left at the bank.

On the Friday before the robbery, Mike LaJoy, Larry Fletcher, both DeLegges, and Lover Boy Mendola met again at Sansonetti's Restaurant.

Fletcher said, "I got this court appearance I gotta do on Monday, so I don't think I can make this job. I hope you guys understand that I ain't getting cold feet or nothin', but it would be really bad for me to get busted missing a court date to rob a bank. I think they'd revoke my parole."

Joe D'Argento said Gerry Tomaszek could cover for Fletcher, so everyone agreed Tomaszek should be taken into the gang. "I'll give him a call right now," Joe said. Within the hour, Tomaszek walked into the restaurant and joined the group.

The gang was growing, so they decided to discuss the roles they would each play in the robbery. DeLegge, Sr. was considered to be the senior member, so he was to drive the crash car. That cop in the parking lot had recognized him a couple days ago, and besides, at his age (fifty), he might not be up to the commotion that might ensue during a chase. So his role was to follow the getaway car, and if there was any pursuit by the police, he was to try and ram the police car, then claim he was confused by all the noise and excitement.

D'Argento and Tomaszek were to scoop up the money into cardboard boxes. Mendola was to place the weights against the bank doors. LaJoy was to run to the front of the bank and announce the robbery. Johnny the Bug would drive the getaway car.

They made masks from old T-shirts, cutting out eyeholes so the rest of their faces were covered. Frank, Sr. passed out pairs of "Groucho" glasses with big noses and black eyeglass frames.

At 9:00 o'clock on Monday morning, D'Argento, Tomaszek, and Mendola met at a bowling alley so they could drive over to Frank's in one car and not draw so much attention. They got to Frank's about 9:45. Mendola and Tomaszek left almost immediately, telling the group they were going to steal some license plates.

While they were gone, D'Argento and Frank, Sr. removed the back seat from the work car, a 1963 Chevy Impala SS with a four-speed transmission and bucket seats. Joe had stolen it a couple of weeks earlier from the parking lot of the International Harvester plant and had stored it in his cousin's garage. He hadn't stolen the car for this job, he stole it "just in case" he needed a stolen car for something. They removed the back seat so the three guys who sat back there could crouch down out of sight. A car with five guys crammed in might stand out more than one with two.

Frank got the lead weights and put them in the front seat where Mendola was to sit.

Just then, Frank heard the phone ringing and ran inside to catch it— it was Johnny Varelli. "I'm not gonna make it," he said. "No offense, but I'm just not comfortable with your kid being involved. He's never pulled a job before; he's an unknown quantity."

When the guys returned with the license plates, Frank said, "The job is off. Johnny the Bug called and said he was out on account of Frank, Jr. being involved. We ain't got enough guys to pull this job."

"Hold on," Joey said, "let me give Pat Schang a call. He'll be in."

Schang was there in twenty minutes, and with Frank in his Studebaker and the rest of the gang in the Chevy, they left Frank's house at eleven o'clock. They drove by the bank and followed the planned escape route to the Dora Street house in a practice run.

They were killing some time while they waited for the train. Finally, at about 11:30, they saw the gates come down at the train crossing and knew it was time to strike. Schang pulled up near the rear of the bank, and Mike LaJoy, Joey D'Argento, Guy Mendola, and Gerry Tomaszek jumped out of the car and headed into the bank.

Mendola placed the two cans in their strategic spots. Tomaszek and D'Argento led the way, calling out, "This is a robbery!" They both hopped over the railing in front of the bank manager's desk and headed back behind the tellers' cages. LaJoy took his position in the middle of the bank lobby and shouted at everyone to be quiet and to stay down so that no one would be hurt. All of the men were armed, Tomaszek with a .38, Joey with a carbine, Guy Mendola with a .25 automatic, and LaJoy with a .38.

Pat Schang was outside keeping the motor running. He was positioned such that he could see the railroad crossing a couple of blocks away. He was excited and could feel the rush of adrenaline. He watched with trepidation as the huge railroad engine lumbered toward the crossing at Rose Street . . . pulling only a caboose.

Several minutes after they entered, the four came running out of the bank and piled into the car, telling Schang to "hit it." Schang pulled out of the bank and was turning right, southbound on Rose, when he saw a Franklin Park police car heading north, directly toward them. "What the hell happened to Junior?" thought Schang, as he made eye contact with the cop bearing down on him.

As it turned out, Junior was just, at that very instant, placing a call to the Franklin Park police to announce that a bomb had been placed in the high school. Since they were already responding to the bank robbery call, they assumed it was a hoax and ignored the call. Nice job, Junior.

Frank DeLegge was in place in the Studebaker, so Schang figured they'd be okay. What he hadn't figured on was the Studebaker being unable to catch the police car to crash into it.

Pat Schang made a couple of quick turns before he realized the squad car was staying right with them. He yelled at Joe, who grabbed the carbine and fired once to shoot out the rear window of the car. Then, he fired a couple of rounds in the general vicinity of the police car. The cop hit his brakes, causing the car to skid out of control. He wrestled the wheel and managed to stop the car without hitting anything.

A second police car passed him almost immediately, taking up the chase.

Schang accelerated to eighty or ninety miles per hour. He could see that another police car had entered the chase. From the bank they headed south on Rose Street to Chestnut, west on Chestnut to Scott Street, north on Scott to Schiller, west on Schiller to Sunset, north on Sunset to Minneapolis, west on Minneapolis to the alley between Sarah and Dora Streets, and north into the alley.

At one point, when Schang slammed on the brakes to make a turn, Joey came flying forward between the bucket seats and broke off the rear-view mirror with his head. Schang cussed him out, saying he couldn't see, but Joey got back in position and told him it was okay; they'd lost the cops.

Schang was a good driver and kept his cool. He was grateful for a fast getaway car. After a series of turns, all of which involved screeching tires and sliding, someone yelled out, "There's the alley!" Schang slammed on the brakes, entering the alley sideways as the car skidded on gravel. He gunned the motor down the alley, and he kicked up a cloud of dust and screeched the tires even more.

It was late morning on a fall school day, so there were no kids around, but every mother's heart stops when she hears squealing tires, and it takes several seconds for her to realize the kids are safe at school. In that several seconds, all the mothers headed toward the sound and got a good look when Schang got to the rear entrance of DeLegge's house. He nearly missed it and locked up the brakes, sliding past the entrance to the garage. When he stopped, everybody piled out of the passenger side of the car before he backed up. The last guy out failed to close the car door, so when Schang backed up past a telephone pole, he hooked it with the door, and the door fell to the ground.

When Sylvia Danato got to the alley, she saw Mike LaJoy standing at the garage and holding the door open. Joey D'Argento was standing in the middle of the alley holding a rifle and the passenger door from a 1963 Chevy Impala SS.

Schang pulled into the garage. Joe followed with the door and then he, LaJoy, Mendola, and Schang headed into the house, leaving the loot in the car. Inside the house they discarded their disguises and exited through the front door. Schang and D'Argento headed straight through several yards across the street until they reached JoJo's Restaurant on Mannheim, arriving there about ten minutes before noon. Schang called his wife to come pick them up. As they sat in the diner waiting for Schang's wife, the owner of the restaurant, who was a woman named Jean, and a distant cousin, remembered him from past family functions. She approached D'Argento and they chatted some about the family but, as Jean would later testify, "Joey, he seemed distracted, like he had something on his mind."

Mendola, LaJoy, and Tomaszek walked off in the other direction, separating from one another and meeting later at the bowling alley.

That night, Schang met DeLegge, Sr. and Guy Mendola for dinner and he asked how much money they had scored.

"Eighteen thousand five hundred dollars," reported Frank, "and I had to burn some of that because the bills were marked."

"But the papers are reporting more than forty-three thousand," Schang piped in.

Guy Mendola said, "There were two boxes of money. There had to be more than eighteen five."

"I only saw one box," replied DeLegge, "and there was eighteen thousand five hundred—that was it."

Mendola got into a shouting match with the senior DeLegge in the restaurant, and the argument got so heated they had to leave. Mendola was so upset he left town, eventually refusing to take any part of the loot from thieves who had cheated their partners.

The next morning, Schang saw DeLegge, Jr. on Mannheim Road and flagged him down. They parked at a fast food joint and young Frank, who was thirty years old at the time, told Schang he had gone over to the Dora Street house after the robbery, where he met his father. They moved the money into the trunk of the Studebaker and stashed the guns and masks under a stairwell inside the house. The neighborhood was crawling with police and FBI agents by then, all racing around trying to pick up the trail. Frank, Jr. started raking leaves in the front of the house. Eventually, an FBI agent questioned him about what he might have seen, but neither Frank nor his father admitted to seeing anything.

The feds seemed already to know Pat Schang was involved and mentioned him by name. How could this be? It had been such a good plan, but it was falling apart before their very eyes.

Within a week, three of the robbers who had actually gone inside the bank, D'Argento, LaJoy, and Tomaszek and the driver, Pat Schang, had all been arrested and charged with bank robbery. Guy Mendola was spared, though he would later wish he'd been busted with the rest of them. The DeLegges arranged with bail bondsman Rocco Montagna to bail everyone out, and that's when the trouble started. Everyone was convinced there was no way the G could have found them all out so quickly unless there was a snitch in the group.

Mendola was the obvious suspect because he had refused his share of the loot, and he hadn't been arrested. Schang thought it was D'Argento. D'Argento thought it was LaJoy. Ironically, these three—Schang, D'Argento, and LaJoy—would later become government witnesses.

Several weeks after his release on bail, Schang met up with Rocco Montagna, who probably ended up with the lion's share of the booty in the form of bail fees. Schang shared with Rocco that the guys were concerned about how quickly they had been arrested. There must have been someone in the gang that gave them up to the G. Word on the street was the "beefer" was Mike LaJoy, but they were reluctant to do anything about him because he was Willie Daddano's nephew. LaJoy had a serious gambling problem and was deeply in debt. Rocco said they should talk with Daddano, and he'd set it up.

Soon after, Schang and Montagna went to meet with Willie "Potatoes" Daddano.

Schang explained to Daddano about his suspicions regarding LaJoy. Willie suggested he arrange lie detector tests for the gang to find out if there was a stool pigeon. If someone failed the test, Willie was okay with him being shot on the spot. "Leave him on the box" was Willie's phrase, no matter who the guy was.

Several days later, Rocco called Schang and asked him to come down to the Riviera Bowling Alley where he met up with D'Argento, LaJoy, Tomaszek, and Willie Daddano. Rocco told the guys the lie detector tests were all set up and would be given right away at the motel next door. They were each ordered to pay twenty-five dollars for the test. The money was paid to Rocco Montagna, and it's unclear whether any of it ever made its way to the polygraph operator.

They all walked next door to the Leyden Motel, where three of the gang got into a car with Willie while Rocco and the fourth went into a room in the motel. There was a Cook County Sheriff's Police squad car parked near them in the parking lot. Each, in turn, went into the room with Rocco and with William Witsman, a deputy sheriff. The lie box was set up on the nightstand so the subject could sit on the edge of the bed while being tested. Instinctively, they all knew the message behind the presence of a .38 that rested atop the portable polygraph machine.

Witsman advised each of them to relax and said that he was going to ask them five or six questions, and they could answer however they please, tell the truth or not, just answer the questions:

What is your name?

Are you married?

Where do you live?

Did you rob the Silverleaf Savings and Loan Association on Madison Street in Chicago?

Have you given any information to the FBI in recent months?

Following the administration of the tests, Schang, LaJoy, and Montagna drove to a restaurant at Twenty-second and Central and delivered the graphs from the lie box to Daddano, who had left the motel earlier.

The next day they were told they had all passed the test, but Guy Mendola hadn't been there, so arrangements were made for Mendola to show up a week later at Willie's house, where Witsman had set up in the basement. Mendola had some trouble with the test and took it a second time. He was eventually cleared, but the cloud of suspicion stayed with him.

On June 29, 1964, attorney George Bieber called the FBI advising that Mendola would surrender the following day, which he did, making bail right away. Several weeks later, when he arrived home late one evening, someone waited for him in his garage. When Lover Boy stepped out of his car, he was felled by five shotgun blasts.

The murder of Guy Mendola was investigated by the chief of the Special Investigations Unit, Cook County Sheriff's Department, Richard Cain. It was never solved.

On February 4, Gerald Tomaszek appeared at the office of the FBI with his attorney and demanded they return seventeen guns that had been confiscated from his home at the time of his arrest. Inexplicably, all seventeen of the guns were returned to him. Certainly no one was more surprised than Tomaszek himself. On February 7, a teletype was sent to the special agent in charge of the Chicago office from the office of the director.

It said: "You are instructed to immediately advise Bureau full facts and circumstances concerning the return of guns to Gerald Tomaszek. Advise whether prior approval of the U.S. Attorney was obtained for the return of these weapons."

There had been no such approval. For days afterward, the tension in the Chicago office of the FBI was palpable.

On February 17, D'Argento, La Joy, Tomaszek, and Schang appeared before the judge, and their case was continued until May 4. Then it was continued to September 14; finally, the trial was set for November 23, and actually began in February 1965.

On April 27, 1965, following a two-month trial, a federal jury convicted Joseph D'Argento, Mike LaJoy, Patrick Schang, and Gerald Tomaszek of the robbery of the Franklin Park Bank on September 23, 1963. They were each sentenced to fifteen years in the federal penitentiary.

Throughout the entire process of securing these convictions, the FBI had attempted to develop one or more of the defendants as a cooperative witness. Patrick Schang was the first to flip. He actually testified against his partners in the trial. The others held out.

Two years later, in October 1967, Joseph D'Argento contacted the U.S. Attorney's Office to say he wanted to meet. He was at the federal prison in Leavenworth, Kansas. One of his fellow prisoners, Paul "Peanuts" Panzko, a Chicago-area jewel thief, had told D'Argento that he was to be killed by another inmate on instruction of the Chicago Outfit. The FBI seized the opportunity to flip D'Argento. They arranged to have him moved out of Leavenworth and housed with several county sheriffs in Northern Illinois and southern Wisconsin under an assumed name in their local jails. He would spend most of the next year moving periodically from one county jail to another.

With Schang and D'Argento now cooperating, the feds had what they needed to move on Willie Daddano and Richard Cain. For good measure they added in both DeLegges, Johnny "the Bug" Varelli (who was later removed and tried separately), and Rocco Montagna, the bail bondsman. The plums of this case, though, were clearly Daddano and Cain—Daddano because he was a high-ranking member of organized crime, the kind that is hard to get off the street because they rarely commit crimes directly, and Cain because he was known as a corrupt police officer and a made member of the Mafia.

They had to work fast in order to beat the statute of limitations, so they brought D'Argento and Schang before the grand jury and secured indictments against four new defendants in the Franklin Park Bank robbery. Indictments were returned on December 20, 1967, and agents were dispersed across the city to make the arrests. All four men were arrested that same day. All made bail before nightfall.

Richard Cain was charged with misprision of felony, which is failure to notify a law enforcement official that he had knowledge of a felony committed by others, and conspiracy to aid a known felon.

CHAPTER

13

Dick was short of cash and moderately crippled in his ability to earn money, so he made a decision to represent himself in this trial. He felt it could be futile to hire a lawyer anyway; it was well known that the feds wanted badly to get a conviction against Dick Cain. They had known about his dealings with the Outfit for years and, since they had been unable to do anything about it, they weren't going to let this opportunity get by. Dick knew that a good lawyer could get a pass from the U.S. Attorney's Office for a future case if they didn't put up such a big fight on one that was important to them. This was one of those cases, and he figured representing himself might really be his best shot.

He was a pretty smart guy but, given that he'd dropped out of high school in the tenth grade, this was probably not the best decision he'd ever made. Dick was an insatiable reader and had learned a great many things on his own, but he hadn't learned the law well enough to try this case. He knew the other lawyers well, though, and figured that he could follow their lead and work the rest out on the fly.

Following his arrest in December 1967, Dick was ordered to stay within the confines of Cook County or risk forfeiting his bail. If he found it necessary to leave town, he had to petition the court for permission. He did, on a couple of occasions, ask to leave for the purpose of conducting business for Accurate Laboratories, the private detective agency he owned. He promised to return to stand trial and was granted leave to go, once to San Francisco and once to Las Vegas. In both instances, the local office of the FBI was notified to meet him at the airport and make sure he knew he was to be followed. Dick never worried about being followed, it rarely took him more than a few minutes to lose the tail.

Throughout the spring and summer of 1968, Dick and his co-defendants made numerous appearances in court to address requests by the government and to file a slew of motions themselves. The one motion that Dick needed to win his case was a severance of his trial from that of his co-defendants. Judge Hoffman; Tom Foran, the federal prosecutor; and Cain himself knew that if Cain were tried separately he would have a good chance of winning the case. The only one that mattered, though, was Judge Hoffman, and he repeatedly denied the request.

The DeLegges wanted a severance from Dick's charges because of his association with Richard Ogilvie, who was then a candidate for governor, charging that "if the defendants, Frank DeLegge, Sr. and Frank DeLegge, Jr. were on trial in the above captioned case with Richard Cain as a co-defendant, it is felt that the press coverage would involve this case in the area of politics." Denied.

Dick filed a motion to transfer his trial to another district, citing prejudicial press coverage. Denied.

A motion to compel the government to disclose existence of electronic eavesdropping. Denied.

At an August hearing before Judge Julius Hoffman, George Callahan, an attorney for Willie Daddano, stated to the court, "They (the prosecution) have filed an answer (to an earlier motion) which I hope your Honor won't take seriously."

Judge Hoffman responded, "You want me to take yours seriously, but not the response of the United States government, sir? I can't agree to do that. I will take them both seriously; I have thus far. I always do."

That exchange between them set the stage for the relationship throughout the trial (which included numerous light moments), revealing Judge Hoffman's respect for both sides in the proceedings. For the lawyers, if not the defendants. He was even complimentary of Dick's handling of his own defense on several occasions.

By September, everyone was called before Judge Julius Hoffman and informed that the trial was to proceed. No one on the defense team was pleased about drawing Hoffman. He had a reputation for being incorruptible. They remembered it was Hoffman who heard Tony Accardo's case back in 1960, and Hoffman certainly remembered that Dick Cain had played no small part in that case.

Because he remembered the Accardo case and how Accardo's people had worked the list, looking for friends, Hoffman was careful not to request a jury pool until the day jury selection began and was careful to caution the defendants not to make any attempts to contact members of the jury.

Dick's co-defendants included Willie "Potatoes" Daddano, a senior member of the mob who was pretty much in charge of the West Side. Willie's alleged role in the crime was asking Dick to arrange the polygraph tests. He played no role in the bank robbery, which the government acknowledged, and only got involved after the fact.

Frank DeLegge, Sr. and Frank DeLegge, Jr. had been involved in the robbery and had evaded prosecution the first time around because no hard evidence could be found against them. Frank, Sr. had actually been the instigator of this robbery, having expressed a need to get some cash to pay his loan shark. They were the only ones in this trial charged with bank robbery; the others were conspirators after the fact.

The final defendant was Rocco Montagna, the bail bondsman who bonded the gang out back in 1963 and then acted as sergeant-at-arms during the subsequent polygraph exams.

A couple of weeks before trial, Dick contacted Bill Roemer, the FBI agent who had arrested him, and asked that he set up a meeting between Dick and Tom Foran, the U.S. Attorney who was in charge of the prosecution. Roemer knew better than to act as a go-between (and he was later reprimanded for it), but he liked Dick and agreed to place a call. Foran showed up at the designated meeting place and was surprised when Dick approached him. He was wearing a hideous disguise: a woman's wig, huge dark glasses, and a fedora. Foran struggled not to laugh.

Dick told him that he and Willie were prepared to stand mute to the charges if the government would deport them to Italy and not give either of them any jail time. Again, Foran struggled not to laugh and acknowledged that Daddano, as an immigrant, could be deported, but he was pretty sure Dick had been born in the U.S.A. and was, therefore, not eligible for deportation.

This is where Dick's longtime policy of lying about his age almost paid off for him. Foran was pretty sure Dick had been born in the United States but, at that particular moment, he couldn't have proved it because they were searching the records based on a phony date of birth, and they were further slowed by the fact the indictment had been issued in the name of Ricardo Scalzetti, believing Richard Cain to be an alias. Eventually, they found his birth certificate, though, and when they attempted to verify its accuracy with Dick's grandmother in Owosso, Michigan, she threw them off the property, refusing to give any information to people who only wanted to hurt her Richard.

Since the government had three witnesses who had actually participated in the robbery, the case against the DeLegges was a slam-dunk. The other gang members, because of their positions in the Outfit, knew both Willie and Rocco, so their case was pretty solid as well.

The one weak link in the chain was Dick Cain. He was said to have sent Bill Witsman out to give the polygraph tests. He had not participated in the robbery. He was not present at the time of the tests; in fact, he was in Spain. There was no physical evidence linking him to the crime. There was only the testimony of the guy who ran the lie box, and for testifying against his former boss, he was given immunity from prosecution. The case against Dick was totally dependent on the fact he was being tried with four other people whose guilt could not be challenged. The prosecution was counting on their ability to declare Dick guilty by association. They knew if he were successful in getting a severance from the rest of the defendants, they hadn't a prayer of convicting him.

U.S. Attorney Thomas Foran and his team made it clear to Judge Hoffman that this linkage was critical to getting Cain. Hoffman agreed and steadfastly refused all of Dick's attempts to have his case severed from the others. Foran told me they had loads of evidence against Dick they did not present at trial because they didn't have to. Aided by Dick's decision to represent himself, they were confident they had him caught up in the wave, though it's curious they didn't present any of it.

The trial lasted two weeks and, predictably, most of the evidence presented centered around the bank robbery. When Bill Witsman was called, Dick had his only real opportunity to defend himself. He and Witsman had been good friends at one time. Moreover, Witsman was then dating one of Dick's ex-wives. The focus of Dick's case was to establish that Witsman had access to a portable lie box and didn't necessarily use the one owned by the sheriff's department.

In the end, each of the lawyers delivered a weak closing argument, hoping for a sympathetic ear in the jury box. When it was Dick's turn, he faced the jury and began with a quote from Sir Walter Scott's *Marmion*: "Oh what a tangled web we weave, when first we practice to deceive."

On October 3, 1968, Dick was convicted of misprision of felony, aiding and abetting criminals, and conspiracy to obstruct justice. His co-defendants were ahead of him on the indictment, so their sentences were read first. Dick listened impassively as Judge Julius Hoffman read the sentencing order into the record. He fully expected to receive the maximum term.

He was sentenced to two concurrent four-year terms, one-concurrent three-year, and fined a total of thirteen thousand dollars. Hoffman also rejected the request for bail pending appeal, and added for effect, "I would point out that the evidence in this case shows clearly, and the verdicts of the jury indicate not a reasonable doubt but beyond a peradventure of a doubt, that all of these defendants are a menace to the community. They are dangerous, and I would not want to be one that turned them loose on the community."

Dick believed Judge Hoffman was talking about the others and continued to press for bail. Hoffman was not amused as he replied, "Mr. Cain, I don't want to say unkind things to a man who was honored by a public official of this county by being appointed to a very responsible position, and, by the way, you defiled that office according to the verdicts of the jury and according to the evidence which I heard, but I have to tell you that you are a threat to the safety of the citizens of this community and dangerous to property to have you . . . [released] on bail after the jury has found you guilty. I deny your motion."

Dick was disappointed, but he wasn't surprised. The trial had drained him mentally, and he was beginning to think it might be beneficial to have some time to recoup his strength. Jail isn't the best way to do that, but he was going to make the best of it. Turned over to the custody of the U.S. Marshal, his first stop was the federal tier of the Cook County Jail.

Following the trial, Foran had a huge issue to resolve with Schang, LaJoy, and D'Argento. They had been very cooperative, testifying in what Foran considered his biggest trial. They were still serving out fifteen-year sentences for their role in the bank robbery. He knew returning them to the prison system would be a death sentence for them all. For almost a year leading up to this trial, he had kept them in a series of county jails in Illinois, Wisconsin, and Iowa under assumed names. Now he was through with them, and he had to re-introduce them to prison. He had, however, agreed to help them get a reduced sentence for their cooperation and had, in fact, provided some minor financial support to their families during this time.

The next step in Foran's plan was to convince the governor of Illinois to commute their sentences. He called Governor Shapiro and was told in no uncertain terms that Shapiro wouldn't touch it with a ten-foot pole. He had just lost a hard-fought election and any commutation of jail sentences for mob-connected felons would guarantee a future in the political graveyard. He'd be forever marked as a puppet of organized crime, regardless of how right and proper it was. Perception is reality in the world of politics and, in this case, Shapiro believed a move like this would hang like a millstone around his neck.

Shapiro told Foran to contact the governor-elect. The bad news was Shapiro had just been defeated by Richard B. Ogilvie, former sheriff of Cook County, Dick Cain's boss and good friend at the time the of the bank robbery.

There were two immense obstacles to getting Governor-elect Ogilvie to cooperate. The first was that Foran, a Democrat, was a member of Ogilvie's political opposition. The second was this trial had nearly cost Ogilvie the election because of his association with Dick Cain. The crime was actually committed while Ogilvie was sheriff and Cain was chief of the SIU. Shapiro had spared no effort in the campaign to tag Ogilvie with "the Mark of Cain." It was the one black mark on Ogilvie's nearly spotless career in law enforcement and politics, but it was a big one.

Foran felt he owed it to these three guys to try, so he contacted Ogilvie and arranged a meeting. He told his story and, when he was finished, Ogilvie told him he would be concerned about making such a move because it might look like he was in on the plan from the start. Ogilvie talked about the price he paid for trusting Dick Cain and how that nearly cost him the election.

In the end, though, Ogilvie saw Foran was right. They did owe a debt to LaJoy, D'Argento, and Schang for making this case, and they would surely be killed if they returned to prison. So he granted Tom Foran's request, one of his first official acts as governor and certainly one of his most courageous.

CHAPTER

14

Like many big cities, Chicago processes a lot of federal prisoners. At the time of Dick's trial, there was no federal facility for housing these people, so they rented space in the Cook County Jail. The federal tier was segregated from the general population but, aside from that, the facilities were pretty much the same, and the county provided all the staff.

During his two-plus years as chief investigator for the Cook County Sheriff's Police, Dick had made the acquaintance of several people at the Cook County Jail. He was known to inmates and staff alike; some knew him personally, some were friends, and some were enemies. To ensure he did not receive favorable treatment, the warden ordered Dick placed in solitary confinement until he figured out what to do with him.

The cells used for solitary were about six feet by eight feet, with twelve-foot ceilings. In each cell a single bare bulb hung from the ceiling. It could be illuminated when the jailers wanted, but rarely was. There was a small cot, securely anchored to the wall and, in one corner, was a stainless steel device that functioned as both a sink and a toilet. The sink was at the back, where the tank would be on a traditional toilet, so you had to straddle the toilet to use it. There was no seat to raise or lower; anything that could be removed and used as a weapon was simply never installed in a jail cell.

Prisoners in solitary were allowed only limited access to outside exercise areas, so their physical activity was pretty well restricted to whatever they could do in a cell: push-ups, sit-ups, or running in place. They were allowed outside of their cell for only one hour per day and were required to spend that time alone as well. Back in the cell, there were no sheets, no blankets, and no toiletries.

Dick had asked for permission to use his electric typewriter to prepare his appeal. The warden had flatly denied the request, so Dick had petitioned the court to issue a court order compelling the warden to allow him to use his electric typewriter. To Dick's delight, he won this one and the court ordered the warden to allow Dick to have access to an electric typewriter.

Soon after the court granted his petition, Dick's wife brought it to him on visiting day. He was ecstatic. He hated writing longhand. Also, he believed, even though the courts occasionally waive the requirement for typewritten documents when a prisoner is defending himself, handwritten documents wouldn't have the same impact as typed ones. The typewriter was inspected and searched, and Dick was allowed to take the typewriter back to his cell.

That was when he first realized there were no electrical outlets in the cells in solitary.

The warden was back in control; Dick could not have an extension cord, especially in solitary, because he might hang himself with it or, worse yet, hang someone else. He speculated that the warden expected to be indicted if anything good happened to Dick.

He had his first lesson in how the system maintained complete control over its guests, despite occasional intervention by the courts. For his three remaining weeks in solitary, Dick borrowed a manual typewriter that was available only after 11 P.M. Its owner used it during the day, but could not use it in the dark because he couldn't type without seeing the keyboard. Dick was an accurate touch typist and so could type in the dark. He was not allowed any light because there was but a single switch for all the cells; lights out meant lights out. So, he typed in the dark, at least until he was released from solitary.

The typewriter incident deepened his conviction that they would do whatever they could to make his life uncomfortable. Not only was he not granted any special privileges, but also he would have to fight for what most prisoners took for granted. He resigned himself right then to do his time quietly, but with no hesitation to fight for his rights. Because of the stigma associated with the designation of "OC" (organized crime) stamped on his file, he was treated differently than the other prisoners. On many occasions, he wrote and speculated about how he might have been treated if he were a murderer or a drug dealer or had committed a "respectable" crime.

When he was finally released from solitary, he walked into the day room. One of the first comments he heard was a guy referring to him as a "copper." "I knocked him twenty feet across the room and, while they waited for the guards to take him to the infirmary, Will (Willie Daddano) explained what would happen to him if he said anything about how he got his broken nose." It was an unfortunate comment for the guy with the broken nose, but it was fortuitous for Dick to have been able to deal with such a comment early on, to let the other inmates know not to fuck with him.

Judge Hoffman had denied bail, but Dick had the right to appeal that denial to the U.S. Court of Appeals and the U.S. Supreme Court, independently of the appeal of his conviction.

A friend of Dick's offered to pay legal fees for his appeal, so one of the first things Dick accomplished after the trial was to hire an attorney, Dom Rizzi. His attorney advised him to hold off on filing an appeal bond until after the upcoming elections, which were about a month away. Rizzi lasted about that long before Dick fired him and, temporarily, went back to defending himself.

Dick had maintained throughout his trial that his indictment had political overtones: that among other things, the Democrats were scrambling to defeat Richard Ogilvie in the governor's race, and one of the best tools available to them for discrediting Ogilvie was to associate him with Dick Cain. As sheriff, Ogilvie should have known about his chief investigator's activities. Ogilvie's opponent ran full-page ads in the Chicago papers, branding Ogilvie with the Mark of Cain. Dick laid low until after Election Day, just in case.

When the votes came in, Dick's old friend and former boss, Richard B. Ogilvie, was elected governor of Illinois by a narrow margin. Dick didn't bother to send congratulations, knowing he had burned that bridge. Dick put Ogilvie out of his mind altogether. He hadn't spoken to his old friend since the day Ogilvie fired him in December 1964. Dick's behavior had nearly ended Ogilvie's career.

Life in jail is boring at best. Dick worked on his appeal and, once he was released from solitary, he spent time with the rest of the jail population, smoking Chesterfields (he could no longer afford the Dunhills), telling stories, and playing pinochle. He said he was approached almost daily by at least one jailhouse informant who hoped Dick would say something incriminating.

Reading consumed a large portion of his available time. Prisoners were allowed two books in their cells; additional books were confiscated as contraband. Lydia sent Dick two books a week while he was at Cook County, so he became a primary supplier of reading material on the tier. When he got a new title, his neighbors signed up to borrow it. A few books were available from the jail's library, but Dick's books were generally more current and came with his critique, since he read everything that was sent to him.

Dick could have been transferred out of Cook County anytime after his conviction, but he was kept around because the authorities hoped that he would break and agree to cooperate on other cases.

During his more than nine months in the Cook County Jail, Dick was hauled before the grand jury five or six times to face questions about mob activities in interstate trucking, gambling, and organized labor. He consistently refused to cooperate.

The grand jury is a unique investigative body that has the power to force a witness to testify by granting immunity. If, after the promise of immunity from prosecution, the witness continues to refuse to answer questions, the grand jury can declare the witness in contempt and jail the witness for the remainder of the grand jury's term (usually a maximum of eighteen months) or until the witness decides to cooperate. There is no trial; no lawyers are present; no defense is allowed. At the end of the grand jury's term, the witness is released from custody with little or no fanfare, though there is always the chance a newly-empaneled grand jury will also call the same witness.

This tactic was used in May 1965, when Sam Giancana was subpoenaed to testify about mob activity in Chicago. He first agreed to the terms of immunity, but later changed his mind and claimed his Fifth Amendment right against self-incrimination. The court held Sam in contempt and placed him in the Cook County Jail. Sam held out, continuing to refuse to talk. He quietly did his time—twelve months' worth in jail. Sam's stutter-step at his opening appearance with the grand jury cost him his job as boss of Chicago organized crime. His initial agreement was all the mob needed to declare Sam a loose cannon. When Sam was released in 1966, Tony Accardo explained to him that his days were over. Sam thought about standing up to Accardo, but on reflection realized he could never win. He would only be killed. So he moved to Mexico.

When the grand jury brought Dick in, they attempted to convince him he should talk and threatened to grant him immunity if he refused. But Dick was already in custody with a four-year sentence. A contempt citation would not affect his status as the grand jury was not empowered to assess consecutive time, so they didn't have their accustomed leverage. They could only jail an uncooperative witness during the term of the grand jury, not for any time beyond their expiration, giving them a maximum threat of eighteen months. Dick laughed at their threats and refused even to give his name.

Another prosecution tactic is to keep bringing an uncooperative witness back before the grand jury, so even if the witness is not talking, it might look as though he is. Since all grand jury testimony is secret, the witness might be suspected of talking and could be subject to retaliation by the mob, even if he wasn't talking. That plan worked with many witnesses, but Dick had used it too many times himself to be intimidated by it now. He was contemptuous of snitches. Even when he was a cop and regularly employed them, he had considered them the lowest form of life.

On February 7, 1969, Dick wrote, "I was down to the Federal Grand Jury again Thursday—spent a grand total of one minute before that august body (I won't even give them my name—claim the 5th, and justly so—everything they ask me is intended to result in an indictment)—I think that it was the last time they'll call me."

"My state case (the perjury case) has been continued until May 16th. Now the Gov't will either keep me here, or put me 'on the send,' and if it's to Tacoma, Washington, it'll indeed be quite a trip (stopping off for a few days at every County Jail on the way). One fellow here spent eight weeks travelling between California and Chgo—tho if they do, I'll have to be brought back at Gov't expense in May—We'll see."

Dick's days dragged on. He played pinochle for hours, read as many books as he could get his hands on, and was escorted on endless trips downtown to appear before the grand jury or for other court business. "I was downtown yesterday, and, of course, the trip is like a ditch-digging contest—strip searches four times, sitting in a bull pen, on a steel bench for 8 hrs etc—when you return, one is tiredissimo." (February 19, 1969)

On the 25th, "I was called downtown by the gov't today unexpectedly—it seems [Judge Julius] Hoffman is upset that I am still in Chgo—the G asked me if I wanted to stay here until May 16 or go to Washington state, and return for that date. No matter what I said, the opposite would have been done, in addition to the possible twisting, so I said, do your duty. They were not satisfied with my attitude. I therefore had to explain that I am not satisfied with the continuing miscarriage of justice, and that as far as I was concerned, I would not become a part of any part of its directives. So I still don't know what's happening."

He wrote regularly about the things that irked him there, the destitute state many prisoners endure. He wrote about one poor shmoe who had been in jail for three months because he couldn't post a twenty-five-dollar bond. He shared his cigarettes with guys who didn't have any. He hired inmates to do his laundry and clean his cell, paying them in cigarettes, as much to help them as to avoid doing the work himself.

He told his mother how he hypnotized incoming drug addicts to get them through a cold-turkey withdrawal. Dick had studied hypnosis years earlier and was happy to have discovered this very practical application for his talents. He would explain he only did it to "shut them up." His expertise became so well known that incoming prisoners began "asking in the receiving room as they arrive to come to the tier where I am, so they can take advantage of the socialized medicine. I suppose they'll accuse me of something or another because of it, but it seems to me that if it helps them, and keeps the little darlings quiet, it's better than nothing at all."

Dick usually complained about something in every letter he wrote, but he rarely complained about the same thing a second time. When he registered a complaint, he was stating a fact; he didn't like this or that, no big deal, just thought you might like to know. He didn't whine.

In February 1969, Dick wrote a letter to Attorney General John Mitchell offering to become an undercover investigator for the federal government in exchange for his release from jail. It was a bold move but a decidedly deliberate one. Dick never really felt a part of the family of organized crime, so his allegiances were few, and the opportunity to work with the government to bring them down was not out of the question for him.

He offered to deliver up convictions against the leaders of organized crime in New York, Detroit, Los Angeles, New Orleans, Tampa, and Chicago. As a bonus, he would help to bring down mob operations in Mexico, Equador, Brazil, Argentina, Chile, England, France, Iran, and the Caribbean.

He offered to submit to a debriefing interrogation, with the proviso that it be for intelligence purposes only and not for any future testimony. That was too good an offer for the government to pass up. So, knowing full well they would never let him out early, they played him along.

The letter was handed to Assistant U.S. Attorney Lawrence E. Morrissey and, three months later, the debriefing was conducted by Morrissey and Cook County State's Attorney Edward V. Hanrahan.

In the debriefing, Dick was asked about the hierarchy of the Chicago mob and his role in it. He explained he had never wanted a leadership role. He was content being Mooney's guy. This arrangement afforded him maximum flexibility without limiting his opportunities.

Dick volunteered to Morrissey and Hanrahan that he'd been told of his impending indictment by mob attorney George Bieber, who learned it from one of the government witnesses in the case. Dick then met with Felix "Milwaukee Phil" Alderisio, the boss in Chicago at the time, to seek his advice.

Eager to know more about the inner workings of the mob, the two interrogators asked Dick to explain how things work. Dick went on to explain the boss is responsible for sitting in judgment over disputes as they arise. The many factions in Chicago operated fairly autonomously, but a portion of their profits were sent "out West" to the boss. Collections were made during the first two days of the month, usually by Dominic "Butch" Blasi. Blasi would then distribute his collections to the boss. Then on the third of the month, payouts were made to corrupt politicians and police. These payouts were handled by various bagmen, a job Dick himself had held in the fifties with the Chicago Police Department. He told them that back then Giancana's benefactors included the commander of the robbery detail, commander of the burglary detail, commander of the narcotics section, the Chief of Detectives, and the chief of traffic, which pretty much covers it.

The FBI summary of this debriefing is about thirty pages and reveals Dick had a great deal of knowledge about operations in Chicago and elsewhere around the country. He detailed how he managed to move Sam, and himself, into and out of Mexico without being detected and how their participation in the drug trade was strictly forbidden in Chicago, though they became major suppliers to the New York mob. Still it wasn't enough to convince them to buy into his plan to work as an undercover agent.

After Dick had been in the federal tier of the Cook County jail for about five months, he reflected on how his time was probably a tad easier to do than it was for other inmates. He didn't have to deal with sexual advances because he was a "name," which meant he was treated with respect. The other prisoners demanded nothing of him because they feared they would be killed if they did. Dick didn't do anything to discourage that line of thought.

In April 1969, Dick was optimistic for a change. He was encouraged that he might be granted a new trial, if the prosecutors could find a way to save face. The "face saving" would be the federal prosecutor's attempt to explain away the tactics used to convict Dick (the lone witness without corroboration and no link between Dick and the bank robbery). He maintained the entire process had been instigated to hurt Ogilvie in the gubernatorial race. If Dick Cain were granted a new trial, he believed the prosecutors would have to justify their actions.

Dick usually gave the impression of being very much in control. But eventually his mood became grim and his patience wore thin. The long stretch in the county jail was taking its toll. As a temporary facility, it did not have the resources of a long-term institution. The library was mediocre; there were very few inmate jobs available.

Dick didn't dare let his depression show, especially to his fellow inmates. "And presently, I sit here in my Island on the Federal tier, listening to Andres Segovia and the String Quartet on FM, while six feet away the fires of racial hatred, sexual aberration, robbery, larceny, rape and maybe even Misprision of Felony are being lit. Through it all, I remain aloof and non-comprehending, noncompusmentes. I may wake up one day, look around and say, 'where the hell am I, anyway?' Meanwhile, everyone calls me Mr. Cain."

In the spring, he got company. When Sam "Teets" Battaglia arrived at the federal tier of Cook County Jail, following two years of appeals for a 1967 conviction on federal charges of extorting money from a construction firm, the inmates got a chance to see another side of Dick Cain. Battaglia was one of the current bosses of the Chicago mob, having taken over in 1966 with Accardo and Alderisio when Sam Giancana was exiled to Mexico. When the inmates saw Dick Cain and Sam Battaglia were pals, there were no more doubts about Dick's authenticity.

About Battaglia, Dick said, "He got framed even worse than I. Fifteen years and the G witness (only one) against him said that he never met the man. Guilty. Ho hum, next case."

Teets was about sixty when he stopped in at Cook County on his way to pull fifteen years at Leavenworth, but he could have passed for forty-five. Always keen on fitness, his stocky, solid frame and bulging chest had earned him his nickname back in the old days when he was an "unofficial" member of the 42 gang—"unofficial" because his older brother was in the spotlight as one of the original 42s. Big brothers can't accept little brothers as peers, so Sam had to be content to hang out with the big guys and by the time he had made his bones, the 42s had been absorbed into Capone's organization.

The 42s were too young, in the 1920s, to be associated with Al Capone's mob. They ranged in age from early teens to mid-twenties. What set them apart from other neighborhood gangs was their ruthlessness, their unhesitating willingness to pull out a gun and shoot someone with little or no provocation. Sam Giancana and Sam DeStefano were among the most ruthless and heartless of the 42s. Both saw prison time before they turned twenty, and both survived to make a career of crime. Battaglia was a little more refined and younger than the other two Sams, but a serious gangster nonetheless.

Once Dick got busy again with his appeal and with the overturned perjury conviction in the Zahn Drug case, he was more upbeat, more confident. It didn't matter what happened, just that something was happening. He could involve himself in his defense. He could harass the prosecutors who dragged him downtown for strip searches and endless hours of waiting. They wanted him to plead guilty on the Zahn Drug case. They offered him a concurrent sentence, which wouldn't have increased his jail time, but he still felt he could beat it. Also, if he gave them a guilty now, he felt that would lessen his chances of getting bail on the federal conviction.

By July, Dick had been in the federal tier of the Cook County Jail for nine months. His only opportunities to be outdoors had been short walks from the prison van to the courthouse on his many visits to the grand jury and to the state and federal courts. He wanted out; he wanted a more reasonable "home." As the deadline neared for the Zahn Drug case to be retried, Dick was trying to get his affairs in order. It was clear he would be moved soon, and he couldn't wait.

When Dick went to state court on July 8 to begin his retrial on the overturned perjury conviction, he learned that his co-defendants, Sergeant John Chaconas, Lieutenant James Donnelly, and William Witsman had pleaded guilty to reduced charges and paid fines of $250. He also learned that the evidence, which the state had used against the others, would be admitted at his trial, even though Dick would be on trial alone and that evidence did not relate to him. Bill Witsman showed up with four policemen as bodyguards and was introduced as a new state witness against Dick. It looked like a stacked deck so, on the advice of his attorney, Julius Echeles, Dick pleaded guilty to a misdemeanor and was sentenced to six months to run concurrently with his federal time. Had he fought the charge, he could have been sentenced to three years at Stateville Prison, time to be served after his federal debt. It was a small moral victory for him and lifted his sprits some.

With the state case resolved, the feds were free to move Dick. On July 18, he learned he was going to Texarkana, Texas. Dick was convinced he was going to Texarkana because that was the farthest prison from Chicago where he could be sent that didn't currently house other organized crime figures. He would have preferred Marion so he could be near his family and friends. Despite having four wives and six children, his current family circle consisted of a relatively small group of people.

Ordinarily, the bureau of prisons attempts to keep an inmate in the prison that is closest to home, believing they have a better chance at rehabilitation if they are near family and can have regular visitors. Organized crime figures are considered incorrigible and beyond rehabilitation, so those rules don't necessarily apply.

At 6:00 A.M. on July 19, Dick was taken from his cell in handcuffs and leg irons by two burly federal marshals who didn't look happy about having to be there. He was ushered out, stopping only to sign papers outside the warden's office. Before they left the building, the marshals picked up another prisoner, Guido Fidonzi, also bound for Texarkana. The first day, they traveled as far as Springfield, Illinois, about three hours south of Chicago. Once in Springfield, Dick and his traveling companion were delivered to the county jail to spend the night. The marshals went out to dinner and stayed in a motel.

On day two, they didn't leave the jail until mid-morning. Then they stopped for lunch around 1:30. The marshals didn't stop during the normal lunch hour because they felt vulnerable to escape attempts when restaurants were crowded, and it was very intimidating to civilians. The prisoners were not permitted out of the car without handcuffs and leg irons. When they went to the bathroom, they were permitted some freedom, though not much in the way of privacy. A marshal was with them, gun drawn, to ensure against escape.

They arrived in Jefferson City, Missouri, about 4:00 P.M. on Sunday, July 20. Usually, it takes about an hour to process a transient prisoner who's spending the night in a county jail, but being a Sunday, the sheriff was out and had to be tracked down to sign the forms. The marshals didn't check into their motel until after 7:00 P.M. Because of the late hour, there was no decent food for the prisoners. Dick was offered stale crackers and a soft drink, which he refused. He fumed over the treatment, but knew if he complained, it would only get worse.

Monday morning, his escorts picked Dick up about ten o'clock. They'd had a leisurely breakfast, far better than Dick's, and they were in good spirits and talked freely with Dick throughout that day. One town they passed through was Springfield, Missouri, and Dick couldn't resist telling his guards about his job nine years before when he had been hired to investigate the police department, and his investigation had resulted in the firing of the chief of police and thirteen patrolmen. The marshals couldn't believe they were getting a lecture on police corruption from a former cop they were taking to a federal penitentiary.

They spent Monday night in Little Rock, Arkansas. The jail was a little better than the one in Missouri, but Dick couldn't stand the way the staff treated him. They tried to provoke him. They knew very little about him except that he was a former cop, but that was enough to get them started. He feared he was starting to get a taste of what it would be like in Texarkana. Being from Chicago, Dick had formed opinions about the south and about southerners that were less than flattering. He was now discovering southerners had opinions about Yankees as well. The Bible Belt he'd heard about was real.

The next morning they began the final leg of the journey. Passing near Hot Springs, Arkansas, Dick recalled hearing his mother tell about the trip she took there with his father the year before he was born. He told the marshals the story and about how his father had hated the trip because Vincenza had come along, as well as Lydia's brother, Al.

As they approached the prison walls, the marshals, who were starting to like Dick, kidded him good naturedly about his new home. Over the next couple of years, whenever they were back at Texarkana to pick up or deliver an inmate, they would always stop and say hello.

The huge walls and surrounding fence with its long spirals of concertina wire gave the place an ominous look. So this was it. "This place is a Paradise compared to Cook County," Dick wrote. "I've been eating like an Armenian with a tapeworm; the food is certainly better than that served in restaurants! What a difference."

Dick was processed and assigned a caseworker. Their initial interview included a review of the post-sentence report prepared by a U.S. probation officer. Somewhat abridged, it gives an overview of how they attempt to classify their prisoners:

Education

As discussed in the post-sentence report, Scalzetti claimed that he took language and/or psychology courses at the University of Mexico City in 1961 and at the University of Madrid in 1954. The University of the Americas, formerly the University of Mexico City, was unable to locate a record for him and the University of Madrid failed to respond. Thus, there has been no evidence forthcoming, showing that Cain achieved any college level education.

In keeping with his apparent need to fabricate, Scalzetti reported to a former employer that he was a Doctor of Psychology and a graduate of the University of Loyola. Since he made no such claims to the writer, an investigation in this area was not made.

Details of the Offense—Defendant's Version

The defendant emphatically denied any guilt or involvement in respect to the instant offense. He maintained that he, himself, was the victim of a conspiracy, a political vendetta, resulting from his refusal to furnish certain information, albeit false, to government officials, which could be used to jeopardize political careers of others.

A lengthy account was given by the defendant of how his major difficulties with the law coincided with important political elections. It was his contention that the sergeant of the Sheriff's Police, who reportedly administered the polygraph examinations in the instant matter, lied when he claimed that he acted at the direction of the defendant. He maintained that the sergeant had acted without his knowledge and passed the blame to the defendant, simply to evade the responsibility and punishment. For the political implications, the defendant was then expected to involve his own superior, Richard B. Ogilvie, who was his party's choice for the governorship of Illinois at the time of the indictments, and the Sheriff of Cook County when the instant offense occurred. Since such an accusation on his part would have been false, defendant said, the defendant became the target for government action. This is always the case when an individual alleged to be involved in some wrongdoing does not involve a superior in the hierarchy.

The defendant pointed out that his state conviction in 1964, concerning conspiracy to commit perjury, occurred during the major political elections then and for essentially the same reason.

Prior Record

Excepting the instant matter, it appears that the defendant incurred only one conviction, which was later reversed. He was one of four members of the Cook County Sheriff's investigative unit who were convicted on December 9, 1964, of conspiracy to commit perjury.

This charge arose in connection with an investigation of the burglary in 1963 of $240,000 worth of drugs form the Louis Zahn Drug Company in Melrose Park. Defendant had been indicted with three others, after the State's Attorney charged they lied to a grand jury when they testified that one of them was not present at a motel raid where $40,000 of the merchandise was recovered, and in denying that the same party had rented the motel room. The State maintained that the defendant had conducted a fake raid on the motel to create the impression that, through his efforts, a substantial portion of the merchandise was recovered, while in reality, he had secreted loot there. The implication was that he was somehow involved with the theft, or the perpetrators.

As a result of the convictions, the defendant was sentenced to one to three years at the Illinois State Penitentiary. This decision was reversed by the Illinois Supreme Court on February 15, 1967, and a new trial was ordered. The high Court was of the opinion that the defendants' trial had not been properly conducted.

The Assistant United States Attorney in the instant matter described the defendant as being a pathological liar, often under suspicion for various crimes and thought to have been involved in several murders. In addition, authorities were of the opinion that he had been involved in some narcotic activities in Mexico. In 1961, he was reported to have been the chauffeur and bodyguard for the Syndicate leader, Sam Giancana.

It should be noted that the balance of this report reflects the defendant's refusal to answer many question, or give specific details, based on his claim that the United States Attorney's office threatened him with deportation and could use certain information against him. Background data has been received piecemeal and, although some areas have not been fully explored, now with a supplemental report, the defendant was able to furnish some information, only with the understanding that relatives were not to be interviewed, with the possible exception of his present wife.

Family History—Defendant

The defendant stated that he was born on October 4, and was forty-four years old, although he would not give the year of his birth. He would not give any identifying information about his parents, and whether he had brothers or sisters. He claimed United States citizenship, but chose not to disclose the locale of his rearing.

The defendant inferred that he was reared in a home, which had considerable marital discord. He related that a divorce occurred between his parents when he was between five and seven years old. Thereafter, he lived with each parent on a rotating basis for approximately six months at a time. He felt that he was not accorded proper parental treatment, and his rearing was unsatisfactory, but he would not be more specific.

At the age of fourteen, the defendant said, he dropped out of school, left home, and was on his own thereafter. His family did not know where he was, and he thought they were not that concerned.

After departing from his parental homes, the defendant traveled extensively, living at places like New Jersey and the Bahamas. He maintained himself by working as a dishwasher, pool hustler, bartender, and otherwise, generally living in flophouses. He considered these years to be very trying, due to his youth, but valuable, from the standpoint of helping to shape his personal philosophy and code of ethics from practical experience.

At the age of eighteen, he said, he entered the Unite States Army, and between the years of 1942 and 1950, he was in the military service or engaged in work as an espionage agent. During the latter year, he returned to Chicago. He added that he spent some of this time trying to educate himself.

Parents and Siblings

As noted above, the defendant refrained from giving any specific information of an identifying nature about his parents and whether he had brothers and sisters. He admitted that his mother was living in Chicago at the present time, however.

Marital History

The defendant states that he is presently married for the third time. His wife is an entertainer.

A Chicago newspaper file on the defendant contains an article from 1967, concerning the fact that license plates on the car of Chicago hoodlum Sam Giancana, in Mexico, had been issued to the defendant's wife, who was the secretary of Blake Productions and defendant was the president. The article mentioned that she was a professional singer and former beauty shop operator.

Home and Neighborhood

As the defendant's wife would not consent to an interview, a visit could not be made to the home. The defendant said that he and his family live in a five-room apartment, one of four flats in the building.

The defendant stated he had been living at this apartment for four years. He claimed that he was living in Chicago between 1956 and 1960, in Spain between 1954 and 1956, where he had a home and in Mexico between 1960 and 1962, where he was working for the Mexican government. He said that he lived at the Marina City Apartments in Chicago between 1962 and 1964. In addition, he lived part of the time between 1964 and 1966 at locations in Mexico and Argentina.

Education

Other than the fact that he left school at the age of fourteen, the defendant would not give any information concerning elementary or secondary schools that he attended. He did mention that, while in the Army in 1947, he took the high school equivalency test. At the time he applied for admittance to the institute named below, he gave conflicting information on two separate applications in respect to having attended high school in Carson City, Nevada, and in Michigan.

In the early 1950s, the defendant took a complete six-week course at the Keeler Polygraph Institute, 161 East Grand Avenue, Chicago. The defendant claimed that the course had been of twelve week's duration. Further, he credited himself with taking language or psychology courses at the University of Illinois in 1958, the University of Mexico City in 1961, and the University of Madrid in 1954. A report from the University of Illinois shows no attendance by him, and it appears that a request for information from the school in Mexico was not received. No information has been forthcoming as yet from the University of Madrid.

The defendant related being able to speak in number of languages, having proficiency in Pitman and Gregg shorthand and being able to type 100 words per minute.

Religion

The defendant stated that he was an agnostic and objected to much religious doctrinaire[sic]. He discussed having self-developed sense of morals and religious views. As an example, he feels that disloyalty (informing) is a very serious wrong. He considers many laws as being impractical and has a deep aversion to individuals being forced against their will to lead their lives in certain prescribed ways, either by direct force or by subtle means, both of which he believes are used in our society.

The defendant expressed considerable interest in reading, writing, and teaching. He said that he has 12,000 books in his personal library, has written two books concerning narco and scientific interrogation, and a half-dozen articles on interrogation, using hypnosis. He described having taught nurses, anesthesiologists, and dental technicians at the Chicago Institute of Hypnosis, 11 South Michigan Avenue, for two years between 1956 and 1958. The balance of his time is spent earning a livelihood, he said.

Health—Physical

The defendant is of medium stature and build, standing 5'7" and weighing 175 pounds. He has brown hair and green eyes, with well-formed facial features, making a comely appearance. He said he bears a bayonet scar on his right side and has recurring malaria, both of which stem from his service in the Orient. In addition, he has a bullet scar on his stomach, head wounds, and an assortment of fractures, including cuts and scars from fights. He would not discuss the circumstances surrounding the bullet wound. He mentioned having had an operation on an eye while in the Army and again in 1964.

Mental and Emotional

There are no records of intelligence testing known to the writer, but it seems that he has a high average to high intelligence, based on his mode of expression, communicative skills, and his fund of knowledge. He said that he had been tested in the past and was found to have an intelligence quotient of between 148 and 150. He considers himself to be emotionally stable, though he created the impression with the writer of suppressing considerable hostility and, from indications, a sub-culture, and anti-establishment orientation.

According to the present director of the Keeler Polygraph Institute, Leonarde Keeler, a polygraph examination of the defendant, while he was a student at the institute, revealed violent reactions and deception in the areas of integrity and morals, such as compliance with the law and concerning his feelings about Communism. It was discovered that his claims of having been a Warrant Officer and a counter-intelligence agent were not true. The director remarked that, had he been in charge of the institute at the time, the defendant would not have been admitted, based on his examination results.

Employment

The defendant maintained that, after completing his polygraph training at the Keeler Institute, he was self-employed (1955 or 1956 to present) on a full- or part-time basis, doing investigative and polygraph examinations work. He said that his business was known as Accurate Laboratories, although it had several other names and a number of addresses for financial and legal reasons. His activities in this line included wiretapping, political and other investigations, much of the time in other countries, often taking the form of espionage. His clients or contractors included the Republican Central Committee, the Central Intelligence Agency, the Justice Department, Luce of Time, Inc. and Hefner of Hugh Hefner Enterprises, he said.

Between May 16, 1956, and May 16, 1960, the defendant was a member of the Chicago Police Department, serving in the capacity of a detective after February 1, 1958. His annual salary was $6,240 ($7,500, according to the defendant), when he resigned to accept other employment, according to a report from this department.

When the defendant resigned from police department in May 1960, he was with the Police Sex Bureau Squad. At that time, he had been accused of spying on City Commissioner Irwin N. Cohen, being paid $1,700 by the State's Attorney's chief investigator. Newspaper articles show that the defendant stated at the time that he was innocent of such activity, but was resigning from the police force, as the notoriety had destroyed his future value as a detective. It might be mentioned that the defendant, in discussing this incident with the writer, referred to the then City Commissioner Irwin N. Cohen as being Mayor Daley's "bagman."

Sometime after defendant's resignation, it was discovered that certain files on cases investigated by the defendant were missing from the police records.

The defendant stated that, after he resigned as a police detective, he worked for the Banco De Mexico, Mexican Treasury Department, in Mexico City between 1960 and 1962. His duties consisted of teaching government-personnel sabotage and espionage work. He said that he was deported form Mexico in 1962 by presidential mandate, after a "Bobby Kennedy man found out I had been wiretapping the Czechoslovakian Embassy there." This agency has not replied to date to our request for information.

The defendant was the chief investigator of the Cook County Sheriff between 1962 and December 1964. The Sheriff's personnel files were not available at the time of the preparation of this report, though it is a matter of record that the defendant held that position. He was given considerable publicity in the newspapers at the time for his numerous vice raids and arrests. Concurrently, a feud existed between the defendant and the State's Attorney's office, the latter charging then that he had not been obtaining properly executed warrants and, as a result, many of the court cases, following his arrests, failed to produce convictions. The same office charged that the defendant was primarily interested in gaining publicity, rather than in law enforcement. As the result of a conviction later reversed and a new trial ordered, the defendant was discharged from his position by the Sheriff. The defendant stated that he had been earning $12,000 annually in that position, although newspaper reports show his monthly salary was $835.

The defendant stated that his employment after leaving the above position has consisted of his private investigation, exclusively. Whereas he maintained that his annual income during the past decade has fluctuated between $12,000 and $20,000, the Assistant United States Attorney said that information of a financial nature concerning the defendant shows that his income was considerably less.

The defendant expressed his intention to be a writer, after he is permitted to return to the community, inasmuch as his reputation would make other legitimate means of earning income extremely difficult. At first, he agreed to produce a list of his published writing, but later declined, claiming that, should the same become a matter of common knowledge, his future potential in this area could be retarded.

Military Service

The defendant declined to give any information about his military service, other that the fact that he was in the United States Army for a period of time and that he had two names and engaged in secret assignments in the service. The military personnel Records Center was able to locate his file and reported that he served in the Army between July 31, 1947, and June 23, 1950, two years, two months, and twenty-six days being in foreign service. He was given an honorable discharge and attained the rank of private first class. It was stated on the report that he did not have any special assignments while in the military.

Evaluative Summary

This is the case of a thrice-married, forty-four year old man who has received a sentence of four years and a fine of $13,000 for conspiracy to conceal knowledge of a bank robbery and assist the perpetrators thereof, and the actual concealing of the knowledge and assisting the participants. He continues to maintain his complete innocence in respect to the instant offense and presents a detailed description of how he has been the victim of a political vendetta.

There is little or no verifiable information available concerning his formative years. If his account has validity, it would appear that he was exposed to considerable marital discord between his parents and shunted between them after their divorce, until he went on his own at the onset of his adolescence. Thereafter, he survived by his wits and hustling ability. He credits these experiences as helping to shape his personal philosophy of life, which gives evidence of resentment toward the generally accepted social and legal processes. It is interesting that, in spite of these feelings, he chose to involve himself vocationally in law enforcement and private investigative work, although he was quite controversial, and under suspicion at times, while performing his duties as a Chicago Police Detective and later the chief investigator for the Cook County Sheriff.

The defendant seems to be a highly intelligent individual who has educated himself to a large extent. He claims to be an expert in the interrogation field and to have exceptional ability in languages, shorthand, and typing. Further, he credits himself with a number of published articles and books, expressing an intention to earn his livelihood by writing in the future.

He served honorably in the United States Army for three years between World War II and the Korean conflict, although falsely claiming, it appears, to have engaged in special secret assignments during his military career. In addition, he describes a rather involved life as an investigator and as an espionage agent in this country, Latin America, and Europe, his services being utilized by prominent private citizens and persons in high governmental positions. It would seem that he is inclined toward self-glorification, with at least some fabrication and/or exaggeration of his affairs and ability.

The defendant has had two unsuccessful marriages and feels that his present marriage is precarious, due to the adverse notoriety he has received. He can be personable, but gives indications of harboring considerable hostility, with the likelihood that he can be easily provoked. Though his record shows no standing convictions, except the instant matter, he has long been reported to be associated with Syndicate figures, and suspected of a number of criminal offenses, including murder. One would have to wonder whether he will lead the sedentary type of existence he claims to be planning on his return to the community.

Respectfully submitted.

Arthur M. Afremow
United States Probation Officer
January 29, 1969

The report is fair and as accurate as possible under the circumstances. During orientation with his case worker, Dick respectfully declined to confirm or even discuss any information about his date or place of birth, stating there was a potential deportation hearing in his future and he didn't want to provide any information that the government might later use against him. His caseworker told him he understood and simply noted it in is file.

Religion is an important part of prison life, and the caseworker was interested in knowing where Dick stood on the subject. Dick told him, "Although raised a Catholic, I have studied all religions as an avocation through the years and have developed a philosophy which, for want of a more concise term, can be referred to as agnostic. I am uncommonly interested in all forms of religions, their history, leaders, and adherents, and have studied them extensively. Although I am sympathetic as well as interested in all religions, I cannot as yet classify myself as a follower of any particular dogma."

Translation: I know what you want me to say, but I'm not going to give it to you. However, I am going to let you know I am educated enough about the subject not to be called a heathen if I refuse to attend services. You can't hold that against me because I'm smart enough to have made an informed decision not to participate.

Knowing this was going to be an ordeal, Dick was determined to be cooperative, yet not give up his dignity. If he showed any weakness with either the administration or the other inmates, it was going to be a tough time. He had to learn how to strike a balance between assertiveness and being a troublemaker. He had to define for himself what the limits were and he had to be consistent about them.

His first test happened in the first month at Texarkana. Having arrived on July 22, he was given a few weeks to settle in, get through the orientation process, and get the lay of the land. On August 14, he was assigned to the Food Services Department. He quietly, respectfully declined the assignment. He was told this wasn't an offer of employment. He was required to go where they sent him. He held his ground, explaining that in his career as a police officer he had put more than six thousand men behind bars, and he was not going to start cleaning up after them.

This bit of assertiveness cost him three weeks in solitary, but he took the time without complaint. He hadn't refused to work, he told the warden, he'd refused to work in the kitchen. Eventually, the administration blinked. They released him from segregation and, in mid-September, he was assigned to the clothing room (laundry) where he worked for the balance of his term.

Round one went to Cain, but he was about to learn that winning a skirmish doesn't mean shit in the long run.

Dick settled in and became a regular correspondent. He tried not to involve himself in the lives of the other inmates. He wished only for the passage of time. There were escapes, stabbings, rapes, and all sorts of general depravity going on around him, which he tried to ignore. The FBI interviewed him once about a stabbing that happened just a few feet away from where he'd been sitting. He declined the opportunity to be of assistance.

In 1971, Chicago was preparing for the coming governor's race. Ogilvie was seeking re-election, and the machine was working hard to present its candidate. Mayor Daley's hand-picked man was to be Thomas A. Foran, the prosecutor who put Dick away. "I expect Foran will cite his prosecution of me as one of his credentials for nomination."

Foran lost the race, but it's interesting to note that nearly thirty years later, before his death, Foran's Web site listed his prosecution of Richard Cain among his greatest accomplishments. He was also quite proud of his prosecution of the Chicago Seven, but managed to ignore the eight Chicago policemen he persecuted as scapegoats in Mayor Daley's riots at the 1968 Democratic Convention in Chicago.

Dick related a story about a fellow inmate named Guido Fidonzi with whom he became close. "We're the only two Italians here, and of course, are subjected to quite a bit of needling. We have been offering to enroll all comers into the mob for two packs of cigarettes, providing we can get a candle, stiletto, parchment and all the usual trappings. But no matter how much we joke about it, guards and cons alike believe the myth."

One of the best tools a prison has to motivate its prisoners to behave and to cooperate is the awarding of "good time." An inmate has two routes to reduce his sentence. Statutory Good Time (SGT) is usually awarded automatically unless there is a disciplinary issue allowing the warden to revoke it. Once revoked, it can be reinstated after six months if conditions warrant. Dick had seven days revoked in August over his refusal to work in the kitchen.

The second is Meritorious Good Time (MGT), which is a bonus to recognize performance, attitude, and contributions exceeding normal and expected requirements. The inmate's supervisor has a checklist of items related to work performance and attitude with a 1–3 ranking (3 being good). If an inmate scores mostly 3s, he would likely be recommended for MGT. This was where they had Dick Cain by the short hairs and they'd make him pay the price for his assertiveness.

The warden refused to consider Dick for MGT until May 1971, despite his being recommended for it on every report. He was furious when he realized what they were doing. He complained to his caseworker, to the warden, and finally wrote this letter to the director of the bureau of prisons.

Mr. Carlson:

I am corresponding with you in hopes that you will take some action to rectify what I consider to be an arbitrary and unfair policy pertaining to Meritorious Good Time, exclusively instituted against myself, at the apparent behest of the Bureau of Prisons.

Having been in Federal custody since October 3, 1968, I spent almost ten months in the Cook County Jail before being sent to F.C.I. Texarkana. On Sept 12, 1969, I was assigned as clerk in the Clothing Room at this institution. Since that time, on every even month, a work report has been submitted to the Record Office. I believe that every work report indicates that my duties are performed at least satisfactorily. I have had no disciplinary or other adverse reports submitted against me in the past fourteen months.

Yet I have been informed by both my caseworker, Mr. Woods, as well as the Associate Warden, Mr. Dickson, that I have been, and am, ineligible for MGT benefits, due to the fact that the Bureau has classified me as in the Organized Crime status. Should I be given MGT, as is every other prisoner whose actions, like mine, merit it, there would be "criticism from the Bureau."

If this is indeed the case I must maintain that such a Bureau policy is selectively prejudicial, and contrary to the basic precepts of the MGT program.

Can it be possible that the Bureau exerts a fearsome influence over its administrators in the field, preventing them from dispensing equal and equitable benefits? I doubt that this is the intention, although it is the end result, in this case

My release date, as it stands, is November 1971. This would mean that I will have served three years and one month of a four year sentence. I was deprived of the opportunity of even eligibility for MGT by being kept in the Cook County Jail (O Bastion of Luxury) for the first ten months of my custody.

I have been given to understand that each and every one of my "co-conspirators" have been granted MGT: Daddano (Atlanta); Montagna (Sandstone); DeLegge (Leavenworth) and DeLegge (Terre Haute), all convicted in the same trial with me, and all classified as Organized Crime, all are receiving MGT.

In addition, I believe that such popular Organized Crime luminaries as Battaglia (Marion); Amabile (Leavenworth); Tornabene (Sandstone) etc., are all receiving MGT. Please do not misunderstand, I have no objections or resentment against anyone who is receiving MGT; my viewpoint is not negative, it is positive. If there are provisions for such benefits as MGT, and they be given to inmates who are classified OC, and to my co-conspirators, I fail to understand why I must suffer a greater proportion of imprisonment than they. I wish neither superiority nor inferiority, only equality. Is that an "Impossible dream?"

Mr. Woods kindly suggested that were I to provide "information" it might be "possible" to obtain MGT. I gratefully declined such a solution to this problem, believing that the Quid Pro Quo for MGT relates to behavior, not to data.

Mr. Dickson agrees that my behavior has been in accordance with the standards of F.C.I. Texarkana. Understandably, however, he abhors Criticism from the Bureau. I don't believe he or anyone in the Government service should be criticized for treating me, or anyone else, with evenhanded justice. Mr. Dickson stated that he would try to do something, but I do not want he or anyone else to have to place themselves in jeopardy in order to allow me what everyone else gets.

My requests of the Bureau of Prisons for whatever amount of time I spend in durance vile, are slight. I ask that I be fed and clothed and boarded and treated as is everyone else; I wish to be contemporary. In return, I will not escape, engage in illicit activities, agitate, terrorize or antagonize my fellow inmates, and will reasonably follow all the rules of custody. I realize that such a contract was not signed between us; yet is not such an agreement implied? I cannot complain about food, clothes or cell; I receive the same as everyone else. And in treatment, only in the matter of MGT do I feel that I have cause to complain. I have earned MGT, as have others; they receive it, I do not.

I respectfully request that I be granted MGT retroactive to January 1970. Every other inmate assigned to the Clothing Room, barring disciplinary or poor work reports, has been given MGT within sixty days of assignment.

There is an old saying: "All men are created equal, only some are more equal than others." I hope that in regard to MGT, this adage will not mean that I will be singled out and disenfranchised. It would simply be unfair.

Thanking you for any consideration in this regard, I am

The Notorious
Richard Cain

Dick's letter was returned with a form letter, suggesting he discuss the matter with the staff. Associate Warden Dickson reprimanded the staff in the clothing room for allowing Dick to use the typewriter to write this letter. He eventually would receive MGT, but not retroactive as he'd hoped.

He was very frustrated by this incident and wrote many other letters, as did his lawyer, Julius Echeles. He continued to cry "OC" as though it were a race card, but by his own admission, other OC inmates all over the country, including his co-defendants, were receiving MGT. The staff at the prison continued to tell him it was due to bureau policy, but probably just to deflect his frustrations. Most likely he had been denied the time because of his refusal to take the kitchen assignment, perhaps because he had been a cop, but certainly not because he was organized crime.

Aside from the early incident over his work assignment, there are no disciplinary issues documented in Dick's prison record. By all indications, he did his time quietly, making few friends or enemies. He was approached regularly by inmates who tried to get him talking about his past. In some cases it was just curiosity about a so-called celebrity inmate, but in many more the questions were designed to elicit information that could be used as a bargaining chip to get sentence reductions for themselves. Dick was on to that strategy, though, having benefited in his cop days from information from jailhouse informants. He didn't like them, he didn't trust them, and he certainly was not stupid enough to be taken down by one of them now.

He did befriend some of his neighbors, though. In one instance, he leaned on an old friend in Chicago to write the prison offering a job to an inmate who could be released early if he had a job waiting. Dick would ask his mother for a magazine subscription in the name of an inmate with a long sentence, so if Dick got an early release, the magazine would still get some use. In another instance, near his own release date, he asked that money be sent to an inmate who had no one on the outside to care for him—a simple gesture of kindness.

Dick believed being stuck in the Bible Belt was part of his punishment. He frequently mentioned their attitudes, but tried to keep it light. On February 2, 1971, he wrote to his mother, "Happy Groundhog Day. I looked this morning and some bucktoothed hillbilly caseworker stuck his head out of the records office, saw his shadow, and told me I'd have to do another six months!"

He once became the reluctant pal to an Italian sailor, Luigi from Genoa, because the guy spoke no English, and Dick was the only person there who spoke Italian. These gestures were just part of getting by for Dick. He neither sought nor expected anything from them in return.

His marriage was slowly disintegrating while he sat behind bars. His wife professed her love, but complained the publicity about him was hurting her singing career. It sure couldn't have helped. So she dragged it out for three years, and just before he was to be released, she sued for divorce.

Dick was a prolific letter writer and while he always seemed to have plenty to say, he was ever vigilant of the censors who reviewed everything, incoming and outgoing, for signs of illegal activity. So, he talked about family, about the news in Chicago, and frequently about his contempt for the paddy pig, Thomas A. Foran, the federal prosecutor who had put him away. He was adamant in his continued claim that his was a political persecution. The Democrats, he insisted, saw prosecuting Dick Cain as a useful weapon in smearing the gubernatorial campaign of Richard Ogilvie. He portrayed himself as a victim, but it's not likely anyone ever bought it.

This is not to suggest Dick was innocent, but it helps explain why Dick felt victimized by the system, because he knew they didn't have enough evidence for his case to be won by the government on its merits. They were totally dependent on strategy. Theirs was a team effort, involving the U.S. attorney, the FBI, and of course, a sympathetic judge. They had done their homework, but *boy* did that piss him off.

I had a discussion with Tom Foran, before his death, about the case against Dick and mentioned to him that I had read the trial transcript and it seemed to me that they had presented no direct evidence of Dick's guilt. I wasn't suggesting that he was innocent, but wondered if Foran would comment on what seemed to me to be a stacked deck. Trying Dick with the guys who actually robbed the bank would lead the jury to conclude that he must be guilty just because he was in the courtroom with the rest of them. Foran insisted that he had included direct testimony from one of the cooperating witnesses who overheard a conversation between Dick and Willie Daddano while they were all riding in a car together. Maybe so, but I couldn't find it. He also claimed to have had additional evidence that he hadn't presented at trial, but wouldn't tell me what that was.

His relationship with the censors at the prison was a constant source of aggravation for him. Occasionally, they would return mail to his mother or his wife they thought outside the bounds of their rules. It seemed to him to be inconsistent and arbitrary. He was careful about his own correspondence, careful not to name people he'd denied association with. "Will" for Willie "Potatoes" Daddano, "my friend" for Sam Giancana, "Philly" for "Milwaukee Phil" Alderisio, "O" for Dick Ogilvie, "Sam" for Sam Battaglia and "Vito" from New York for Vito Genovese.

In his only direct reference to Sam Giancana, he responds to his mother's inquiry about receiving a golf magazine: "Funny you should be getting those golf magazines—my friend never did read them, substituting practice for theory, as the Idle Rich are wont to do. He <u>is</u> my friend, and as you may have gathered, that type is a rare breed. Although I always knew that fact, I had further evidence of it when I was in Cook County Jail, and from a very unlikely personage who remarked (when trying to break me to his/their will) that he turned down the fortune offered him to leave me alone! I truthfully denied knowing anything about that, and when the realization struck home that I *really* didn't know anything about it, the turkey understood that he had gobbled too much and had provided by his own words the exact standard by which any expectation of cooperation on my part was doomed. I had a good laugh at his stupidity, and at the best place, in front of him."

In a rare moment of contrition, Dick actually confessed to a crime while writing from prison, though he was never charged with it. He was frequently quite hateful toward the Irish, with whom he associated most of the bad things in his life. Beginning with the fact that his father was Irish, continuing through the domination of Mayor Daley's machine by the Irish, and of course his prosecution by the hated Irisher Thomas Foran.

Reaching back to the mid-sixties when Dick lived in the Marina Towers, he wrote, "When Murray Humphries and I were living in Marina City, we dumped a barrel of orange dye in the river just as the St. Patrick's Day parade was crossing the State St. Bridge, making the water Orange instead of green. The gnashing of teeth was really something to behold. They were screaming about the insult at City Hall for a month afterward."

Dick was scheduled to be released at 8:00 A.M. on October 20, 1971, with a bus ticket to Chicago on Continental Bus Service and $135 in cash. Lydia had arranged for an airline ticket, but there were only two flights out—one at 7:30 A.M., the next at 4:30 P.M. His final confrontation with the administration was over his being allowed out early to catch the earlier flight to Dallas so he could connect into Chicago and be home in time for lunch. He won that last battle.

On balance, his three-plus years in the prison system went well. He stayed out of trouble, and he was left alone. He came out knowing that he might have to return one day, accepting the realization that he could never make a living now in the legitimate world with a prison record and an undeniable connection to organized crime. He was resigned, though, to make the most of it, and live as good a life for himself as he could manage.

CHAPTER

15

Jack Mabley had written and offered to pick Dick up at O'Hare, but Dick told him that he'd make his own way. Knowing the heat that Mabley would have taken for his trouble, he responded with an uncommonly unselfish refusal. It was his erstwhile papa, Scully Cozzone, who picked him up at the airport. Scully and Lydia had rekindled their relationship quite by chance shortly before Dick was arrested back in 1968 and they bonded right away. Scully knew the life, and never questioned Dick's decisions, unlike his real father. Scully and Lydia would be lifelong companions, but they never married. Lydia told me it was because she had been divorced and his Catholicism forbade him to marry her. Family lore has it that he avenged the death of Ole Scully, his mentor and great friend, by killing the men who had killed him, and Scully Cozzone believed he couldn't marry because of the gravity of those sins. Whatever the reason, they were happy together and took care of one another.

Dick returned to Chicago feeling dejected and as close to beaten as ever in his life. He needed a plan, something that would set him apart from his peers, provide an income, and help him to leave his mark.

He took a room at the Sherman House. The ink was barely dry on his divorce papers, but he knew staying with his ex- was not an option. His mother lived in a one-bedroom apartment and, while she had offered the couch, that would have been too difficult—for them both. He couldn't afford the Sherman House, but that was surely temporary. On his first night back, he had dinner in the hotel dining room with Lydia and Scully

Cozzone. Hots Michaels, one of his best friends, was playing the piano in the dining room at the Sherman House and joined them between sets. Dick savored a couple of bottles of his favorite wine, a Zinfandel, and rounded out the night with a half-dozen scotches. Zinfandel and Scotch were the two things he missed the most while serving his time in Texarkana. On his first night back, he was going to enjoy them both.

The next day he met with Pat Marcy, whom he'd called from the airport in Texas. Pat told him Sam was expecting to hear from him and wanted Dick to come to Mexico as soon as possible. It was heartening for Dick that Sam made the request and, though he couldn't leave the country just yet, he'd get there as soon as he could.

Next on Dick's agenda was a meeting with Ben Meeker, head of the U.S. Probation and Parole office. He had not been paroled, he believed, because of his organized crime status, so he still owed the government six months of his life, and while mandatory good time allowed him to leave Texarkana, he would still have to report to a parole officer until his sentence expired in April 1972.

Giancana had put out the word that Dick was to be allowed to "earn" a living. To the Outfit guys, this meant they were to exempt him from the general rules about territories and to help him find a way to generate income. He wasn't exempted from the "street tax" however, and would be required to share, like everyone else.

A year earlier, Frank Pierce was approached by a group of black gangsters who, because of theft and generally bad management among their ranks, were barely breaking even in their numbers games. The concept of breaking even or possibly losing money on the numbers rackets is inconceivable to any of the Outfit guys. Numbers is a sucker's game, easy to fix, nearly impossible to win. And the blacks had figured out a way to add risk to the game. Unbelievable, thought Pierce. When the Outfit guys ran a numbers game, the payoff might be based on the last dollar digit of the daily total handle of the win, place, and show bets at a local race track, read from top to bottom. For example, if the daily handle was:

Win . . . $986.45
Place . . . $437.99
Show . . . $32.66,

then the daily number was 672.

The way the Outfit might play this game is to wait until most of the bets had been placed, figure out where their risk is, then call their friends at the track and fix it on that end. The blacks didn't have options like that, so sometimes they'd lose their asses through plain dumb luck. Often as not, though, their losses were internal. The draw for this kind of numbers game in the poor black neighborhoods was that, when you won, the payoff could be as high as 500 to 1. The real odds were much higher, so the opportunity to profit at the game is phenomenal—if you're the one with the book—and better still if you can rig it. The other thing that set them apart is that the size of the bets was much smaller than elsewhere; bets might be as small as a penny for the blacks, though usually it was a five or ten cent game.

The discipline required to run a numbers game is critical. If the runners are trying to carry some of the action themselves, or simply pocketing some of the money and not reporting it, the punishment has to be swift and sure. In the Outfit everyone knew that such an infraction would likely cause the death of the runner in a violent manner. Everybody knew that, but of course there was much more money involved in the Outfit bets, and that might have been part of the problem. Even if you're a tough guy, it's hard to whack a kid for stealing a couple of bucks; that's where the discipline would have broken down first.

In the black neighborhoods, justice of this sort was neither swift nor sure. People just got away with it, and consequently the guys running the games were barely getting by. They needed help.

They knew of Pierce's mob connections, and they were aware that he ran the South Side gambling for the Outfit. Ever since the Capone days, the blacks had their own thing and fought to keep it that way. When Sam Giancana did time at Terre Haute years ago, he met a guy named Eddie Jones who bragged about how lucrative the numbers rackets were in the black neighborhoods. He bragged and Sam encouraged him to talk, eventually learning all the particulars of the process. When Jones was released from prison, after Giancana was, Sam had him kidnapped and convinced him to leave the country. With Jones out of the way, Sam used this new-found racket as a stepping stone to improve his own position in the Outfit and he did very well with it until he ran up against Theodore Roe. Roe had successfully taken the Black rackets back and defied the Outfit guys until he was killed in August 1952, leveled by five shotgun blasts.

Now, though, none of the Outfit guys wanted to go into the black neighborhoods and take it over. There was money to be made, but it would have been a bloody mess, and no one had the stomach for it.

The leadership in the black gangs proposed a partnership. Pierce wanted nothing to do with it, but just as he was about to say no, word came down that Dick Cain was getting out of prison and needed a way to earn money. Problem solved. Through Gus Alex, Pierce turned the whole thing over to Dick. After studying the situation, Dick realized he'd been handed a gold mine. All he had to do was train the runners; they'd do everything else. He would have none of the security issues; they would take care of enforcement. He would have to run the counting house and take his cut, but little else.

He had agreed to take on what he called the "Negro rackets" on the South Side. He scheduled training during December 1971 and planned to kick things off the first week of January 1972. The runners, about fifteen hundred of them, had to be trained in the proper ways of a numbers runner. This was going to be a professionally-run operation, and it was going to be done his way. The numbers rackets in the black sections of South Chicago had been around for years, but had recently gotten completely out of control for reasons Dick was not going to try to understand or explain. He was just going to change how they worked. The deal they made was that the blacks would keep forty percent of the profits, with sixty percent going to the Outfit. Dick would have to spread his take wide and far to take in the district cops and several levels of mob hierarchy.

The training agenda would include a serious talk about the consequences of stealing. There's an interesting dichotomy among thieves—that it's okay to steal from your victim, but heaven help you if you dare steal from a thief. There would be enforcers on the payroll—from the Blackstone Rangers, a black gang on the South Side, whose job would be to punish theft. Since these rackets involved tens of thousands of relatively small bets, few larger than a quarter, the security issues were vastly different from a typical Outfit gambling operation. Everybody seemed to know that somebody was "gonna steal some money," and it was Dick's job to make them understand that when it happened, "somebody was gonna die." It seemed a harsh penalty for petty theft but, from Dick's point of view, you've got to look at the bigger picture and establish enforceable ground rules. He expected they would test the system but, after a few of them got whacked, they'd get the picture. He structured the organization so that none of the runners would ever know who he was; he would deal only with the leaders.

Dick was told the FBI would not "countenance" this type of illegal activity on his part but, on further reflection and, no doubt a sales job by Dick, they agreed to allow his participation in hopes of gaining valuable information about police corruption. But they wouldn't stand for violence.

Like most Outfit guys, Dick was a racist and not at all thrilled about doing business with these guys, but it would be easy money and he needed some of that. My sister went to Chicago to visit Dick during this time and he tried to recruit her to work as a liaison with the blacks, figuring that her liberal Ann Arbor roots would help her to understand them and be more empathetic than he could be. Also, it would keep him from having to deal with them directly, but he couldn't quite sell her on turning to a life of crime.

On his second day home, Dick called Special Agent William F. Roemer of the FBI and asked for a meeting. They had met three times before, when Roemer first tried to recruit him in 1967, when Roemer arrested Dick in front of the Sherman House late in 1967, and again when Dick called him to request a meeting with federal prosecutor Thomas Foran. Roemer had asked to be the one to arrest Dick because he'd worked so hard to build a prosecutable case against him with smoke and mirrors. They had waited to indict him until six weeks before the statute of limitations would have run out on his crime because they knew they had a weak case and kept hoping for more evidence.

The FBI knew its case against Dick was extremely unstable. Roemer also wanted to be in on the arrest to be sure no one spoke out of turn, that nothing went wrong in the arrest that would cause their house of cards to fall.

Agent Roemer was a large, affable man who had been a champion boxer during his college days at Notre Dame. He talked with Dick for several hours the night of Dick's arrest, mostly about issues unrelated to the case. He was surprised at how easy it was to talk with Dick and how educated and intelligent he seemed to be. Roemer had been working almost exclusively on organized crime cases since arriving in Chicago eight years earlier and had learned some of these guys were actually due some respect. Not that he was going to tolerate any illegal behavior from them, but he felt compelled to treat some of them better than others. Roemer had first attempted to recruit Dick as an informant back in 1967. They'd had dinner at the Sirloin Club on West Madison. Roemer was reimbursed nine dollars and eighty cents and reported to SAC Marlin Johnson that "this expenditure was for dinner for Richard Scalzetti Cain and SA during which time Cain furnished substantial info on Giancana and status of organized crime today."

In a memo from Roemer to FBI headquarters on October 31, 1967, he advised that Dick had been "designated as a target under the UECIP (Upper Echelon Criminal Informant Program) for further development." His efforts to recruit Dick dated to at least August 1967, and were temporarily suspended after Dick won his appeal on the Zahn Drug case and was waiting to be retried. They were delayed again in December because of Dick's arrest on charges stemming from the Franklin Park Bank robbery.

Now it was three-and-half years later. Dick was making the overture. He remembered that Roemer had been quiet and respectful during their talk that night, an easy guy to talk to, a guy who knew a lot about the mob, but he had more questions than answers. Bill Roemer was, to Dick Cain, the perfect mark for his plan with the FBI.

When they met, Dick told Roemer, that having served his time in jail, he now wanted to have a hand in making some changes in the Outfit. He was going to earn a leadership position for himself and he wanted the FBI to come along for the ride. "Who knows," he told Roemer, "we may be able to help one another." A part of Dick's plan as he explained it, was that he wanted the FBI to legitimize him. He'd been successful in Mexico in getting the treasury department there to give him credentials that identified him as one of their own. He wanted to become an undercover agent for the FBI and to help them cripple the mob. If along the way he managed to enhance his own position in the Outfit, so much the better. He wanted a badge and a salary equal to an agent's.

During this meeting, which happened on November 1, 1971, according to Roemer, Dick "offered his services to the bureau in the capacity of foreign intelligence agent with the proposition that he would have an agent's salary and tenure. He felt that by investing money of organized crime for Giancana and others, he could obtain information of considerable investigative interest."

When they next met, on November 3, they discussed the possibility of Dick accepting a position with Giancana in Chicago and working for the FBI in an undercover capacity. Dick replied that he'd consider it with three conditions, "sufficient payment on a C.O.D. basis to make it worthwhile to him, agreement that he will never testify in court as to any information furnished by him, and an understanding that he will be free to travel."

Roemer went on to say that other sources had verified Dick's status in Chicago at the time and that his claims "appear to be unexaggerated." Further, he stated, "He is extremely sharp, intelligent, aggressive individual with Italian background and is undoubtedly LCN [La Cosa Nostra] member who would be eligible for appointment to 'commission' when and if his accomplishments made him eligible for same. It appears reasonable to believe he has potential to eventually be 'boss' of organized crime here and Chicago's representative on 'commission'."

On November 9, the bureau officially granted authority to Bill Roemer to begin paying Dick for his information, but they thought it was "premature to designate him a top-echelon informant." They suggested "if he does supply quality data regarding orgnanized crime matters in the future, you may resubmit your application."

Dick continued to maintain with Roemer that his reason for becoming an informant was that "he considers himself a professional law enforcement agent and that the proposed plan of action is the best way for him to perform law enforcement function." He maintained that the payments made to him by the FBI "are important to him only for expenses and the fact that it indicates to him that the bureau is appreciative of his cooperation."

The idea of Dick having any semi-official FBI sanction was absolutely out of the question, but Roemer was hungry to know what could be done to turn this guy into a government informant. The FBI's recently instituted Upper Echelon Criminal Informant Program was designed specifically for this situation. Dick was clearly well-connected in the mob, and the FBI wanted desperately to know what he knew. After several weeks of negotiating, Roemer got Washington to agree to the money part of Dick's request, but they considered the issue of giving him a badge to be simply laughable.

They started working on a strategy for how they were going to manage the relationship and how Dick was going to talk with the FBI without losing his life. Dick made it clear he was not going to break his relationships within the Outfit. Quite the contrary, he had every intention of using the FBI to help him establish himself in a leadership position in the Chicago Outfit. He was up-front with Roemer on this point. If the FBI was going to benefit from information Dick provided, he had to be free to capitalize on that knowledge as well. Roemer told him he would turn a blind eye to violations of state law that involved victimless crimes, specifically gambling but, if Dick ever crossed the line and involved himself in any violent crimes or major federal offenses, Roemer would take him down.

During the time they took to negotiate their deal, Dick settled into the Brittany apartments at 233 Erie Street, apartment 1401. He had reconnected with his twin daughters who were fifteen by then, and they moved in with him.

Dick and Bill Roemer agreed that the safest place to meet was in Dick's apartment. Roemer could enter a building several blocks away and, through a complicated series of basement doors, underground tunnels, and parking garages, he could work his way into the basement of Dick's building, unnoticed by anyone who might be watching the outside. It would also be virtually impossible for anyone to follow without Roemer's knowledge.

They agreed to meet every Wednesday when Dick was in town. Dick would prepare sandwiches and have some cold beer ready when Roemer arrived at one o'clock sharp. Sometimes they'd meet for up to four hours, usually it was just a couple of hours. Roemer was always quick to remind Dick that he was being paid only for viable information, C.O.D. He wasn't to expect any money until after he delivered the goods.

The twins were told only that Dick had a meeting at one o'clock and they had to be out of the building. When they returned after five, they were to immediately check under the pillow on his bed. If his gun was missing, they were to get out of the building and wait for him to contact them. The gun was always there though, and that gave a certain sense that everything was okay. Sometimes they would make the sandwiches before they left.

They were curious about who Dick was meeting with and suspected (feared, more likely) that it was the FBI, but discounted that because they were sure their father would never cooperate with the feds. These girls, like their father, had virtually grown up on the street and to them the idea of being a snitch was simply unfathomable.

One Wednesday afternoon, Kimberly was running late and was racing out a few minutes after one o'clock. While she waited for the elevator, someone opened the door to the stairway and retreated upon seeing her standing in the hallway. She was tempted to run over and take a look at who it was, but knew her father would be furious with her, and what good would it do if she didn't recognize him? She had never met Roemer and wouldn't have recognized him, but she would have spooked both her father and the FBI agent if she'd gone to the door.

During these weekly visits, Dick and Bill Roemer became quite close, and both men came to look forward to them, even if there was no mob business to discuss. Knowing they were polar opposites on most every imaginable issue seemed only to strengthen the bond. Their bantering on political issues, religion, and every other imaginable topic was clearly something that gave them both a great deal of pleasure.

One day the conversation became extremely strained for both men. Chuckie Carroll, a key lieutenant for Frank Pierce, head of South Side gambling, had been killed in an apparent mob-style hit. Roemer wanted to know if Dick was involved because, if he were, if this killing was how Dick was going to move in on the South Side, Roemer was going to stop it right then and there. Dick denied any knowledge of the killing, but didn't convince Roemer, who kept after him as if he were interrogating a prisoner. Dick felt he was under attack, which of course he was, and tried to give it right back. The inevitable result was the two men wound up fighting in the living room of Dick's apartment. Dick had been quite a fighter in his younger years, but now he was nearly blind due to a degenerative eye disease, facing a guy who probably had close to a fifty-pound weight advantage, not to mention a lifetime of boxing experience. It didn't take long for Roemer to get Dick under control and pinned on the couch. Both men recognized this was not a fight to the death; there was no attempt by either of them to draw a weapon. It was just a fight.

With Dick immobilized, Roemer told him he wasn't accusing him of Carroll's murder. He just wanted to be sure Dick understood the consequences would be huge if Dick were found to be involved.

Roemer was required to file a report after every meeting with Dick and to justify all payments made to him. The bureau was quick to support the idea of developing Dick as an informant, but their demeanor seemed to change from the start, as they questioned every piece of information Dick provided and harangued Roemer for corroboration and solid prosecutable data. Each week Roemer would file his report and each week they would reply with follow-up questions and questions about the validity of the information he was offering. After several months they cut him off, saying that, while his information was interesting and in many cases new, they weren't opening any new cases because of it. Roemer persisted and eventually lost the battle, though he was able to make a final payment in February when Dick appeared desperate.

The last straw for the bureau was the collapse of the numbers rackets, which came to be known as "Black Bingo" in the first few weeks of operation. When Dick first took on this project, he was provided funding by Gus Alex and Ross Prio to get things organized. He put the runners on the payroll during training, then, in mid-December, they pulled the plug and told Dick to walk away. Believing that he had Sam Giancana's blessings, he resisted, then refused and tried to carry on without them. It might have worked, except that in just the second week of operation the players hit it big and Dick didn't have the resources to pay off. He attempted to borrow $50,000 from a couple of shylocks like Sam DeStefano, but was given various excuses for why they couldn't help. In the end he had to shut it down and, while he felt bad about the failure, he was furious with Alex and Prio for leaving him out in the cold.

The memos from the bureau to Bill Roemer were quite pointed at this stage; justify these payments with hard facts and new cases or cut him off. Roemer worked hard, but Dick was determined to draw a line on the quality of information he gave up. Partly because he was concerned for his own safety and partly because he had never intended to help the FBI make cases. He was in this to draw money from them and to potentially lead them to some of his enemies. In the meantime, though, he had to be very careful about what information he gave up. Sometimes it could be traced back to him, which would blow his cover, resulting in his immediate execution.

Roemer was told to get more meaningful information from him. When Roemer would report that Dick had met with so-and-so, the bureau headquarters would reply, "How do you know he met with these people?" Then Roemer would ask Dick for advance notice of a meeting, so they could put agents in place to observe. Dick would comply, and he'd meet with some people they could identify as "upper-echelon" mobsters, so

Roemer could report that he actually saw the meeting take place. He'd feel pretty good about that until headquarters would say, "How do you know what he was talking about?" Roemer was stumped again. Electronic surveillance was not as good in those days as it is today, and Dick would have refused to wear a wire anyway, but it was frustrating for Roemer that whatever he did was never good enough for Washington.

Dick needed the money and hated to admit it. He was counting the days until April, when he could apply for a passport and rejoin Giancana in Cuernavaca. He felt safe there. The Black Bingo had seemed to be a perfect stepping-stone into a leadership position in the Outfit, but when that fell apart, everything fell apart. His leverage with the FBI had been his potential to achieve a leadership position, even to become Chicago's representative to the commission. Everybody recognized however that those things could only happen if he was successful with the blacks. Take that away and the FBI would ask, "Dick who?"

During the fiasco with the Black Bingo, Dick was always alert to other business opportunities. He'd been unable to meet with Sam since his release because of travel restrictions and Sam's commitment to stay in Mexico, but they had spoken on the phone and exchanged messages through Sam's many couriers. It seems that Kuwait and Libya each had substantial oil deals with the USSR, but they also had significant surpluses of oil. They were looking for a less-than-public way in which to sell some of their surplus. As Dick explained it to Bill Roemer, "We'll make a deal with the Chinese Communists to buy the oil at $3.50 a barrel (which was a premium at the time) and make a bundle."

Dick's current problem was that he was not allowed to travel without the blessings of his parole officer and he couldn't exactly ask permission to fly to a communist country to make a deal that had to be kept a secret. He speculated that he might be able to fabricate a reason to go to Canada, to interview for a job maybe, and while there, in Toronto, he could visit the Chinese embassy and ask to meet with their trade representative.

Roemer was skeptical, but listened anyway. Dick explained that Sam and Aristotle Onassis were good friends and that Onassis had already agreed to ship the oil from Kuwait to China. All he needed to do was get in touch with the trade ministry at the Chinese embassy and he'd make it happen. He was concerned that if he had to wait until after

April 5, when his parole was lifted, it would be too late to make the deal. He talked about it for four or five weeks running, but nothing ever came of it. The obvious question here was "why would anyone insert Dick Cain into the middle of an oil deal?" He had no credentials whatsoever in the field. In the long run it didn't much matter, and the whole idea faded away.

CHAPTER
16

In the winter of 1971, a friend of Dick's was seeing a blonde everyone considered a knockout, but who wasn't the brightest kid in town. Dick was busy getting re-acquainted with his friends. Having recently been released from the federal penitentiary it was strategically important that he re-establish himself as a force to be reckoned with.

A Saturday night on the town was to have ended with Dick and few of the guys picking up a musician friend after an engagement at a downtown hotel. Earlier in the evening, they had been to see him perform and had offered to take his girlfriend home. Having made stops at several other clubs along the way, she had ample opportunity to talk them into letting her stick around until later.

The group was traveling in two cars. The people in the rear car thought the woman had been left at the last stop. The cars pulled into an alley behind the Sherman House. When they got out of the car, the woman looked back at the rear car. She heard two gunshots and saw a man fall to the ground. Screaming hysterically, she nearly fainted. Dick quickly got her inside the building and explained it had been a practical joke, just to put her on. Then, knowing she couldn't possibly have seen the face of the man who had just been killed, he pointed to one of the guys just then entering the hotel lobby and said, "See, he's fine. Nobody would have really been hurt out there. We're all friends here."

Quickly, Dick made the rounds of the living revelers and advised them all of the story, so they all teased her for the rest of the evening about the joke they'd played on her, thus avoiding the need to kill her too.

Dick had a reputation for being a ladies' man. He enjoyed their company and knew how to entertain them. During 1972, after his parole had expired, he spent a great deal of his time traveling between Chicago and Sam Giancana's villa outside Cuernavaca. Sometimes he would fly, but frequently he would make the trip by car. He, of course, couldn't drive any longer, so he had a full-time driver, Michael Gilardi. Gilardi was an almost constant companion when Dick was around Chicago, but only traveled with him when he traveled by car. Gilardi was proud of his role as Dick's driver cum bodyguard and was quick to act if he felt a need to protect his boss.

During the summer of 1972, Dick was planning to drive down to Mexico and invited Marlene Kennedy, a friend of the twins, to accompany him. She was excited about the trip and spent weeks preparing for it. Gilardi was very distrustful of Marlene, and Dick seemed to get a kick out of playing that to get Gilardi's goat. She had been invited in order to make the car a tad less suspicious on the long journey. Dick had confided in her that he would rather have taken the twins, but he was uncomfortable about their apparent inability to keep secrets. They were known to talk openly of his exploits at a pool hall they frequented. This trip was going to involve some things he'd rather not have them talk about, so he took Marlene instead.

Dick loved the twins, he loved all his children, but he hadn't a clue how to advise them or discipline them. By the time he stepped back into their lives they were fifteen years old, addicted to heroin, and entrenched in lives of crime themselves. They told me they'd committed their first burglary at the age of nine. Dick had abandoned them, but he thought he was leaving them with a mother who would at least care for them. Rosemary, at that point in her life, was incapable of caring for them, because she was completely consumed with her own life of partying. She'd leave the twins at home alone from the age of eight, so it only took a little while for them to discover life on the outside. Maybe they were bored, maybe they were seeking the company of people who wanted to be with them. Ultimately it doesn't matter how or why; it happened. To her credit, Rosemary eventually straightened out her life and married a terrific, hard-working man before she died. Dick's granddaughter still lovingly refers to Gramps as the rock on which she's been able to build the foundation of her own life.

For Marlene, this jaunt to Mexico was a four-week vacation she wouldn't soon forget. Covering the nearly two thousand miles from

Chicago to the suburbs of Mexico City took more than a week, even on the fastest available routes. Marlene was uncomfortable with Gilardi from the outset of the trip. He was constantly trying to get himself between her and Dick, both verbally and physically. He acted as though her mere presence was an unwanted intrusion to himself and to Dick. Rather than set Gilardi straight, Dick regularly threw fuel on the fire by complaining to Gilardi about her. To Dick it was all a joke, and he thoroughly enjoyed playing the two of them against one another.

When they arrived at the villa, Marlene was exhausted and looked forward to spending the next few days lazing beside Sam's pool. She'd met Sam once before but had never spent any time with him. She was impressed with his politeness and generosity, though she still didn't see much of him. He and Dick played golf every day and, when they were at home, they generally climbed to the top of a large cupola above the third floor of the house. It was big enough for the two of them to be comfortably seated, and it gave them a commanding view of the surrounding area. They weren't so much concerned about looking out for an assault on the property as getting away from everyone else, but they did joke about the possibility of an attack.

When Sam did come down to the pool, Marlene and Gilardi were expected to keep their distance unless Sam invited them over to chat.

As they got closer to their scheduled departure time, Marlene asked Dick if they could take a different route back home. She really wanted to see the mountains in the American West; the Grand Canyon and the Rockies. They had skirted them on the way down in the interest of time, but "couldn't we," she pleaded, "couldn't we please take the long way back?" Marlene was genuinely interested in seeing the mountains, but she was also aware of Gilardi's dislike for the slow, winding roads in the mountains and saw an opportunity to get back at him for all the sniping she'd endured for the previous couple of weeks.

Dick went through the motions of objecting and consulting with his driver, only to hear Gilardi's loud and vociferous opinions on the subject. In the end he consented to Marlene's wishes, again more to irritate Gilardi and agitate the relationship between the two of them than for any genuine concern one way or the other. Gilardi pleaded his case: too slow, fewer options for an escape, and more isolation if the car broke down. Ultimately, none of it mattered. Dick agreed because he was having fun.

Several days into the return trip, Dick brought Marlene to the back of the car during a stop at a motel. He told her he wanted to share with her the reason that it was necessary for him to make this trip by car. He opened the trunk of the car and reached into a small bag at the rear of the trunk and extracted a small shoe box, the size children's shoes would come in. He opened it and revealed to Marlene a box half-full of diamonds. Dick explained this was one of Sam's sideline businesses, smuggling precious and semi-precious stones.

Dick had been traveling almost constantly since the expiration of his parole in April 1972. Sam Giancana was waiting for him in Cuernavaca, and they had business to conduct. It's speculation to talk about what the business consisted of, but certainly there was the smuggling of diamonds and emeralds, and most likely some drug deals as well. The only real evidence that exists from this time period is Dick's passport. He traveled with multiple passports, but the key one is his legitimate U.S. passport, which indicates that he was very busy indeed.

The FBI attempted to locate him on several occasions, sending instructions to the LEGATs in Palermo, Rome, and London, but they never actually saw him outside of the U.S. or Mexico.

In June 1972, he flew into Bogata, Colombia, and then to London, Athens, and back to Colombia. Based on the dates of entry and exit, he had to have used other passports as well because his passport shows him arriving in Bogotá on June 14 and exiting on June 21. The London and Athens stops happened between those dates, indicating he left Bogotá with a different passport.

Over the remaining months of his life, he visited Madrid, where his firstborn daughter lived. Her younger sister was visiting in late 1973 when she was first told that Dick was alive and arranged for them to meet in Rome for the first time. She was sixteen and her mother had told her all her life that he'd died. Dick abandoned her mother while she was pregnant, and left two other children as well when he married Rosemary, who was also pregnant with the twins at the time. Dick spent a week with her, and among the things she saw was a bundle of five or six passports. Dick was legally blind by this time and had a driver to take them wherever they went in and around Rome, but she was surprised to realize the driver came equipped with guns as well.

London, Luxembourg, Malta, Beirut, Colombia, and Greece, all multiple times. Frequently, the dates were inconsistent, indicating his switching to another passport. Through photographic and eyewitness accounts, I know that he visited Switzerland, Italy, and Iran, yet none of these countries appears in his passport. In the early seventies, it was nearly unheard of to arrive at a foreign airport without getting a passport stamped. The final entry in his passport marks his return to Chicago on December 2, 1973.

During this time he was focused primarily on gambling and drugs. The FBI reported their sources indicated Dick was managing a whorehouse in Spain during this time. He had also written a movie treatment about the Bay of Pigs and was attempting to raise money to have it produced as a movie.

He'd gotten pretty adept at negotiating casino deals. He and Sam had opened one in Beirut, where Sam owned a home. They had a commitment from the Shah to allow them to build one in Tehran, and he also applied for a casino permit on the tiny Mediterranean island of Malta. There is correspondence between the government of Malta and the FBI regarding the application Dick filed. They were seeking background information and the FBI was, predictably, less than cooperative. For good or for ill, they simply did not care to share.

CHAPTER

17

Throughout the balance of 1972 and 1973, Dick's travels appear to have been meant to act as a major conduit for heroin coming through Spain and the U.K. into New York. FBI reports indicate they had knowledge that he was using a small hotel/bordello in Spain as a conduit for drugs coming from the Middle East through Italy to Spain and, ultimately, New York.

It seems the old mob policy of staying away from drugs was no longer so important. The usual rackets, specifically in Chicago, had started to dry up. Bookies were regularly busted by the FBI, frequently due to a tip from a gambler who needed some relief from his debts, or from a spouse who was tired of learning she was short of money again. Prostitution was harder than ever to control, and loan sharks were losing out to credit cards. Even Mad Sam DeStefano was branching out and putting his money in real estate.

The FBI was finally starting to have an impact on organized crime, thanks to a string of new directors who were actually interested in doing their job, and thanks in part to new legislation like the RICO, statutes which gave them new ways to go after the mobsters.

Dick explained to Roemer that the new Outfit was vastly different from the old days. There was no longer a boss—not a single boss, in any event. Tony Accardo was sort of in charge, but he had taken to spending more and more time in Palm Springs, California, where he felt safe. Over time Accardo began refusing to make decisions out of fear that he'd be indicted on some sort of conspiracy charge. The old guys began to fear they might die in prison if they were ever arrested again and became very cautious. The concept of territories had gone by the wayside as guys had to reach out for better opportunities, the result being that business opportunities were available on a first-come, first-served basis. You no longer had to get approval to operate in one part of town over another.

Dick recognized that it was best to walk away.

Departing Chicago on May 1, 1972, Dick told many of his friends that he didn't expect to ever live there again. He spent Christmas and New Year's that year in Honolulu with Sam Giancana and Phyllis McGuire. Something happened during that holiday visit that pushed Dick over the edge. He called Bill Roemer in Chicago and asked him to arrange an introduction to the legal attaché (LEGAT) in Mexico City.

On January 2, 1973, Dick met with the LEGAT at the Vienna Restaurant in Mexico City. Dick explained that something happened in Hawaii that made him furious and he was determined to get even with Giancana. He told the agent that he'd considered beating Sam up, or even shooting him, but decided it would be smarter to get even in another way. He told the agent that he'd had a gun with him at the time, the result of that admission was that all future correspondence involving Dick carried the tag line "Armed and Dangerous." Sam, he told the agent, had gone to San Francisco from Honolulu. He implied that he had a contact at the embassy in Mexico City and was aware of their activities relative to himself and Giancana. This was probably a bluff on his part, there's no evidence to indicate he actually had such a contact.

He told the agent that "he considers himself a writer, and he wants to prepare reports of everything he knows about Giancana and his associates. He indicated that Giancana was the top figure in the Mafia and is still active. He promised that he would be able to furnish sufficient information to get an indictment for Giancana within the year. He said this information might be forthcoming in a few weeks or a few months, but he wanted to be assured of a year and wanted this assurance in the form of some kind of written contract. For this year he wanted compensation similar to that of an experienced agent, specifically four hundred dollars a week for an entire year. He advised that he was in contact with Giancana 90 percent of the time, but noted that there would be some weeks when there would be no information and insisted that he not be subjected to any pressure to produce during such periods."

He was told that any such agreement would have to be approved by Chicago. While the agent didn't expect any such offer would be approved, he wanted to string Dick along for a while to see what he could learn from him.

They met again two days later at the Fonda Santa Anita on Mariano Escobedo. The agent reported that he "had intimated to me and to SA Roemer in Chicago that he and/or Sam had a pipeline into the embassy and knew of embassy and legal office activities directed against Sam. He was told that this would have to be resolved, since obviously, if Sam knew of our activities his (Dick's) life would be in jeopardy. He said they had no source in the embassy but just in general were in a position to know of embassy efforts directed against Sam. Throughout the interview he maintained an attitude of omniscience, as if he knew everything that moved, even when his information was quite inaccurate."

The discussion then turned to Dick's offer, which was rejected. Instead, they offered to pay smaller amounts for specific information they deemed to have value to the FBI. Dick was indignant and suggested he might shop his information around to the CIA and the IRS, if the FBI didn't want it.

Dick told the agent he had just returned from Sicily, which he implied was the place of his birth, and that he had recently been to the Dominican Republic to negotiate the purchase of a small hotel for Sam, which would be converted into a casino. Unfortunately, "came the revolution," and Sam lost a fifty-thousand-dollar deposit on the property. He told of hundreds of slot machines in Guatemala that were controlled by Sam through his front men in Miami.

The agent's report went on to say, "He made much nostalgic reference to his days as a policeman and detective with the Chicago PD and later, as Chief of the Sheriff's police. The general tone being that he was one smart, tough, and corrupt cop from the very beginning, and quite proud of all three, particularly the last. Claimed some fourteen killings attributed to him. Contemptuous of cops who settle for petty graft.

"Much name-dropping, i.e., when he was in Monte Carlo with Sinatra (the s.o.b.), met the Prince, was bodyguard for Senator Goldwater when General Wood offered him $4,000,000 for his campaign. Much braggadocio, albeit with some charm." Curiously, that last line "albeit with some charm" was crossed out by someone at FBI headquarters in a knee-jerk reaction to colorful editorial commentary.

He seemed to have patched things up with Giancana, at least on the surface, but eventually decided his best move was to return to Chicago. In April 1973 he was there for a couple of weeks, and perhaps coincidentally he was there when Sam DeStefano was killed in his garage. Some people believe that Dick was the killer, but DeStefano had so many enemies there may actually have been people waiting in line to kill this guy.

In December, he returned to Chicago for the last time. According to his passport, he arrived on December 2. There's no indication where he arrived from, as the previous stamp in is passport indicates he left Bogotá, Colombia, on November 27.

CHAPTER

18

When Dick returned he was determined to make his mark. As before, the first order of business was to earn a living. Marshall Caifano headed up the best burglary crew in town, and Dick wanted in on that. So they collaborated about who to hit. Being more social than Marshall, Dick was often able to get information about a target as well as his partner. The thing that prevents most burglars from hitting the big score is they don't really hang out with people who would become targets. Dick felt he was more adept at that part, at getting to know the targets without drawing suspicion to himself.

He targeted a house in Oak Park once and had his daughter Karla approach the homeowner in the early evening. She rang the doorbell and when the lady of the house answered, she introduced herself, "Hi, I'm Mary Alice. I used to live in this house with my parents and I just came back to Chicago for a visit after living in Paris for the past few years."

"Well, hello Mary Alice, it's so nice to meet you.

"I was wondering if I could come in and look around, you know, just to see the place again, I miss it here so much, this was my favorite place in the whole world." Naturally the lady would let her in, after all what's to fear from a sixteen-year-old girl? Karla would case the place like a pro, making mental notes of the location of valuables throughout the house. She even peeked into the closet in the master bedroom looking for a safe. She wouldn't participate in the actual burglary, but she certainly provided plenty of help to daddy.

* * *

"Hey Ruthie, wanna meet a killer?"

"What in hell are you talking about?" asked Ruth Allen, to the seemingly absurd question from her friend Jackie O'Shea. Ruth had invited Jackie to a Christmas party at her apartment on December 8, 1973. She was startled to hear Jackie open the conversation in such a way.

Jackie explained, "I've been seeing a guy who's in the Mafia, and I thought you might enjoy meeting him, so I'd like to bring him to the party next week. What do you think?"

"Well, I suppose so, I was just thinking the other day how I've never actually met a killer. After forty years in Chicago, you'd think I would have, wouldn't you? Jesus Christ, Jackie, listen to us. Tell me about this guy. No, better yet, just bring him over and let him tell me about himself."

That was how Ruth Allen came to be introduced to Dick Cain and how they began their thirteen-day affair, which she remembers even today with more clarity of detail than any relationship before or since. "I fixed him breakfast on the day he was killed," she explained in a careful way that left no doubt how they happened to be together at breakfast time. His last meal had been poached eggs on whole-wheat toast. As she was telling about Dick, she wanted to play his song, "My Foolish Heart," on the piano. She said it was his favorite, but who the hell knows.

Ruth Allen was one of four women who were "seeing" Dick Cain at the time of his death. They all claimed to be in love with him, taken in by his charm, his risk-taking, his flair for storytelling, and his love for women. They all seemed to know about the others (in the case of Jackie and Ruth, they openly talked about "sharing" him), but each was convinced he loved her best. He only saw other women because of his insatiable appetite for sex.

"He loved the theatre and opera. He took me to see *La Bohème*," Ruth said. The other women saw other things he loved; Jackie O'Shea was a jazz pianist. "He loved music, especially jazz." Dorothy Storch was a columnist for the *Chicago Tribune*. To her, Dick was a lover of literature. He told her that he owned five thousand books. Arlene Turi was a painter in Switzerland. Dick had an appreciation for her art that could only come from a deep-seated understanding of art, and she loved him for it.

Part of Dick's charm was his ability to pass as knowledgeable on a broad range of topics. In fact, he did love art, jazz, opera, and literature. He was able to move each one in turn to the top of his list, depending on whose hand he found himself in pursuit of. In fact he was an incessant reader, though I doubt he ever owned five thousand books. He did have an appreciation for good art; it was much easier to fence. And of course he was a jazz lover—he spent a lot of time drinking in joints that featured jazz groups of the highest order.

"I'm forty-nine years old, and I can't believe I'm still alive," he told Ruth one night after attending the theatre. He was sincere in that thought. Dick had believed, even fifteen years earlier, he had already crossed the line, beyond which he couldn't expect to survive a normal lifetime. He was really forty-two, though, having clung to his decision in the Virgin Islands to add seven years to his age. But that wasn't important now. Dick was in the midst of a major power shift in organized crime in Chicago, and he believed he was in control—a fatal miscalculation.

A few weeks earlier, he was having a night out with Marlene Kennedy, the girl he'd taken on the trip to Mexico. They were sitting on a park bench near Buckingham fountain when someone opened fire on them. "A rookie," thought Dick. The shooter had nearly hit Marlene in the head. She felt the bullet go by, but it hadn't come close to Dick. He allowed himself to discount the seriousness of the attack because of the amateur manner in which it had been carried out. The shooter had apparently used a pistol, not a good idea unless you're up close. So it must have been just a random shooting, or so he told Marlene, not directed at them. Today we would call it a drive-by shooting, no doubt from a car on Lake Shore Drive. Must have been random, after all, he reasoned; a mob hit would have come a lot closer to being successful, another serious miscalculation. They were starting to mount up.

He brushed it off, but suggested to Marlene they take a break from seeing one another for a while. She did not object. Before he left her for the evening, he gave her a cassette tape. He told her, "If anything happens to me, listen to this tape. It's worth a lot of money to you."

Dick was busy. As the year wound down, he became increasingly complacent about the risks involved in the work he was doing. He had never had much respect for the senior guys in the Outfit. They weren't generally very smart, and he felt decidedly superior to them. The night after the shooting incident, he was seen by the FBI in a heated confrontation with Gus Alex on the sidewalk outside Adolph's on Rush. Adolph's was a regular mob hangout and a favorite of Dick's. Fortune Renucci, the owner, was one of Dick's best friends. They all knew they'd find Dick at Adolph's most late nights.

As the days ticked by in December, Dick felt increasingly uneasy. He was considering a broader takeover that would have included multiple hits. He had a plan to take out the key players on New Year's Eve in Chicago, Las Vegas, and Honolulu. He had recruited a team, but there was a non-believer among them, a guy who thought he would be more successful ratting out his friend than standing to fight with him.

On December 17 Dick was leaving Rose's Sandwich Shop at 1117 West Grand on Chicago's West Side. It was his mother's birthday, and he'd planned on having dinner with her that evening. He was about to share his cab when he noticed a car across the street, a nondescript Ford occupied by two men wearing suits. Clearly cops. Dick suggested to his companion that they separate, to determine which one of them was under surveillance. When the cab pulled away from the curb, it was immediately clear that Dick was the target. He gave some hurried instructions to the driver. It was foolish to think they could follow Dick Cain through Chicago's Loop. His years as a cop had led him to discover some very creative ways to lose a tail. Chicago has so many buildings that are connected by underground tunnels that it took him just a few minutes, after leaving the cab, to slip away. The next order of business was to find out who they were and why they had followed him. No doubt they were cops, but from what agency? The Chicago Police Department had pretty much left him alone, but he knew they had Marshall Caifano under surveillance, so it wasn't a big stretch to think they had shifted their attention to Dick. After all, he had just left Marshall. The FBI could be after him, but he didn't think Roemer would have had him followed without some sort of warning. It could have been a mob hit team, but that was highly unlikely since they'd been too obvious.

So, were they good guys or bad guys, cops or robbers? He had blurred the line so thoroughly over the past twenty years it was hard to tell them apart anymore. Still, he thought it more likely they were cops so, when he got to a phone, he called FBI Special Agent William F. Roemer. He told him he wanted to meet, right away if possible. They'd been together a few days before when they had dinner at the Den in the Palmer House. Dick's request had a ring of urgency to it, though, so Roemer agreed to meet him back at the Den.

Without taking time for pleasantries, Dick said, "Bill, are your guys looking for me?"

"No, I don't think so. Why?"

"I just left Rose's, and as I was pulling away, I was followed. The car looked like one of those cheap pieces of crap you guys drive."

Roemer said, "I'll ask around. Are you sure they were agents?"

Dick said, "I can't be sure, but they definitely acted like agents, subtle as a freight train." He tried to put the incident out of his mind, but it was unsettling—damned unsettling! If the two men had been looking for him, it wasn't to treat him to lunch.

The cops knew Dick was a regular at Rose's. He had noticed the tails since he'd returned to Chicago. They started following him from the airport, as soon as he got off the plane. Michael Gilardi, Dick's driver, was getting better at losing them, but he still had plenty to learn. Dick had enjoyed the game when he was younger and could drive himself. Now he wished his eyesight wasn't so bad.

He recalled the time he and Gerry Shallow were driving to Michigan to visit Dick's daughter Karla, who was hiding out after having gotten into some trouble herself. Dick was driving, Gerry riding shotgun, and Karla's twin Kimberly was in the back seat. Heading south on the Dan Ryan Expressway toward the Chicago Skyway, Dick noticed they had picked up a tail. The driver was following quite closely, not trying at all to be discreet. Dick was on parole at the time and was not supposed to leave the state without permission from the court, so he couldn't be seen headed for the state line.

Losing a tail on the freeway is difficult without speeding, but speeding was unacceptable since he was planning to stay on the freeway and would surely get stopped by the highway patrol sooner or later. Getting off the freeway was unacceptable because they had a six-hour drive ahead of them, and they just wanted to be on their way. The only way to lose this tail was to convince its driver to abort, so Dick maneuvered his car, leaving the tail almost directly behind him. Suddenly, he swerved one lane to the left, reached over the back seat, pushed Kimberly to the floor, held her down, and slammed on the brakes. Before the startled driver could react, they were side by side. Shallow drew his .357 Magnum and took aim. When the agent in the tail car found himself staring down the barrel of a gun, he reacted as calmly and logically as any good cop would in similar circumstances. He locked his brakes, went into a four-wheel skid, and completely lost control of his car, not to mention his target. They never figured out just who was tailing them, but it really didn't matter.

Dick and Gerry continued on their way, confident in the knowledge they wouldn't be bothered any more on the trip.

But by now, near the end of 1973, Dick was legally blind and uncomfortably dependent on his driver or, worse yet, a taxi, and mounting anxiety over his status as a target only heightened his frustration.

Dick met with Marshall Caifano regularly at Rose's to talk about what he was doing and, frequently, to give Caifano money. He had been trying to entice Caifano to support his plan to take control of gambling on the South Side of Chicago. He wanted Caifano to deliver the support of the old guard or to put him on the holiday hit list. He had talked and planned for months. He knew the mob guys were still laughing about his failed effort with Black Bingo, but he had a plan that would show them what he could do.

Now it seemed as though none of that mattered. He sensed real danger.

If the cops weren't after him, then Caifano had to be up to something. Caifano was from the old school and had worked with Sam Giancana since the thirties, when his brother, Fat Leonard Caifano, was a peer of Giancana's and a member of the original 42 gang. Caifano had recently returned to Chicago after a stint in federal prison. With Sam on the outs with the mob, Caifano had to count on the generosity of Tony Accardo to make a living. So far that had worked out, but he knew he was on shaky ground with Accardo, and Dick was trying to exploit that. Caifano wasn't having any of it, though. He knew Dick had no respect for him and, if push came to shove, Caifano would get the shove.

But Dick couldn't believe Caifano would be behind a contract on him. Why? They'd had some differences about some burglaries, but he felt they had been resolved. Dick didn't think Caifano was smart enough to have figured out his relationship with the FBI, so he dismissed the idea of it being mob guys who were after him. Therefore, it had to be the cops.

The guys in the mob would have hated knowing Dick had been secretly meeting with the FBI for the past eighteen months, but he was sure that secret was safe. Roemer wasn't going to blow it; he had a lot riding on their relationship. Besides, they had become quite close. Dick had agreed to provide information about machinations within the mob. He was rather proud of that deal. Who else could have gotten the FBI to cooperate in a takeover of the Outfit?

The next morning, December 18, 1973, Dick paid a visit to an old nemesis, Thomas A. Foran, former United States attorney for the Northern District of Illinois. Foran had left his job as a federal prosecutor not long after putting Dick in a federal penitentiary for three years and was in private practice, with offices on the twenty-first floor of 111 West Washington in the Loop. On this date, as he was leaving his office around 4:30 P.M., he pressed the elevator button and waited. When the elevator appeared and the doors opened, Dick Cain was standing in front of him.

"Hello, Tom. Remember me?"

"Of course, Dick. How've you been? I read about your being released last year. I hope you're well."

"I am well, Tom," Dick replied, "but you know, that place you sent me had more rats than prisoners."

They chatted amicably as they descended to the first floor and, once outside, they went in opposite directions. Foran surmised Dick must have been coming to see him, but was puzzled that Dick hadn't made an attempt to engage him in a discussion of any legal matters or, for that matter, anything specific.

Undoubtedly, Dick was trying to learn who was after him and felt if he made a surprise visit to Foran, he would be able to tell if Foran knew anything. Although Foran had left the prosecutor's office, he would likely have been apprised of any pending action on any of his high-profile cases, and Dick Cain had been his biggest. It would have been good news for Dick to learn of a pending arrest. At least then he wouldn't have to worry about being killed. But Foran apparently had no such knowledge, or at least none Dick could detect. Foran may have had a poker face, but surely, Dick thought, even Foran would have given something away upon seeing Dick for the first time since his trial ended more than five years earlier.

Dick tried to put it out of his mind; a distraction like that could throw him off balance. If someone was trying to kill him, there wasn't much he could do to stop it. He wasn't going to run. All he could do was to be cautious, but he knew even that would not protect him if the mob wanted him dead.

The next day, Wednesday, December 19, he met again with Roemer. The FBI was concerned about the death of Fiore "Fifi" Bucieri, who was considered to be a top-level boss at the time. What was Fifi's death going to do to the organization? Roemer paid Dick one hundred fifty dollars for their conversation, which was considered well worth it at the time, because there was so much consternation in town about the potential shake-up. The FBI had only two sources of information at the time, bugs and snitches. You can't have bugs everywhere, and you can't always trust the snitches—they're bound to have an agenda of their own; Dick certainly did.

The only way they were ever going to get quality information was to put one of their own undercover and get him on the inside. Hoover was opposed to the notion; he didn't trust his agents to work undercover without becoming corrupt themselves. It wasn't until several years after Hoover's death in 1972 that the bureau finally put one of their own inside the mob. Special Agent Joe Pistone infiltrated the Mafia in New York, and finally the bureau got their inside view. Donnie Brasco, as he was known to the mobsters, is a law enforcement anomaly, a true hero in the war on organized crime, who put his life on the line and crippled the Mafia with his testimony in numerous trials. It's risky business, though, and where do you find guys with the cajones of Joe Pistone? Maybe they've done it since, but I doubt it. Organizationally, the FBI has trouble with it. They tried numerous times to pull Pistone off the street, fearing that too much under-cover time would certainly corrupt him. He courageously resisted, and the streets of New York are safer today because he did.

In Chicago in 1973, they had to rely on the bugs and the snitches to tell them what was going to happen now that Fifi was dead. Dick wasn't about to tell them about his own plan to take over, and most of the other snitches could only talk about what they hoped would happen. The truth was that nobody knew.

On the night of December 19, Dick met his daughter, Kimberly, for dinner and, as usual, Michael Gilardi was with him. Michael seemed nervous and fidgety to Kim, but she tried not to make anything of it. She and her father talked about having lunch the next day. Michael interrupted, saying, "But you can't have lunch tomorrow; you gotta meet that guy."

Gilardi said "that guy," drawing out the words and gesticulating with a twist of his head as if he were trying to point over his shoulder without using his hands. This made Kim suspicious. Dick immediately acknowledged he did have other plans and apologized. Kim was annoyed at having been so obviously excluded from the conversation, but she bit her tongue. Though she was only seventeen, Kim and her twin sister Karla understood a great deal about their father's "business," possibly even more than Michael did.

Soon Gilardi left. "See ya boss. I guess Kimmie can handle gettin' you home. Is that OK?"

"Right, Michael," Dick responded, "I'll be fine. Just pick me up in the morning."

As soon as Michael was out of earshot, Kimmie glared at Dick and said, "OK, what's this *'that guy'* bullshit? Doesn't he know who I am?"

"Take it easy on Michael. He's just following orders. Never speak names that don't need to be spoken. You never know who's listening. 'That guy' is Marshall Caifano. We've got to discuss some things at Rose's tomorrow."

Kimmie knew about Rose's and had met Dick there numerous times. She remembered her father had made her move to a different chair the first time they ate there together so that his back could be against the wall, enabling him to see the door. The place was small, just eight tables and only one that was suitable for monitoring who came in. To accommodate the mob guys who wanted that table, Jelly Cozzo always left dirty dishes on it so someone just walking in wouldn't sit there. Dick knew just to go to that table, and Jelly would have it cleared immediately.

Just a little Italian diner in a commercial area on Chicago's West Side, Rose's had long been a favorite of Marshall Caifano. Jelly Cozzo, the owner, had been described as a "bad hombre" by people from the old neighborhood, a guy who believed his mob associations were paramount in his life. He catered to the Mafiosi who frequented his diner and relished the attention they gave him. His food was good, but not flamboyant: spaghetti, ravioli, and even great lasagna when his mother was up to it. He always had a little red wine to serve his regular customers. Dick's favorite was Zinfandel, and nobody ever had to ask if he wanted a glass. It was just served.

Changing the subject, Dick said, "Kimmie, if I have to take a long trip, could I count on you to take care of your sister and Mamooch (Dick's mother)? I mean if I were to go far away for an extended period of time, could you handle things here?"

"Of course I can, Daddy. What kind of trip are you taking?"

"I can't tell you any more about it now. Just remember I'm counting on you. You're the one they're going to turn to for help. Anyway, Marshall and I will be through with lunch by one-thirty or so. Why don't we get together then? I'll call you."

Dick didn't know what kind of trip was in his future, but he seemed to sense that something was going to happen. Perhaps that he was about to be arrested. This was how it had happened before, the FBI making a big show of force to bring him in on a weak case. The previous week he must have thought about it a great deal, given the attempt on his life and the increased surveillance. Was he going to be arrested? Or was he going to be hit?

He felt Roemer would help to hold off any federal indictments. He would at least have told Dick if a warrant had been issued, but the Chicago cops had no idea about his relationship with the FBI. Dick could have been wanted by the Chicago PD for any number of offenses, from jaywalking to murder. If Roemer had found out Dick had been involved in any "serious" crimes, he had promised to see Dick was busted—and busted hard. But that wasn't likely to happen without warning, without some signal that it was coming. There were no solid signals here, only some people who seemed to be after him. It would have been difficult not to think about the events of recent weeks. He knew he had to be careful not to lose control, not to lose his edge. He was smarter than his opponents, but that wouldn't matter if they came after him with guns.

On the morning of December 20, 1973, Jerry Gladden's day started with a tail on Marshall Caifano. Gladden was a cop who seemed to truly enjoy his work. As an investigator in the Intelligence Division of the Chicago Police Department, he was able to do the things he most wanted to do, help put the bad guys in jail. He and his partner started following Caifano from his home at 9:00 A.M. and logged each of his stops. Their function was not necessarily to catch him committing a crime, but to gather intelligence about his activities, including who he met and where he met them. This intelligence was extremely important in the process of building future cases against him and his colleagues. At 11:25 that morning, Gladden and his partner watched Caifano enter Rose's Sandwich Shop, a mile or so from the Loop, and noted the time and location in their logbook.

At 11:35, Gladden and his partner pulled away from the curb after deciding to let Caifano eat his lunch in peace. There was never anything interesting about sitting in a car waiting for a mobster to eat lunch, so they left the area.

Michael picked Dick up around eleven; they got to Rose's at 11:40. Often, Michael was invited in for lunch, but on this day Michael said he had to see his doctor, so Dick sent him on his way. As expected, Marshall Caifano was there and greeted Dick in his normal, semi-cool manner. Since Caifano had gotten there first, he had the seat facing the door, which made Dick a little edgy, but he tried not to let it show. Caifano had never liked Dick Cain, feeling he was too cocky and almost arrogant toward the old-timers like himself. He had long been suspicious of Dick, who said he had grown up in the old neighborhood, "The Patch." Caifano had never found anyone who had known Dick in the old days. Once again, Dick's lying about his age had thrown off his enemies; Caifano was asking the wrong people. Dick worked for Sam Giancana though, and Caifano had to respect that and do business with Dick, like it or not. Although Sam was in self-imposed exile and had relinquished most all of his responsibilities, as the former boss of the Chicago Outfit he was afforded the same level of respect as if he still held the job. Marshall Caifano had to deal with Dick Cain, for now.

Dick held Marshall Caifano in the highest contempt. He didn't think Caifano was very bright and, while he had to respect Caifano's position in the mob, he didn't try very hard to get along with him. He thought of Marshall as a rube. They were of like mind in this regard, neither trusting the other, neither wanting to do business with the other, but each recognizing he couldn't always have it his own way.

They talked over lunch and were joined by two others at one point. Caifano asked Dick to go get something. It's not clear what, but Dick left Rose's about 12:30 by cab and returned an hour later. Caifano was gone, but Dick didn't get an opportunity to notice.

Inside the restaurant, a walkie-talkie crackled, "There he is!"

Two men wearing ski masks held four customers, a waitress, and Jelly Cozzo, the owner, at gunpoint against a back wall. Clearly, they knew he was coming back and were waiting for him. When Dick walked in the door, he was immediately confronted by the one holding the sawed-off shotgun; the one with the two gloves: one white, one black. White Hand, Black Hand, Dick would have noticed the irony, two organizations at odds with one another in the twenties and thirties, the good guys and the bad guys.

Ole Scully, Dick's maternal grandfather, had been a leader in the White Hand and had been murdered in 1928 by the Black Hand. Had the Mafia come full circle? Maybe the guy just couldn't find a matching pair of gloves that morning, but sometimes they get off on the symbolism.

It would be over in a matter of seconds; all those years of double-dealing had come to a payoff, the final one. Dick Cain had felt invincible. He had been a cop and was also a made member of the Mafia. His two closest friends were Sam Giancana, former boss of Chicago, and Bill Roemer, special agent of the FBI. He was finally in control of his destiny, or so he thought. Where had he gone wrong? He knew he had woven a precarious web, but he thought he had covered all the weak spots. He knew Marshall Caifano was his archenemy, but clearly he had miscalculated his ability to handle him.

Dick was ordered to stand against the back wall with his back to the kitchen, facing the man with the gun. No words were spoken, only a slight hesitation (recognition?) when their eyes met before the shooter released both barrels of double-aught buckshot upward through the bottom of Dick's chin. The blast tore away the right side of his face. Death was instantaneous. Quickly, the man rifled Dick's pockets and removed a slip of paper before the two of them beat a hasty retreat out to the waiting car.

After the shooting, Jelly knew what to do. When the car left the area, he called the police and said there had been a shooting. Nobody saw anything; nobody knew anything. He had done his part well. Marshall would be pleased.

At 1:35 P.M., Jerry Gladden heard on his radio that there had been a shooting at Rose's Sandwich Shop on West Grand Avenue. "Damn," he thought, "we were just there." The two cops made a U-turn, and in fifteen minutes they were on the scene. The building was filled with cops when Gladden arrived. As Gladden and his partner pushed their way through they recognized the body instantly. Gladden's partner said, "Jerry, that's Dick Cain."

Sam was sad when he heard of Dick's death. Dick Cain had been like a son to him. If he had been stronger, if his own position in the mob hadn't been so precarious at that time, he might have been able to save Dick's life. But this is a tough game; they play hardball. Dick knew the risks, just as Sam himself knew them. Still, he was going to miss him.

Bill Roemer told me he cried when he saw the reports on the TV news. He was stunned. He was at home at the time, exercising in his basement gym. They had become close during the eighteen months they worked together. Roemer once described Dick to me as his best friend.

The day after Dick was killed, Roemer went to the Tribune Tower on Michigan Avenue and visited an old friend of Dick's, Jack Mabley, a columnist at the *Chicago Tribune*. They shared a moment of grief before Roemer spoke: "Jack," he said, "Dick died a martyr; he was working for us."

In retrospect, I can say that wasn't exactly an accurate statement, but it makes an interesting point about who Dick was. That Roemer even cared enough to go out of his way to make that comment is remarkable. But it shows how conflicted Roemer was about his relationship with Dick.

I don't know why Dick Cain was killed. It's safe to say, though, that Dick did very little to ingratiate himself with Marshall Caifano. Caifano could have requested the hit for any number of reasons, not the least of which was Dick's deal with Bill Roemer.

Years later, an inmate at the Illinois State Prison in Joliet referred to Dick's murder as a "police hit," meaning the cops had been made aware something was going to happen at Rose's, and they should be somewhere else. If this were true, and it likely is, it doesn't mean the cops were complicit in his death, only that they were given a heads-up so they wouldn't inadvertently get caught up in something they didn't want to be a part of.

In the end, it all came down to a glance into the eyes of a man with a ski mask, a shotgun, a white glove and a black one. White Hand, Black Hand.

Two seconds, maybe three, was all he had to study the man who was about to take his life. There was no point in trying to run or to negotiate. This guy didn't have any authority to do anything but pull the trigger. Pleading was out of the question. Dick knew this was part of the game he'd been playing. He was surprised to have lived this long, after all, and the tangled web he had woven throughout his life could have ended no other way. He had betrayed so many people in his career on both sides of the law, people on several sides of the law for that matter. It was inevitable someone would say "enough," but who did?

That it was the mob seems to be almost obvious. I'd name the crew, but only one of them is currently dead, and another is in jail for a long time. The dead one was Butch Petrocelli. Butch was killed about six months after Dick was, his body found in the trunk of his car. His mouth and nose were covered with duct tape, to keep him from screaming while his face was melted with a blowtorch. The third eventually held an important leadership position in the mob, but he's in jail now, too.

There's been some speculation that he was killed because of the misfortunes that befell a burglary crew a few weeks earlier. It seems the Chicago cops had been tipped off that a particular house was about to be hit by burglars and were able to make an arrest at the scene. Dick was suspected of setting them up. It didn't happen, but as with Action Jackson, the truth doesn't always matter.

It's just as likely they had been informed of his plan for a New Year's Eve coup. The fact he was an informant was unknown to the mob until Bill Roemer, his FBI contact, stated so in his book *Roemer: Man Against the Mob*. Roemer had to fight an internal battle with the bureau in order to make that statement—as it is against FBI policy to ever name an informant, even a dead one. Roemer won because he convinced the powers at the bureau that Dick Cain wanted it known. Roemer gleaned a great deal of pleasure in telling the story because Dick had provided huge amounts of valuable intelligence about the inner workings of the Outfit, and because he considered Dick to be a friend. His information was background only, not intended to lead to arrests. Dick had insisted to Roemer he would never testify in a trial. He never revealed his motivation for turning on the mob, except to say that Sam Giancana had done something to him so foul he had lost all respect for Sam and wanted to bring down the whole organization.

That explanation pales when contrasted against his obvious plan to run it himself, but that was his only attempt to explain it.

EPILOGUE

In the years since Dick Cain was murdered, organized crime in America has gone through a transformation. The concept of *omerta*, silence, once considered the cornerstone of the Mafia, has all but disappeared. These days, mobsters are tough until they're threatened with prison. They're flipping as informants while still active in order to avoid long sentences. In the twenties and thirties, these guys stuck by one another. If they got busted, they did their time and kept their traps shut; a prison sentence was a badge of honor. Today, they listen seriously to offers of immunity and shortened sentences and witness protection, and they sell their friends down the river, seemingly without a second thought.

I'm not suggesting we should mourn its passing, but the Mafia of today is but a shadow of its former self. When Prohibition started in this country, we entered into a pact with the devil, and the byproduct was organized crime. They had existed, to be sure, before Prohibition, but their reach was limited. With the introduction of speakeasies and bathtub gin, suddenly (and it really was almost an overnight phenomenon) the Mafia touched us all. Worse than that, we didn't seem to mind. We glamorized them, we idolized them, and we respected them; we waited in line to see the movies about mobsters and the seemingly pointless fight against them. They provided the booze to a country that had been fairly ambivalent about booze until told they couldn't have it. Prohibition created explosive growth for two simultaneous cultural tragedies: organized crime and epidemic-level alcoholism.

Average citizens looked the other way when they knew a crime involving the mob took place. After all, they reasoned, they keep their dirty laundry within the group. Sure, they commit murder now and again, but they only kill one another. They don't kill outsiders. We can live with that. Or can we? When the mob got involved in drugs, just like the old timers predicted, everything changed. They couldn't contain the violence within their own ranks because they were forced to do business with outsiders. Worse than that, with easy access to drugs, many of the mob guys started using themselves.

The mob today is not the tightly-knit organization it once was, whose members are "men of respect." They are now a crumbling gang of old men with old ideas, being slowly squeezed out of their positions by a generation of wannabes who have lost the respect of the public and their peers. They are still a threat, though, because they are so deeply entrenched in society. People who are victimized directly by the mob are unwilling to test the viability of the organization because the consequences of a miscalculation are so serious.

During the course of my research I spent some time talking with Bob Cooley, the former mob lawyer from Chicago who chose to become a government witness against the mob, and who almost single handedly brought down the First Ward political machine. Bob didn't see the error of his ways. There was no epiphany of conscience. He got mad. The Outfit put a contract on his life because he stood on principle and refused to identify a snitch and, in effect refused to send a man to his death. His reaction was to first get the contract lifted and then to wear a wire for the G for more than three-and-a-half years before he came in and started making cases for the government. He put a lot of people in jail and today lives his life in a version of the witness protection program. What he did took a lot of courage, but he's pragmatic about it. "It was the right thing to do," he told me, and he'd do it again in a heartbeat. His story reflects how organized crime has degenerated over the years. His book *When Corruption Was King* (2004, Carroll & Graf, with Hillel Levin) is a fascinating summary of how the mob ruled in Chicago "back in the day," and how they've crumbled in recent years.

On a personal note, one of the most troubling aspects of writing this book was dealing with the fact that Dick Cain had crossed the line. My brother was a criminal and most likely a killer. Dick lived a fantasy—an evil fantasy from which he could neither retreat nor recover.

In the early days of my research, I kept hoping for a breakthrough, for some validation of Bill Roemer's statement that he was a martyr. The reality is that Dick Cain was an intelligent, handsome guy blessed with all the best qualities of his Irish and Italian heritage, save one. I have found no evidence to suggest Dick Cain had a conscience. His was a life of absolute self-centeredness.

Dick Cain had no respect for the mob. He held most of the mobsters he knew in the highest disregard. He felt capable of taking control because he was smarter than his peers, but he failed to recognize that being smart isn't what makes a boss; it's being ruthless. He thought he could outsmart them. But when these guys hit a wall, they knock it down. They don't try to climb it, walk around it, or tunnel under it. They blow it up. And so it was with Dick Cain. They didn't know how to deal with him, so they whacked him.

Dick Cain led an interesting life. He made a lot of bad choices, but he made them with his eyes open. He knew the risks of his lifestyle and he embraced them. I'm not proud of my brother—I've spent too many hours trying to pick up the pieces of the shattered lives he left in his wake, from his daughters to his grandchildren. And I don't mean to attach any noble purpose to my own life; I did what I could, when I could, knowing full well that it would never be enough.

Dick was married at least three times, possibly four. He was father to five children and adopted one. His six daughters drifted in and out of his life and, if it was inconvenient for him to care, he simply didn't. Of the six, four survive today, and as I write this one is struggling for her life. It would be easy enough to say that he was a lousy father, but that would be incomplete. He loved his daughters—he just didn't know how to be a father to them. I believe he really wanted to, and there are some shining, if isolated, examples of his doing good things for them. Ultimately, though, he couldn't deliver, and the daughters who did well in their lives did so largely because of their mothers. I hope these four and their children can take some comfort in reading this book, to finally understand what he was all about, and to find, perhaps, some closure.

Dick was a complicated guy, to say the least, and died an unfortunate, albeit predictable, death doing the only thing he knew how to do. His father carried a great deal of guilt, as did his mother, but there isn't any blame for either; Dick made his own choices in life, as we all do.

He never finished high school and yet he was well-educated. He loved to read, and that's how he completed his education. Jack Mabley once wrote a column about his relationship with Dick and referred to him as "Literate, Scholarly and, I Guess, a Killer." Mabley was perhaps the one guy who saw much of Dick's good side, and he had one, despite all evidence to the contrary. Dick tried his best to help his daughters when he could and supported several of Mabley's favorite charities.

His literate side included being a prolific writer. He wrote letters, he wrote short stories, and he even wrote a movie treatment about the Bay of Pigs on the strength of his personal experiences training Cuban exiles in Chicago, Miami, Mexico, Guatemala, and, some say, even in Cuba. He reportedly tried hard to sell it to Hollywood, but was ultimately unsuccessful.

I've read and have copies of most of the things he wrote, and they show a sensitivity that was rarely in evidence in real life.

So, what have we learned from this life? My own hope is, we've learned that no life is beyond redemption, but redemption can only happen from within. It cannot be offered; it must be sought and earned. The choices we make in life may seem personal, but they frequently impact many people. When Dick made the life decisions he made, he gave little consideration to how those decisions impacted his mother, his father, his wives, his children, or his siblings. He went through marriages and relationships with little regard for their impact on his partners. Those of us who survive are left to deal with those decisions, some directly, some indirectly.

This has been an odyssey for me. A journey through a world rarely seen, and it has changed me, changed my perspectives and my expectations. It has helped me to recognize the impact of my own decisions on the lives of those around me, and while I can't change the past, and wouldn't, the future is another story.

INDEX

26th of July Movement, 66, 80
42 gang, 167, 214

Accardo, Tony, 55, 56, 57, 99, 101, 104, 107, 110, 134, 154, 162, 214
Adamowski, Ben, 57, 58, 113
Aiuppa, Joey, 107, 134
Alderisio, Phil "Milwaukee Phil", 134, 136, 165, 185
Alex, Gus, 134, 196
Allen, Ruth, 210
Anastasia, Albert, 67, 68, 69

Batista, Fulgencio, 25, 61, 65, 66, 67, 70, 75, 77, 80, 82
Battaglia, Sam, 134, 166, 182, 185
Bay City, Michigan, 1, 27, 28, 129
Bay of Pigs, 83
Bieber, George, 116, 165
Bissell, Richard, 71
Black Hand, 9, 10, 11, 14, 117, 220, 222
Blakey, G. Robert, 127
Blasi, Dominic "Butch", 136, 165
Bonelli, Nuncio, 14
Bradshaw, David, 119, 120
Brodkin, Mike, 116
Bucieri, Fiore "Fifi", 216
Buenz, William, 24, 80

Caifano, Marshall, 134, 209, 212, 214, 217, 218, 219, 220, 221
Cain, Bill, 4, 30
Cain, Genevieve, 15, 16

Cain, John, 2, 3, 16, 17, 19, 23, 28, 81
Cain, Karla, 32, 61, 194, 209, 213, 217
Cain, Kimberly, 32, 61, 194, 195, 213, 217
Cain, Lydia, 3, 11, 15, 16, 17, 18, 19, 20, 21, 23, 25, 32, 92, 95, 162, 169, 186, 187
Cain, Margaret, 15, 59
Cain, Mark of, 101
Cain, Mary Ellyn, 2, 3, 30, 81
Cain, Michael, 30
Cain, Pat, 30, 32
Cain, Richard "Dick", Throughout
Cain, Rosemary, 30, 31, 32, 34, 60, 61, 88
Cain, William, 15
Callahan, George, 6, 154
Capone, Al, 7, 8, 9, 10, 11, 115, 119, 123, 167, 189
Carroll, Chuckie, 195
Castro, Fidel, 65, 66, 70, 78, 79, 80, 81, 82, 83, 84
Celano, Jimmy, 122
Chaconas, John, 124, 168
Champagne, Tony, 134
Chiari, Roberto, 94
Cloverbar, 43
Cohen, Irwin, 57, 58, 80, 176
Cohen, Scott, 120, 121
Colosimo, Jim, 9, 10
Cooley, Bob, 101, 226
Costello, Frank, 115
Cozzo, Jelly, 217, 220
Cozzone, Scully, 16, 17, 187

Daddano, Willie "Potatoes", 114, 139,
　149, 150, 151, 155, 161, 182, 185
Daley, Richard, 57, 58, 80, 106, 176,
　180, 186
Danato, Sylvia, 147
D'Arco, John, 104, 105
D'Argento, Joe, 140, 141, 142, 143, 144,
　145, 146, 147, 148, 149, 151, 152,
　157
Deeley, Patrick, 52
DeLegge, Jr. , Frank, 141, 144, 155
DeLegge, Sr. , Frank, 140, 141, 142,
　146, 147, 148, 155, 156, 182
DeStefano, Sam, 62, 113, 196, 205
Donnelly, James, 106, 108, 111, 116,
　168
Dooley, Bernadette, 15
Dulles, Allen, 72

Edwards, Sheffield, 71, 72, 37
Eggenberger, Bernard, 121

Ferraro, Frankie, 59
Ferrell, Mary, 129
Fidonzi, Guido, 180
Figel, Harry, 44, 45, 46, 47, 48, 40, 50,
　51, 54, 57
Fischetti, Charles, 134
Fletcher, Larry, 140, 141, 142, 143, 144
Foran, Tom, 154, 158, 180, 184, 186
Franklin Park Bank, 139, 141, 143, 151,
　152
Fuesel, Bob, 100

Genovese, Vito, 185
Giancana, Sam, 30, 37, 44, 56, 65, 68,
　71, 72, 73, 76, 82, 97, 103, 104,
　105, 107, 110, 119, 124, 128, 135,
　162, 166, 167, 172, 173, 185, 189,
　196, 200, 202, 206, 214, 219, 220,
　223
Gilardi, Michael, 200, 201, 213, 217
Gladden, Jerry, 218, 219, 221
Goldwater, Barry, 6, 121, 207
Gorte, Harvey, 16
Gorte, Winifred, 16
Guevera, Che, 66

Hanrahan, Edward V., 165
Hill, Ralph, 133, 134
Hoffman, Judge Julius, 57, 123, 154,
　156, 157, 161, 163
Hoover, Herbert, 7, 8
Hoover, J. Edgar, 115
HSCA, 127
Humphreys, Murray, 119, 123

Jackson, William "Action", 62, 114
JFK Lancer, 128, 129
Johnson, Kenneth, 69
Johnson, Lyndon B., 121
Johnson, Marlin, 120, 192

Kangles, Constantine, 80, 83, 87
Katzenbach, Nicholas, 135
Keeler Institute, 29, 53, 93
Kelly, Edward, 47, 53
Kennedy, Bobby, 80, 92, 120, 128, 176
Kennedy, Joe, 128
Kennedy, John F., 82, 84, 127, 128, 130
Kennedy, Marlene, 200, 211
Kroupensky, Pierre, 84, 85, 90, 91
KUBARK, 117, 118

LaJoy, Mike, 140, 141, 142, 143, 144,
　145, 146, 147, 148, 149, 150, 151,
　157
Lansky, Jake, 69
Lansky, Meyer, 65, 69, 82, 115

Little Al, 100, 123
Lohmann, Bill, 73, 80, 82, 117
Lombardo, Anthony, 12, 13
Lownes, Vic, 87

Mabley, Jack, 4, 34, 39, 55, 60, 61, 87, 95, 113, 120, 187, 221, 227
Machado, Gerardo, 65
Mahue, Robert, 71, 72
Malcotte, James, 106, 108, 129
Marchone, Pasqualino, *See* Marcy, Pat
Marcy, Pat, 101, 104, 105, 110, 119
McGuire, Phyllis, 134, 206
McGurk, Virginia, 1
McSwain, George, 68
Meeker, Ben, 188
Mendola, Guy, 143, 147, 148, 149, 150
Mendosa, Roberto, 69
Meo, Jimmy, 134
Mineta, Norman Y., 5
Montagna, Rocky, 149, 150, 151, 155, 182
Morrissey, Lawrence E., 165
Mulvey, Thomas, 47

Newey, Paul, 57, 58, 61, 80, 113
Nixon, Richard, 128

O'Shea, Jackie, 210
O'Connell, James P., 71
Ogilvie, Richard, 55, 56, 57, 87, 88, 89, 90, 96, 97, 99, 100, 101, 103, 120, 121, 136, 158, 161, 166, 171, 180, 184, 185
Onassis, Aristotle, 197
Oswald, Lee Harvey, 130
Owosso, Michigan, 15, 18, 19, 58, 59, 156

Panzko, Paul "Peanuts", 116, 151
Pape, Frank, 59
Parsons, D. J., 59
Percy, Charles, 120, 121
Petiti, Angelo, 14
Pierce, Frank, 188, 189, 190, 195
Pistone, Joe, 216
Prio, Ross, 116, 196
Prio, Ross, Jr., 116

Ranieri, Billy, 12, 13, 14
Ranieri, Frank, 12, 13, 14
Ranieri, Teresina, 12
Rasco, Jose Ignacio, 84
Republican National Convention, 121
Ricca, Paul, 134
Rice, Downey, 69
Rivas, Suarez, 69
Rizzi, Dom, 161
Robards, Sam, 87
Roe v. Wade, 108
Roe, Theodore, 189
Roemer, William F., 6, 100, 114, 123, 127, 128, 137, 155, 191, 212, 213, 215, 218, 220, 226
Roselli, John, 71, 82
Rosen, Alex, 59, 67
Rose's Sandwich Shop, 212, 217, 219, 221

Sain, Frank, 99
Sansonetti's Restaurant, 141, 143, 144
Scalzitti, Olimpio, 12
Schang, Pat, 143, 145, 146, 147, 148, 149, 150, 151, 152, 157
Scully, Al, 17
Scully, Larry, 15
Scully, Lydia, 11, 15, 16
Scully, Ole, 7, 11, 12, 13, 14, 15, 17, 220
Scully, Vincenza, 11, 15, 16, 17, 18, 169
Shallow, Gerry, 38, 39, 40, 41, 42, 43,

44, 45, 47, 53, 57, 58, 88
Shapiro, Governor, 158
Sierra, Paulino, 118
Sinatra, Frank, 207
Siragusa, Charles, 119, 120
Smith, Al, 7, 8
Smith, Sandy, 120
Spencer, Roswell, 99, 100

The Patch, 12, 219
Thompson, Bill, 8
Tieken, Robert, 47
Tisci, Anthony, 119, 120
Tolan, Philip, 117
Tomaszek, Gerry, 144, 146, 151
Top Hoodlum Program, 123
Torrio, Johnny, 7, 9, 10, 11
Torrio, Victoria, 10
Trafficante, Santos, 65, 67, 69, 71, 73
Turi, Arlene, 210

Van Scoyk, Grace, 42

Varelli, Johnny "The Bug", 143, 144, 145, 151
Vasisko, Vincent, 68
Verona, Tony, 82, 87

Ward, Daniel, 124
Warren Commission, 127
White Hand, 11, 13, 220, 222
Winter, Dale, 10
Witsman, Bill, 39, 88, 109, 124, 150, 168

Zahn Drug Company, 123, 167, 171
Zwillman, Abner "Longie", 67